INTRODUCTION
TO JAVA
PROGRAMMING

2ND EDITION

BY
NAGARAJ RAO AND JOHN YOON

Indo American Books

2261, Ground Floor, Hudson Line, Kingsway Camp, Delhi-110 009
(INDIA) E-mail: sales@iabooks.com, www.iabooks.com

2nd Edition

Book Team
President : Vijay Sharma
Sr. Vice President : Puneet Singh (London)
Vice President : Kanika Sharma (London)
Pre-Press : Purna Kant Mishra
Vice-President Marketing : Agnel Henry

ISBN : 93-82661-54-9

Published and Digitally Printed in India in 2016
with permission from the copyright holder by:
Indo American Books (IA Books)
2261, Ground Floor, Hudson Line, Kingsway Camp
Delhi 110009, INDIA. Ph.: 91-011-42870094
Email: sales@iabooks.com
Web: www.iabooks.com

Contents

Preface   vii

Chapter 1 – Introduction   **1**

1.1   Introduction   1

1.1.1   Install JSE, aka JDK   1

1.1.2   Download IDE Eclipse   4

1.1.3   Creating and Running Java Programs   7

1.2   First Java Programs   8

1.2.1   What is Java Language?   8

1.2.2   Create and Run Welcome Program   10

1.2.3   Examples   10

1.3   Graphics   13

1.3.1   Chapter Exercises   19

1.3.a   What did you learn?   21

Chapter 2 – Data Types, Assignment, Output   **23**

2.1   Introduction   23

2.1.1   Data Types and Identifiers   23

2.2   Expressions   25

2.3   Assignment Statement   28

2.4   Input from the Keyboard   31

2.5   Chapter Exercises   39

Chapter 3 – Conditional Statements   **43**

3.1   Introduction   43

3.1.1   Case for variables   43

3.2   If – else Statement   46

3.3   Switch Case Statement   51

3.4 Comparison between if…else and switch…case statements 54

3.5 Chapter Exercises 59

Chapter 4 – Repetition Statements 63

4.1 Introduction 63

4.1.1 for Loop 63

4.2 while Loop 72

4.3 do-while Loop 76

4.4 Formatting Output Data 77

4.5 Reading from a Text File 80

4.6 Chapter Exercises 84

Chapter 5 – Java Application Programming Interfaces (API) 91

5.1 Introduction 91

5.2 Math Class 92

5.3 String Class 95

5.4 Reading From and Writing to a Text File 98

5.5 What did you learn? 100

5.6 Chapter Exercises 101

Chapter 6 – Classes and Objects 105

6.1 Introduction 105

6.1.1 Importation of Class 106

6.1.2 Construction of an Object 106

6.1.3 Invocation of a Method 106

6.2 User-Defined Classes 107

6.2.1 User-Defined Methods 109

6.2.2 Scope Identifier 113

6.2.3 Accessing Visibility Modified Values 117

6.3 Accessors and Mutators 119

6.3.1 Class with the main() method   122

6.3.2 Overloaded Methods   125

6.4.   Chapter Exercises   140

Chapter 7 – Arrays   **143**

7.1   Java Arrays   143

7.2   One-dimensional Arrays   144

7.2.1 Creation of Arrays   144

7.2.2 Visibility   148

7.2.3 Accessing Arrays and More   149

7.2.4 Reading Arrays   150

7.2.5 Writing into Arrays   152

7.3   Arrays as Parameters and Invoking Methods   154

7.4   Multidimensional Arrays   158

7.5   Exercises and Course Project   161

Chapter 8 – Inheritances   **167**

8.1   Introduction   167

8.1.1 Class Hierarchies   167

8.1.1 Composition Relationship (has-a)   168

8.2   Inheritance Relationship   171

8.3   Visibility and "protected" Modifier   186

8.4   Abstract Classes and Interfaces   189

8.5   Chapter Exercises   189

Chapter 9 – Polymorphisms   **193**

9.1   Polymorphic References   193

9.2   Polymorphism via Inheritances   197

9.3   Polymorphism via Interfaces   204

9.4   Chapter Exercises   207

Chapter 10 – Exceptions   **211**

10.1   Why Exceptions   211

10.2   Exception Class Hierarchies   216

10.3   Exception Handling   217

10.4   Creating Exception Classes   220

10.5   Chapter Exercises   231

Chapter 11 – Graphical User Interfaces   **233**

11.1   GUI Components and Class Hierarchies   233

11.2   Layout Managers   238

11.3   Event Handling   241

11.4   Revisit GUI Components   245

11.5   Chapter Exercises   253

Chapter 12 – Introduction to Recursion and Graphics   **257**

12.1   Introduction   257

12.2   Recursion   258

12.2.1 Recursive requisites   261

12.2.2 Towers of Hanoi   263

12.3   Graphics   266

12.4   Chapter Exercises   275

Appendix A   279

Preface

Introduction to Java Programming is an attempt to introduce Java as an interesting coding language to bring alive simple everyday problems. We are presenting the material as a mixture of Object Oriented Programming with procedural programming, graphics, and GUI (Graphical User Interface). We will continue to add more meaningful problems. The content of this book could be covered in either one semester or in two depending on the level of the student body. If it is covered in two semesters, we recommend that chapters 1 – 7 be covered in the first semester and chapters 8 – 13 in the second semester.

Chapter 1: First, this chapter explains how to install all the applications necessary for running java programs. It then introduces coding with a simple code to print a string. It also introduces simple codes in drawing graphics. We start with a skeletal template of a simple class and a skeletal class of a graphics class. We avoid detailed explanation of packages and methods required for graphics at this introduction of coding.

Chapters 2 – 7: These chapters introduce data types, input and output of data, arithmetic expressions, conditional statements, loops, APIs, user-defined classes and objects, and arrays. We have introduced reading data from the keyboard and text files. We have also introduced a basic output to text files. Object Oriented Programming (OOP) is implemented through user-defined classes. Unified Modeling these chapters will form the foundation for the chapters 8 – 13.

Chapters 8, 9: These chapters introduce the real benefit of OOP. It introduces inheritance and polymorphism. Several examples are included to clarify the is-a and has-a relations. Some examples with graphics are included as well. Inheritance allows you to build and expand classes and helps to reduce coding.

Chapter 10: This chapter deals with exceptions – errors that could occur in programs. Many of these are built into the language and we will be creating user-defined try and catch exceptions.

Chapter 11: Graphical User Interface (GUI) is an important feature of computing. This chapter has several examples on creating GUI components and corresponding actions to be taken. Some of the graphics packages we used in the earlier chapters to do graphics applications are used in this chapter as well.

Chapter 12: This is a kind of fun chapter which uses recursion and graphics. Recursion could be a powerful tool to solve complex problems but also could create interesting graphics.

Appendix A: We have listed several problems for course projects. Students could work in groups of 2 or 3, or individually. These problems will solve some applications and present as a GUI application.

Introduction

1.1 Introduction

Java is a high-level programming language. Every computer will have its own machine language. So, we need to translate Java code into machine code before the computer could execute our program. This translator could be either a compiler or an interpreter. In order to accomplish this, we first set up the programming environment in our laptop or PC. Two software packages should be downloaded: Java Standard Edition (JSE) and an Integrated Development Environment (IDE). JSE will allow us to compile Java programs and an IDE will allow us type, save, and edit programs. We can create Java programs in several ways: typing in Notepad (or similar application) and running at the command level; an IDE that will allow us create, compile, and also execute in a GUI environment; use Eclipse IDE which is a development application which provides more support for creating programs. JSE should be installed for all the three methods. The eclipse IDE can be unzipped. All the three methods will be explained below.

1.1.1 Install JSE, aka JDK

Java Standard Edition (JSE) can be downloaded from the following website:
http://www.oracle.com/technetwork/java/javase/downloads/index.html

Step 1: Download

The version of Java SE is JSE Development Kit 8 (Java SE Development Kit 8u5 or after). Depending upon the system of yours, whether 32-bit or 64 bit-processors, you should download the correct version.

The **Java Development Kit** (**JDK**) helps you to install with some tutorials. The URL is
https://docs.oracle.com/javase/8/docs/technotes/guides/install/install_overview.html#CJAGAACB
Java tutorial: http://docs.oracle.com/javase/tutorial/index.html

Step 2: Installation

Click on jdk-8u5-windows-x64.exe file to start installing. Start by clicking the Next button	Select or unselect as you wish If unsure, do not do anything but click Next
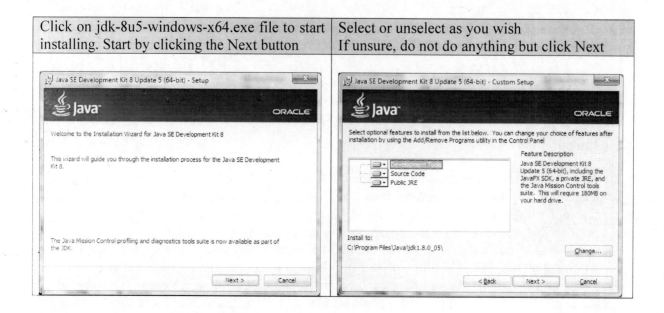	

Downloading the source files takes a while to install on your system. Then, you will see the following:

If successfully installed	If "Next step" is clicked, you may learn more from the website
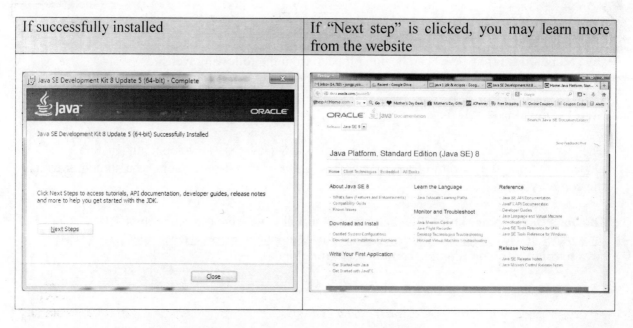	

Now, you may check the version of your installed java virtual machine.

Bring up a command-line window by typing "cmd" in the Search box after clicking on Start

Type `java -version` at the command line and press enter. You will see java version.

Type `javac -version` at the command line. You will see javac version. Probably both of them will be the same. If there are any error messages, they could be fixed as below:

The "bin" folder of jdk should be added to the PATH of user environment variables as detailed below. You will take the benefit of setting the environment variables.

How To Set Environment Variables		
	1.	Click on "Advanced system settings" on the System Control by right-clicking on "Computer" of "Start" button on the bottom of your computer, then another pop-up windows has the tab "Advanced".
	2.	Click on the "Environment Variables" button to open another windows where "User variables for xxx" appears. Note xxx is your login name of your PC. By clicking PATH variable, edit to add the fully qualified address to the folder holding the "bin" directory of your jdk.
	3.	If there is no PATH variable, then create it by clicking on the "New" button. An example of the PATH is ;C:\Program Files\Java\jdk1.7.0_25\bin; Note that it starts with a semi-colon.
	4.	Finally, click on the OK button.
Tip	Remark	1. Any commands (or the executable programs stored in the directory "C:\Program Files\Java\jdk1.7.0_25\bin") are available to run from any folder of the PC. 2. Your java sources can be stored at any folder of the PC. Hence, you can create a folder at any location of your PC and save your java source. Then, in that folder you can compile and run your java program since the commands of compile/run are set for you to execute from anywhere.

After setting the PATH, we are ready to code a java program.

Open a notepad and start editing.	Save as a file with the name "Sample1.java" in the type of "All Files". In this way, the java source can be saved as plaintext.

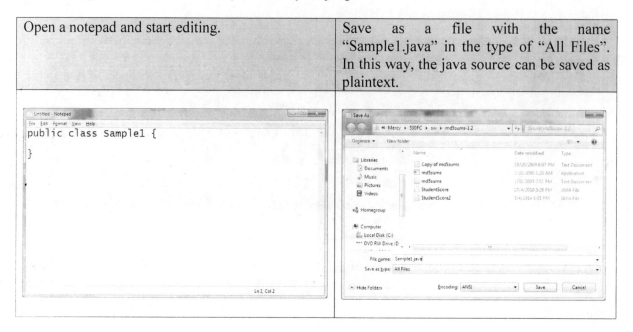

After a java class file is saved, we can compile the file.

In a command-line, type javac <file name with the extension>

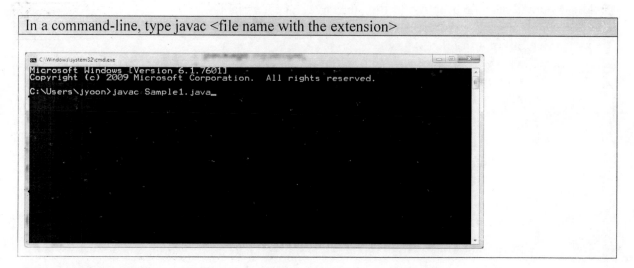

1.1.2 Download IDE eclipse

With the location of jdk set in the PATH variable, the software eclipse will be unzipped after downloading from http://www.eclipse.org/downloads/.

You have to choose the Eclipse Standard version depending on whether your operating system is 32-bit or 64-bit. To find this information, click Start ->right click on computer -> Properties.

Now, click the Eclipse icon to open the IDE where you can start programming.

Java Tutorial on eclipse: http://www.youtube.com/watch?v=xO5DpU2j-WE

Enter a directory where you want to save your java programs	First create a new project from the "File" menu at the upper left corner: File > New > Java Project
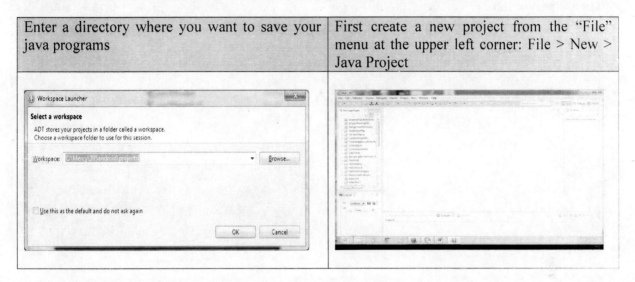	

Then, there will be a pop-up window, where you can create a java project. Enter Project name and go Next as follows:

Enter the name of your Project name. You name it! Then, either click "Finish" or "Next"	If the "Next" is clicked, the below appears. Here you may click to finish.
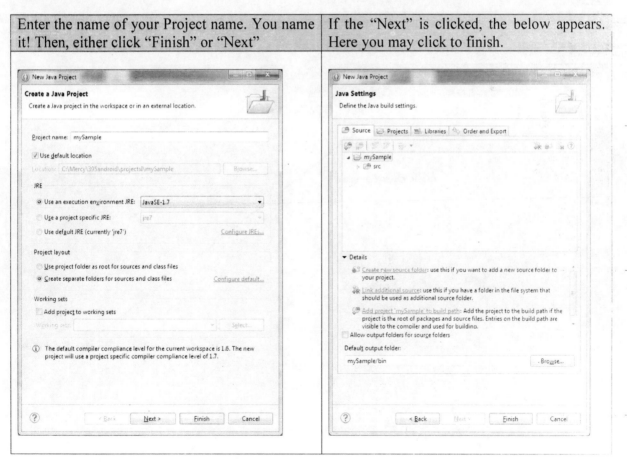	

Once a java project is created, we need to create a class for that java project.

Right click on the project from the left pane of eclipse to choose New > Class	In a pop-up window of Java Class, enter the name of a class. For now, click "Finish"
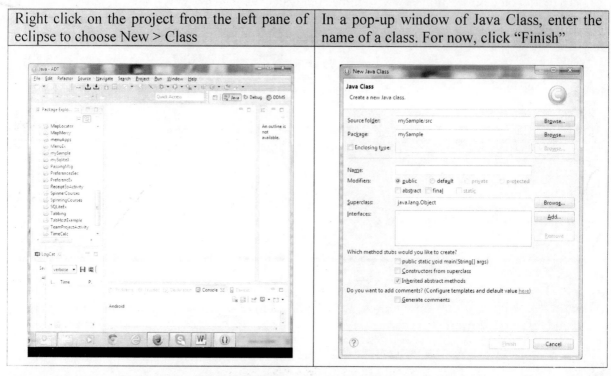	

Then, the editor of java class will be available with a template as seen below:

In the editor, now you are ready to code in the body of the class Sample1.

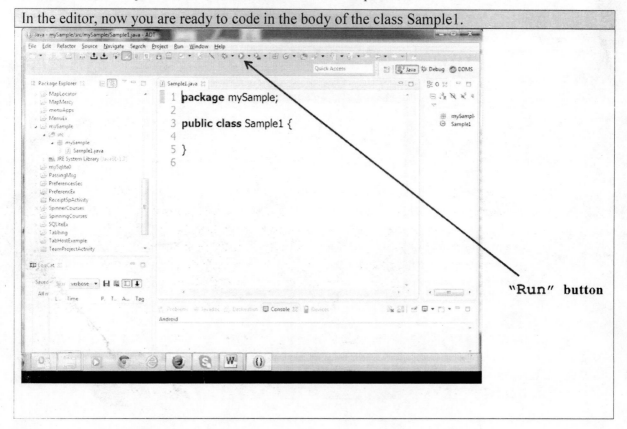

After typing a java class, Sample1.java in our case, we can compile the class (program) by clicking the green triangle in the menu bar at the top and run if no error is found. In the next section, a sample java class will be created and executed. Good luck!

1.1.3 Creating and Running Java Programs

Computer programming requires a compiler and an editor. Between a compiler and an editor, there are basically three approaches: 1) no-binding approach, 2) loosely-binding approach, and 3) integrated approach.

1)   No-binding approach uses a general editor, e.g., notepad, to edit a java coding list and to save it as a file with the "java" extension. Then the java file, e.g., MySample.java, is compiled on OS command-line. In this case, the command is

```
C:\> javac MySample.java
```

Then, the outcome of this compilation is obtained:

```
C:\> dir
MySample.class
MySample.java
```

Finally, this class file can be executed by the command,

```
C:> java MySample
```

Note that when a class file is executed, no extension is needed as shown above. Note also that both javac and java are available in the "bin" folder of jdk.

2)   Loosely-binding approach provides an editor which internally links with jdk. Usually, Graphical User Interface (GUI) is available in this approach. By clicking on a button of GUI, e.g., green triangle button, the java compiler automatically compiles the java file which is loaded on the editor, and it further executes its class file, if no error occurs. Depending on GUI, there may be another button for executing the class file.

3)   Integrated approach provides all available in the Loosely-binding approach plus automatic assistance tools to meet the programming language grammar. For example, as being edited, all possible languages are suggested for a programmer to pick up. The assistance tools avoid programmers from memorizing the detailed language syntax but also the tools teach all potential options of the language. This approach is called IDE (Integrated Development Environment). In this programming lesson, the eclipse IDE is used. There are several open source IDEs with varying features. Eclipse is a popular development tool.

In summary, programmers who use the first and second approaches should keep looking up the java API whenever needed. The API is available in the Internet or can be downloaded for local computer. However, in the third approach the API is already embedded in the IDE and the IDE provides the programmers with the proper API at coding of each Java statement.

1.2 First Java Programs

1.2.1 What is Java Language?

Java is a programming language. Languages like English and German are used to communicate between humans. Java is used to communicate with a computer and make the computer perform tasks a problem specifies. Since we are communicating with a machine, we need to be exact in the Java vocabulary (instructions and definitions) and syntax (grammar). Without further expanding on how this communication takes place, we will delve into programming.

Every type of computer (PC, Mac, main frames, supercomputers, and gadgets) will have its own instruction sets. These languages that computers (machines) understand (in zeroes and ones) are called "machine languages". Java is a high-level language which is very similar to a speaking language. So, we need Java (and similar languages) translated to the specific machine language (details are skipped for simplicity at this point). Some of these "translators" are called compilers. So, every Java program has to be compiled (translated) first and then executed to perform the indicated task.

If one wants to become proficient in any language, one should practice reading, writing, and speaking consistently. The same requirement applies to learning Java. You will have to spend a few hours every week for these courses. Just like one would acquire language vocabulary, one would start learning java vocabulary slowly and steadily, building on previously acquired skills.

Example 1:

Here is a Java program which will just print the sentence "Welcome to Java" to the monitor:

Coding List 1.1: Welcome

```
1 /* Author:
     Date:
     Input: none
2    Output: prints the sentence "Welcome to Java"
3 */
4
5  public class Welcome
6  {    public static void main(String args[]) {
7   // the standard statement for the "main" block, same always
8          System.out.println("Welcome to Java");
9     } // closing bracket for the main method
10 }   // closing bracket for the Welcome class
Output:
Welcome to Java
```

When you compile and run this program, it will print "Welcome to Java" on the monitor. Observe and memorize the following points regarding this program. The statements are numbered for the following explanation.

Lines 1-3: These are multiple-line comments. Compilers will skip these lines. They start with "/*" and end with "*/".

Line 4:   A blank line for clarity

Line 5:   Every program we write should have the words "public class". "Welcome" is the name we gave for this class. A standard practice among Java programmers is to start class names with a capital letter as in "W" in "Welcome". Observe the open bracket "{". This is to indicate that the class block starts from here. To indicate the end of the class we have the close bracket "}" on line 10.

Line 6:   The statement "public static void main (String args[])" is required in all executable Java programs. You will reproduce this line in all your executable programs. At the end of the line, "{" opens the block for the main method. This is closed on line 9. The symbols "{" and "}" should be paired and so every open bracket must have a corresponding close bracket. If you practice indenting all instructions inside these brackets, you will reduce syntax errors.

How To Set Code Blocks		
	Opening Block: 1. Use a separate line for the class block 2. Place "{" at the end of a method or any other java statement. Please see the examples in the Remark block Closing Block: use a separate line in any case	

Tip: Java Convention	Remark	For example
		  • Class Block
		     `public class Welcome`
		       `{`
		  • Method
		     `public static void main (String [] args) {`
		  • If Statement
		        `if (x > 10) {`
		However, in any specific situation, you do not need to follow this java programming convention.

Line 7:   A single-line comment.

Line 8:   This is the line which will print "Welcome to Java" on the monitor. Observe "Welcome to Java" is in double quotes. Anything in double quotes will be reproduced or echoed as it is when used in "System.out.println". So, if we want to print "*", we need to write "System.out.println("*");" Note that the semicolon (;) at the end of this line indicates that this instruction ended at that point. It should be at the end of each completed Java statement.

Line 9-10: Closing a bracket: Line 9 closes the main bracket and Line 10 the class bracket.

1.2.2 Create and Run Welcome Program

1. Type the above program (code) using any editor, e.g., Notepad or in IDE and save it as Welcome.java. Keep in mind the directory where the java file Welcome.java is stored. Suppose that the file is saved in the directory, **C:\Mercy\java131**.

2. Go to Command-line Prompt (if you do not have it on desktop, click on Start and type cmd in the search box)

3. Change the directory to the folder where your java file is stored. If it is stored in `C:\Mercy\java131`, type the following command to go to the directory:

    ```
    Prompt_wherever_you_are:>cd C:\Mercy\java131
    ```

    After this command, your prompt will be

    ```
    C:\Mercy\java131\>
    ```

4. Compile the java file by the following command. Note that the extension, java, should appear for compilation.

    ```
    C:\Mercy\java131\>javac Welcome.java
    ```

    The outcome of this compile is the file called Welcome.class.

5. If there is a compile error, it should be fixed. The language syntax is primarily verified. If there is no syntax error, then, the following command will execute the program.

    ```
    C:\Mercy\java131\>java Welcome
    ```

    Note that the execution of java bytecode does not need an extension. The file expressed above in the command line is not the file, Welcome.class, but simply the class name Welcome.

6. [Challenge] The class Welcome can be used as a type in your future java implementation.

1.2.3 Examples

Example 2: Write a program to print one of your favorite quotes.

a) Select a name for the program (class name). We will call it Quote. So, the class statement is

```
public class Quote
{
```

We have included the open bracket for the class. What is the next statement? It is the main method. It is always the same statement:

```
public class Quote
{
public static void main(String args[]) {
```

Again, we have included the open bracket for the main block. Now we are starting the body of the main method. For some time all our java statements will be in the main block. Now, we need to type the statement to print our quote. Our quote is "Eye for an eye makes the whole world blind. – Gandhi". Here is the statement to print it:

```
public class Quote
{
public static void main(String args[]) {
  System.out.println("Eye for an eye makes the whole world blind.
  - Gandhi");
```

Observe the quote is in double quotes. Also observe the open parenthesis "(" and the corresponding close parenthesis ")". Finally, we end this statement by the semicolon. So, we have the statement to print our quote. Now we are going to close the main method first and then the class. NOTE: The whole print statement must be on the same line. The complete program is

Coding List 1.2: Quote.java

```
/* Author:
 * Date:
 * Input: none
 * Output: prints the quote to the monitor
*/
public class Quote
{   public static void main(String args[])
    {
      System.out.println("Eye for an eye makes the whole world blind. -
Gandhi");
    }
}
```
When you execute this program, it will print the following:

```
Welcome to Java
```

NOTE: If text wraps in `System.out.println` statement, as in

```
System.out.println("Eye  for  an  eye  makes  the  whole  world  blind.  -
Gandhi");
```

either all of that should be on the same line or the wrapped around text must be preceded with a "+" as in

```
System.out.println("Eye for an eye makes the whole world blind. - "
+"Gandhi");
```

Type the code in Notepad. Save it as `Quote.java`. Compile and run. You could also use an IDE.

Example 3: Now write a program to print your quote one word per line.

This is the same as example 1 above except that we need to print one word per line. So, we need to type 10 `System.out.println` statements, one per word. Here is the program

Coding List 1.3: Quote2.java

```
/* Author:
 * Date:
 * Input: none
 * Output: prints a quote on one line and then prints one word per line
 */
public class Quote2
{
public static void main(String args[]) {
System.out.println("Eye for an eye makes the whole world blind. - Gandhi");
    System.out.println("Eye");
    System.out.println("for");
    System.out.println("an");
    System.out.println("Eye");
    System.out.println("makes");
    System.out.println("the");
    System.out.println("whole");
    System.out.println("world");
    System.out.println("blind");
    System.out.println("- Gandhi");
  }
}
```

```
Eye for an eye makes the whole world blind. - Gandhi
Eye
for
an
Eye
makes
the
whole
world
blind
- Gandhi
```

Exmple 4: Print a box of asterisks "*".

We will call this program (class) `StarBox`. Here is the program:

Coding List 1.4: StarBox.java

```java
/* Author:
 * Date:
 * Input: none
 * Output: prints a box of asterisks.
 */
public class StarBox
{
    public static void main(String args[]) {
        System.out.println("********************");
        System.out.println("*                  *");
        System.out.println("*                  *");
        System.out.println("*                  *");
        System.out.println("*                  *");
        System.out.println("*                  *");
        System.out.println("********************");

    }
}
```

```
Here is the output:

********************
*                  *
*                  *
*                  *
*                  *
*                  *
********************
```

1.3 Graphics

We will introduce only a small part of graphics to enable us to have some fun. Just like we need the main() method to execute a class, we need the paint() method to draw some graphics. Since graphics will show up in frames of windows, we need to extend JFrame class and set up the frame. Since we will be drawing images, we need to have axes of reference. In mathematics, we will have the origin at the center and will have negative sides of x- and y- axes. Since we will be placing pixels on graphs, we cannot have negative coordinates. The resolution of the graphics system will determine the resolution of the monitor. We will assume 1800x1200 for these simple graphics examples. In these graphics systems, the origin (0,0) will be the top-left corner. So, the x-axis goes 0 – 1800. The y-axis grows going downwards from the origin, in our case 0-1200. NOTE: the windows origin (0,0) is the top-left corner of the window and the y-coordinate increases downward. Explanation on classes and their objects are skipped. You are asked to just use the template by adding appropriate statements in the paint() method. We will create a simple boilerplate program that can be used for all the problems in this chapter. Here is the boilerplate with comments:

Example 5:

| Coding List 1.5   TEMPLATE TO USE FOR ALL GRAPHICS PROBLEMS |

```java
import java.awt.Graphics; // needed to draw graphics
import java.awt.Color;    // needed to use different colors
import javax.swing.JFrame;// needed to create the window

public class IntroGraphics extends JFrame  // create your class
{ public IntroGraphics()    // set up the window in the constructor
   { setTitle("Introduction to Graphics");
     setSize(1200,1200);
     setVisible(true);
     setDefaultCloseOperation(EXIT_ON_CLOSE);
   }
// THE paint() METHOD IS NEEDED TO DRAW GRAPHICS
  public void paint(Graphics g)
  {
    // PLACE ALL YOUR DRAWINGS HERE.
  }

// main() method to execute. JUST CREATE AN OBJECT OF THE CLASS
  public static void main(String args[])
  { IntroGraphics ig = new IntroGraphics(); // object of the class
  }
}
```

Without much details let us look at the code to draw a line in red, a rectangle in blue, an oval in green. We will copy the boilerplate above and add new code to it, the new code is in red to make it explicit and to show how simple it is to write your programs. The java statements are intuitively understandable. For example,

Straight line: We need the coordinates of two points to draw a straight line. Hence the statement to draw a straight line requires 4 integers, the first two being the coordinates of the first point and the last two integers being the coordinates of the second point. The java statement is

> `g.drawLine(x1,y1,x2,y2).`

Rectangle: A rectangle requires the coordinates of the top-left corner of the rectangle, the length, and the width of the rectangle. The java statement is

> `g.drawRect(x1,y1,length,width).`

If the length and the width are the same, we get a square. If we replace "draw" to "fill" in "g.drawRect()", we will fill the oval with the specified color.

<u>Oval</u>: An oval is an ellipse, inscribed in a rectangle. So, it requires the coordinates of the top-left corner of the imaginary rectangle in which the oval is inscribed, then the length and the width. The statement is

```
g.drawOval(x1,y1,length,width).
```

Following color codes are available (https://docs.oracle.com/javase/7/docs/api/java/awt/Color.html):

Color.BLACK	Color.LIGHT_GRAY
Color.BLUE	Color.MAGENTA
Color.CYAN	Color.ORANGE
Color.DARK_GRAY	Color.PINK
Color.GRAY	Color.RED
Color.YELLOW	Color.WHITE

Example 6: Here we will draw several lines with different colors:

Coding List 1.6 DrawColorLines.java

```java
/* Author:
 * Date:
 * Input: none
 * Output: This program draws several lines in different colors.
 */

import java.awt.Graphics; // needed to draw graphics
import java.awt.Color;    // needed to use different colors
import javax.swing.JFrame;// needed to create the window

public class DrawColorLines extends JFrame  // create your class
{ String response;
  public DrawColorLines()         // set up the window in the constructor
  { setTitle("Color Lines");
    setSize(1800,1800);
    setVisible(true);
    setDefaultCloseOperation(EXIT_ON_CLOSE);
  }
 // THE paint() METHOD IS NEEDED TO DRAW GRAPHICS
  public void paint(Graphics g)
  {    g.setColor(Color.RED);
     g.drawLine(0,100, 500,100); // red line

     g.setColor(Color.BLUE);
     g.drawLine(0,200, 500, 200); // blue line
```

```
        g.setColor(Color.GREEN);
        g.drawLine(0,300, 500,300); // green line

        g.setColor(Color.MAGENTA);
        g.drawLine(0,400, 500,400); // magenta line

        g.setColor(Color.CYAN);
        g.drawLine(0,500, 500,500); // cyan line

        g.setColor(Color.DARK_GRAY); // dark gray line
        g.drawLine(0,600, 500,600);

    }
// main() method to execute. JUST CREATE AN OBJECT OF THE CLASS
  public static void main(String args[])
  {
    DrawColorLines dcl = new DrawColorLines();
  }
}Here is the output
```

Example 7: Here we are drawing a straight line, a rectangle, and an oval.

Coding List 1.7 FirstGraphics.java

```
/* Author:
 * Date:
 * Input: none
 * Output: This is an introduction to java graphics. This introduces drawing
 * a straight line, a rectangle, and an oval in different colors.
 */
import java.awt.Graphics; // needed to draw graphics
import java.awt.Color;    // needed to use different colors
import javax.swing.JFrame;// needed to create the window

public class FirstGraphics extends JFrame  // create your class
{ public FirstGraphics()        // set up the window in the constructor
  {  setTitle("Introduction to Graphics");
     setSize(1800,1800);
     setVisible(true);
     setDefaultCloseOperation(EXIT_ON_CLOSE);
  }
// THE paint() METHOD IS NEEDED TO DRAW GRAPHICS
  public void paint(Graphics g)
  {  g.setColor(Color.RED);
     g.drawLine(100,100,300,300);//(100,100) is first pt, (300,300) end pt
     g.setColor(Color.BLUE);
     g.drawRect(350,100,200,400);//(350,100) top left corner, 200=l, 400=w
     g.setColor(Color.GREEN);
     g.drawOval(600,500,200,400); //oval inscribed in a rectangle with
       //(600,500) top left corner, 200=length, 400=width
     // PLACE ALL YOUR DRAWINGS HERE. IT COULD BE METHOD CALLS
  }

// main() method to execute. JUST CREATE AN OBJECT OF THE CLASS
  public static void main(String args[])
  { FirstGraphics fg = new FirstGraphics(); // object of the class
  }
}
```

We drew the figures in the paint() method. All our graphics statements will be in the paint() method until we learn about methods. Whenever you want to draw an oval, you should work with the corresponding rectangle. To create new images, you should draw them on graph papers and then translate them to the coding. Just to show how this works, we will draw a rectangle and an oval with the same arguments so that you will see the oval inscribed in the rectangle. We will also draw a circle at the center of the rectangle, of course the radius is the smaller side of the rectangle.

```
g.fillRect(100,100, 300,100;
```

will fill a rectangle at (100.100) as the top-left corner, 300 being the length (horizontal length) and 100 being the width.

```
g.fillOval(100,100,300,100);
```

will inscribe an oval inside the rectangle with the same numbers. Now, to draw the circle inside the rectangle and at the center of the rectangle, we need to do some math with the coordinates. Let us figure out how to draw a circle with radius=100 and centered at the center of the rectangle. But, a circle is an oval with equal length and width. So, we need the coordinates of the top-left corner of the square at the center of the rectangle. If the radius is 100, it should be 50 to the left of the center and 50 to the right of the center. The length of the rectangle is 300 - 150 to the left of the center and 150 to the right of the center. Hence the x-coordinate of the corner of the square will be 100+100=200. I suggest you draw the figures on graph paper and figure out the coordinates. It will all make sense. The y-coordinate will stay at 100. Here is the code:

Coding List 1.7 RectOval.java

```
/* Author:
 * Date:
 * Input: none
 * Output: This program draws a rectangle and then inscribes an oval and
 * a circle. Some calculations would require to center the circle to make
 * it fit into the circle.
 */
import java.awt.Graphics; // needed to draw graphics
import java.awt.Color;    // needed to use different colors
import javax.swing.JFrame;// needed to create the window

public class RectOval extends JFrame  // #1 class name RectOval
{ public RectOval()         // #2 constructor name RectOval
  { setTitle("Introduction to Graphics");
    setSize(1800,1800);
    setVisible(true);
    setDefaultCloseOperation(EXIT_ON_CLOSE);
  }
// THE paint() METHOD IS NEEDED TO DRAW GRAPHICS
  public void paint(Graphics g)
  { g.setColor(Color.RED);
    g.fillRect(100,100,300,100);//(100,100) is the corner, l=300,w=100
```

```
      g.setColor(Color.BLUE);l=
      g.fillOval(100,100,300,100); //(100,100) top left corner, l=300, w=100
      g.setColor(Color.GREEN);
      g.fillOval(200,100,100,100); //Circle at (200,100), l=100, w=100

  }
// main() method to execute. JUST CREATE AN OBJECT OF THE CLASS
  public static void main(String args[])
  { RectOval ro = new RectOval(); // object name RectOval
  }
```

```
}
```

1.3 Exercises

Concept Understanding

Note: These questions are to test your understanding of concepts. Some of them may need some exploration to answer them.

1. List five real-world applications that you think can be managed, controlled, and communicated by computer programs.

2. Explain a couple of differences between compilers and interpreters.

3. A Java program consists of one or more coding blocks. What is the name of the block that every Java program needs to execute?

4. Is the coding block "main()" required to all Java programs? If not, why not, in what cases? Is it possible to change the name "main"?

5. The following program has five syntax errors. Identify them. Copy this into an IDE, compile and run by fixing these syntax errors.

```
public class StarBox

{ public static void main(String args[]) {

    System.out.println("*                    *");
    System.out.println("*                    *");
    System.out.println("*                    *);
    System.out.println("*                    *");
    system.out.println("*                    *")
    System.out.Println("*                    *");
    System.out.println("*                    *");


}
```

Programming

6. Write a program to print your name, email address, and phone number on three lines.

7. Write a program to print your initials (or a robot or a house or any figure of your choice) using one or more special characters (like *, #, @, or &). You could use graph paper to design your initials. For example, NSR is

```
*****              ***        *************        *************
*** **             ***        *************        *************
***   **           ***        ***                  ***       **
***     **         ***        ***                  ***       **
***      **        ***        ***                  ***       **
***       **       ***        ***                  ***       **
***        **      ***        *************        *************
***         **     ***        *************        *************
***          **    ***                  ***        *****
***           **   ***                  ***        **  ***
***            **  ***                  ***        **    ***
***             ** ***        *************        **     ***
***              ** *****     *************        **      ***
```

8. Write a program to print 45, 56, 98, and their sum. Label each output value.

9. Write a program to draw x- and y- axes.

10. Write a program to draw three circles of different sizes, from smaller to the largest, in two ways: a) vertically one below the other, and b) concentric – smallest the inner-most circle to the largest as the outer-most circle. Fill all the circles with different colors.

11. Write a program for #3 above with graphics this time. The image could be your initials, a robot, a snowman, a house, or any figure you can think of. Your grade for this project depends on the complexity of the image. It should have at least two figures and two colors.

12. [Self Study, not introduced but you should understand the following questions]

a. The outcome of successful compiling a java program, MyFirstDemo.java, is the file _____, which is a Java bytecode.

b. Java bytecode is executed in _____.

c. Java Virtual Machine is a virtual operating system and there is only one open source implementation available [True/False].

Answer:

a. MyFirstDemo.class

b. JVM (Java Virtual Machine)

c. False since there are numerous implementations. Some of the implementations can be found in http://en.wikipedia.org/wiki/List_of_Java_virtual_machines

1.4 What did you learn?

1. Writing the "class" statement

2. Writing the "main" method

3. Writing System.out.println("character string");

4. Matching open and close brackets "{}" and open and close parentheses "()".

5. Closing statements with semicolon ";"

6. Creating some simple graphics designs.

Data Types,
Assignment, Output

2.1 Introduction

Computer software is a collection of instructions, more specifically a sequence of computer language-specific instructions. Development of a software program is basically solving problems. A problem, if not small, can be decomposed into smaller sub-problems, each of which can in turn be decomposed into smaller problems that will then be manageable. Thus, programmers take care of a small problem at a time.

.2.1.1 Data Types and Identifiers

Let us consider a small problem: A student has a name ("John"), a major ("CS"), and a GPA (3.75). Let us write a small program to just give these values to a Java program and make the program print them. Let us give a name to this small program. Let us call it StudentInfo. We can give the program these values in three different ways:

- Entering the values in the program itself

- Entering the values from the keyboard like you would do in entering passwords, filling out forms, etc.

- Entering the values in a database and reading them from the database. This is how all of large data sets are processed (like your information in your college computer system).

Let us start with the first option, which is the easiest to do at this point. Data for a computer program are similar to appliances and objects to a house: You need to "reserve" appropriate spaces for different appliances - larger space for a refrigerator, smaller space for a dishwasher, and even smaller space for a microwave. Similarly, a decimal number (like 3.5) needs a larger space than an integer (like 23), and even a smaller space for a character (like 'A'). Just like we would tell a builder to build appropriate spaces for the appliances, we need to tell the Java compiler to reserve spaces for different data types (decimal, integers, characters, etc.). We need to identify each of these spaces by their names, like we use room numbers for your classrooms. You find the right classroom by the room number. Similarly locations for these storage spaces are identified by the names we give them. The steps to do all this are:

- Choose names for each of the values: We need a variable name to store "John". Let us call it *name*. Let us use *major* to store "CS" and *gpa* to store 3.75.

- Determine the data types that you want to use for each of the variable names: "John" is a string of characters or a word. So, its type is String. "CS" is also a word, so its type is String as well. 3.75 is a decimal. Its type is double.

- Write the Java statements to define these variables:

```
String name, major;
double gpa;
```

What happens when you execute the definition statements?

- The compiler allocates spaces in the main memory with sizes appropriate to the type of the variable

- The compiler identifies those memory spaces by the corresponding variable names.

How do we put the values in these memory spaces?

- These are called assignment statements. They are used to "assign" the values to the variables and store those values in the memory spaces allocated to each of the variables.

- The Java statements are

```
name = "John";

major = "CS";

gpa = 3.75;
```

Observe that string values are in double quotes and numbers do not have any quotes. Values are on the right side of the equal sign and variables are on the left side of the equal sign. The right-side values are assigned to the left-side variables and those values are stored in the corresponding memory spaces already allocated to them.

In java, there are pre-defined primitive data types, each of which has its own size of memory space. The primitive data types are

char, boolean, byte, short, int, long, float, and *double*

Each primitive type variable holds a single value in a single memory space. *String* type is not a primitive type as it points (references) to several values (several characters). In the `StudentInfo.java`, *name* and *major* are non-primitive and *gpa* is primitive type. A variable is declared in the following form:

type variable;

Table 2.1: Values Permitted to Typed Variables

Type	Storage	Min Value	Max Value
boolean	8 bits	false or true	
byte	8 bits	-128	127
short	16 bits	-32,768	32,767
char	16 bits	0	65,353
int	32 bits	-2,147,483,648	2,147,483,647
long	64 bits	-9×10^{18}	9×10^{18}
float	32 bits	$+/- 3.4 \times 10^{38}$ with 7 significant digits	
double	64 bits	$+/- 1.7 \times 10^{308}$ with 15 significant digits	

Selecting a name for an identifier:

- Should begin with an alphabet or underscore (_), or $ sign

- Can have a combination of digits and alphabets

- Alphabets could be either upper-case or lower-case

- Java is case-sensitive, like passwords: 'A' is different from 'a', for example. "America" is different from "america". Pay special attention to the cases of the alphabets

- Multiple-word names are generally connected by underscores

- It is Java convention to start every word after the first with a capital letter. For example, "weekly salary" could be named as *weeklySalary* or *weekly_Salary*

- It is Java convention to start the name of a class by a capital letter

- NO BLANK SPACES ARE ALLOWED IN IDENTIFIERS

Any Additional Data Type?	
Challenge	We may be able to use a class as a variable. For example, variable String is a class already defined and provided by jdk. In many other cases, we define classes and use them as variables, which are called user-defined variables. User-defined variables will be discussed later.

2.2 Expressions

Most of the problems we encounter in real life involve arithmetic calculations. So, we need to study the arithmetic operators and their order of operations. You are familiar with the precedence of arithmetic operators, but here is a reminder, listed in the order of priority from the highest to the lowest:

1. Parentheses (in Java, we use only parentheses () in arithmetic expressions)

2. Multiplication (*) and divisions (/ and %. % operator gives the remainder. 13%5 will give us 3 as when you divide 13 by 5, you will get 3 as the remainder)

3. Additions (+ and ++) and subtractions (- and --).

NOTE:

1. If you have more than one operator of the same level, the order is left-to-right.

2. There is no exponentiation operator in Java.

3. ++ is an increment operator. It increases the value of the variable by one. If x=5, x++ will increment x value by one. After executing x++; statement, the value of x will be 6. Similarly, -- is a decrement operator, which decrements the value by one.

4. x++ is called the post-increment. If we use x++ in a print statement, it will print 5 first and then will increment x to 6. Similarly, ++x is a pre-increment operator. If you have ++x in a print statement, it will first increment x to 6 and then print 6.

Examples:

1. 4+3*5 is 4+15 = 19 (multiplication before addition)

2. (4+3)*5 is 7*5 = 35 (parentheses before multiplication)

3. 4/2-3*5 + 3%4 = 2-15+3 = -10 (3%4 is the remainder when 3 is divided by 4)

4. 4/(2-3)*5+3%4 = 4/(-1)*5+3%4 = -4*5 + 3 %4 = -20 + 3 = -17

5. 10/4 = 2 (Both 10 and 4 in the expression 10/4 are integers – no decimal point. Java returns only the integer quotient. When you divide 10 by 4, the quotient is 2 and remainder is 2. So, 10/4 is 2, 10%3 is 1, 10.0/3 = 3.333333333, and 10/3.0 is also 3.33333333. **10/3 =3 is an integer division and will truncate the decimal part**)

6. If x=5 and y=x++, then y will be 5 and then x becomes 6 (post-increment). If we now execute z=++x, x will change to 7 first (pre-increment) and then that value will be assigned to z. So, z will be 7 also. – – will work the same way.

7. If a = 2, b=-3, and c = 4.0, evaluate each of the following (Note: If there is no decimal point, it is an integer value)
   a. 4*b/a
   b. 4*b/c
   c. a+c+2*a/b
   d. a++ +5
   e. ++a +5

8. if test1 = 80, test2 = 90, and test3 = 70, evaluate
   a. test1+test2+test3/3
   b. test1+test2+test3/3.0
   c. (test1+test2+test3)/3
   d. (test1+test2+test3)/3.0

9. Write a program to test each of the sections in problem #6.

10. Write a program to test each of the sections in problem #7.

11. Write a program to test each of the sections in problem #8.

The evaluation rule of expressions is summarized in the following table:

Table 2.2: Precedence of Operators

Priority	Operators	Operation	Association
1	[ ]	Array index	left
	( )	Method call	
	.	(dot notation) member access	
2	++	Pre- or post- increment	right
	--	Pre- or post- decrement	
	+ -	Unary plus, minus	
	~	Bitwise NOT	
	!	Boolean (logical) NOT	
	(type)	Type case	
	new	Object creation	
3	* / %	Multiplication, division, remainder	left
4	+ -	Addition, subtraction	left
	+	String concatenation	
5	<<	Signed bit shift left	
	>>	Signed bit shift right	
	>>>	Unsigned bit shift right	
6	< <=	Less than, less than or equal to	left
	<= >=	Greater than, greater than or equal to	
	instanceof	Reference test	
7	==	Equal to	left
	!=	Not equal to	
8	&	Bitwise AND	left
	&	Boolean (logical) AND	
9	^	Bitwise XOR	left
	^	Boolean (logical) XOR	
10	|	Bitwise OR	
	|	Boolean (logical) OR	
11	&&	Boolean (logical) AND	left
12	||	Boolean (logical) OR	left
13	? :	Conditional	right
14	=	Assignment	right
	*= /= += -= %= <<= >>= >>>= &= ^= !=	Combinated assignment (operation and assignment)	

Values Permitted to Typed Variables		
More to Know	— Consider Table 2.1 and recall the operator ++ illustrated in Example 0 above.	
	Given	Suppose an integer variable x is initialized to hold 2147483647.
	Question	What is the minimum and maximum values that can be held in an integer variable?
	Challenge	Answer the following: • The value held in the variable x after ++x • Continually, --x, after that the value held in the variable x Explain why the value in the first bullet is negative. Explain why the value in the second bullet is positive.

2.3 Assignment Statement

Almost every application will have some kind of calculations. For example, if we calculate the average of three grades, we need to store that value in some memory location. That is done in a variable. If we use gradeAve to store this average, then we can write

```
gradeAve = (test1+test2+test3)/3;
```

Here we are assigning the value of (test1+test2+test3)/3 to the variable gradeAve. This is an assignment statement where we assign the value on the right side of the equal sign to the <u>variable</u> on the left side of the equal sign. In Java, the assignment statement is written as below:

type variable = constant value or expression of the type of the variable;

type on the left is needed only if the variable was not defined (created) before this statement.

Example 1: Create an integer variable test1 and assign 95.

This can be done in two ways:

#1. Two-step method (observe the semicolons at the end of the statements)

```
int test1;
test1 = 95;
```

#2 Single-step method (you do this if you already know the value of the variable, to initialize)

```
int test1 = 95;
```

12.   Create the variable pay of type double and then assign it $23,078.75.

```
double pay;
pay = 23078.75; // observe we cannot use $ and comma in numbers
```

13. Weekly salary is calculated by multiplying the number of hours worked and rate of pay. We will include all the statements needed for this expression. We will assign some values to the variables to make sense. Observe when we define more than one variable of the same type, we can do so in a single statement by separating the variables by commas and of course semicolon at the end of the statement. We can assign the expression as below:

```
double hours=25.5, payRate=15.75, weeklySalary;
weeklySalary = hours*payRate;
```

As programming logic is developed and java statements are coded, the whole coding list should be stored in a file and the file name should be the same as the class name. If the class name is StudentInfo, then the file name of that class should be StudentInfo.java.

Example 1: Here is the program.

Coding List 2.1: StudentInfo.java

```
/* Author:
 * Date:
 * Input: none
 * Output: This program prints a student information. Two escape keys are
 * used: "\t" to insert a tab and "\n" to insert a new line.
 */


public class StudentInfo
{ // no variables for the class StudentInfo

  public static void main (String[] args) {
// variables declaration and initialization
     String name;
     name = "John";
// together, it can be rewritten:
// String name = "John";

     String major = "CS";  // declaration with initialization
     double gpa = 3.75;

// display the variables
     System.out.println (name);
     System.out.println (major);
     System.out.println (gpa);
     System.out.println ("----------------------------------------");
```

```java
// we are printing lines of dashes to separate different outputs
// another way of display is to print data on the same line"
    System.out.println (name + "\t" + major + "\t" + gpa);
    System.out.println("-------------------------------------");

// now let us use the escape character "\t" to tab data
// also, let us label the data. Observe that labels are in quotes
    System.out.println("Name: "+name +"\tMajor: "+major +"\tGPA="+gpa);
    System.out.println("--------------------------------------------");

// now, we will use "\n" escape key to insert returns. We will place
// them instead of "\t". Data will be displayed on different lines.
    System.out.println("Name: "+name +"\nMajor: "+major +"\nGPA="+gpa);


    }
}
```

```
Here is the output of the program:
John
CS
3.75
-------------------------------------
John    CS      3.75
-------------------------------------
Name: John      Major: CS       GPA=3.75
-------------------------------------
Name: John
Major: CS
GPA=3.75
```

Dot Notation for Method of Class

As discussed so far, it is known that our coding describes a sequence of Java instructions. Note that Java instructions are available at the website, http://docs.oracle.com/javase/6/docs/api/. An instruction can be in the form, object.method() or Class.method(). There are dots (.) in between the concepts which are hierarchically organized. For example, look up the class Scanner and get some idea from the website: http://docs.oracle.com/javase/1.5.0/docs/api/java/util/Scanner.html

and System fromhttp://docs.oracle.com/javase/1.5.0/docs/api/java/lang/System.html

and http://docs.oracle.com/javase/1.5.0/docs/api/java/io/PrintStream.html

(the latter URL can be accessed by clicking the field "in" from the former URL).

Challenge

2.4 Input from the keyboard

There are several occasions in which we need to enter data from the keyboard. Java allows us to do so. Let us create an object called `keyboard` which will point to the keyboard of your computer. Here is how such an object can be created to point to the keyboard:

How To Create an Object of Keyboard		
Tip		Challenge: • An object keyboard is instantiated from the class Scanner. • The keyboard is denoted by the object called System.in.
		`Scanner keyboard = new Scanner (System.in);`
	Remark	First, consider the right hand side of the above statement. 1. An operator 'new' is used to instantiate an object. 2. The class **Scanner** is explained in http://docs.oracle.com/javase/7/docs/api/java/util/Scanner.html 3. Scanner() looks like a function, which is particularly called a constructor in Java. 4. Scanner() takes an input 'System.in' and returns an object that can scan the keyboard. 5. The input stream object, **System.in** is explained in http://docs.oracle.com/javase/7/docs/api/java/lang/System.html#in
		Note: we can call the Scanner object with any name we want. Here we have called it keyboard to explicitly mean what the object is. Some people call it scan, kb, scn, etc.
		The returned object is then assigned to the right hand side of the above statement. • The variable keyboard, which is an object of System.in, can invoke any methods defined in the class Scanner. • Some of the methods defined in Scanner are `nextDouble()` and `nextInt()`. Notice capital I and capital D in them.

A few of the methods from `Scanner` and `System.out` are used in the `StudentInfo2` class. Reading methods `nextLine()` and `nextDouble()` from Scanner class and output methods `println()` and `print()` from `System` class are used in the following examples.

The method `keyboard.nextLine()` is an instruction that can scan to read the text of the object `keyboard`. `System.out.println(xx)` is an instruction that can return (display) the value of *xx* on the terminal. The standard output (`System.out`) is the computer terminal. In System.out.println(*xx*), where *xx* can be either an atomic value (like 25) or an expression (like hours*payRate). For example,

```
    System.out.println(gpa);   // gpa is a single value
```

or

```
    System.out.println (name + " in " + major + " earns " + gpa);
```

In the latter case, there is a special symbol '+' sign, which is a concatenator. Two given strings can be concatenated (attached together) with a +. For example, `System.out.println(name + major)` displays `MercyCS` where the two variables `name` and `major` hold respectively "Mercy" and "CS". The + sign is not only a concatenator but also a addition operator. **If both the operands are numbers, the + sign will be an addition operator.** For example, `System.out.println(gpa + bonus)` displays 3.95 where the two variables `gpa` and `bonus` hold respectively 3.75 and 0.2. If a `String` value appears before the sum of two numbers, then all the values will be treated as String for printing. `System.out.println(gpa+bonus+major);` will print 3.95CS after adding 3.75 and 0.2. If you have "major" first as in `System.out.println(major+gpa+bonus);`, it will print CS3.750.2.

Example 2: Here is the code to illustrate it:

Coding List 2.2: PrintTest.java

```
/* Author:
 * Date:
 * Input: none
 * Output: This program is again showing how concatenation effects printing
 * numbers and strings.
 */
public class PrintTest
{ public static void main(String args[])
  { double gpa=3.75, bonus=0.2;
    String major="CS";
    System.out.println(gpa+bonus+major);
    System.out.println(major+gpa+bonus);
  }
}Here is the output of the program:
3.95CS
CS3.750.2
```

What is the Output?		
Example	What about the output of the following statement if name, major, gpa hold respectively "Mercy", "CS", 3.75? System.out.println (name + " in " + major + " earns " + gpa);	
	Answer	Mercy in CS earns 3.75.

As mentioned earlier, a better way of getting values into the variables name, major, and gpa is to make the user enter those values from the keyboard. You have used many applications where you will be asked (prompted) to enter your name, or password, or phone number, etc. A value read can be assigned to a variable, which means that the value can be stored in memory and accessed by the label to the memory. The label is called a variable.

Value assignment is made to variables name, major, and gpa as well. As an extension of StudentInfo, we want to read user inputs from the keyboard in the class StudentInfo2. StudentInfo2 is to get the values entered at the keyboard and store them in the variables. The statements needed for reading from the keyboard are numbered in the program below. The program will print these stored values, as in StudentInfo program.

Example 3:

Coding List 2.3: StudentInfo2.java

```
/**
 * Author:
 * Date:
 * Input: Read name, gpa, and major from keyboard.
     #1 We need to import the Scanner class
     #2 We need to create an object of Scanner (kb) to access keyboard
     #3 We need to get the values through kb
     kb.nextLine() will get everything entered on a line, including spaces
     kb.next() will receive only the first word entered
     kb.nextInt() is for reading integers
     kb.nextDouble() is for reading double numbers
 * Output: display the student info
 */
1   import java.util.Scanner; // #1 needed to read from keyboard
2   public class StudentInfo2
{

    // no variables for the class StudentInfo2


3   public static void main (String[] args) {
        // variables declared
4       String name;
5       String major;
6       double gpa;


        // use an object of the class provided by jdk
7       Scanner kb; // "kb" to denote "keyboard"
```

```
8       kb = new Scanner(System.in);
9       // together, it can be rewritten as
        // Scanner kb = new Scanner (System.in);   // #2


// To read user input, we need to ask the user to enter value:
10      System.out.println ("Enter your name: ");


   // As user enters, we should take it and hold it in a variable
11      name = kb.nextLine();   // #3


        // Repeat these instructions for major and gpa:
12      System.out.println ("Enter your major: ");
13      major = kb.nextLine();
14      System.out.println ("Enter your gpa: ");
15      gpa = kb.nextDouble();


        // display the variables
16      System.out.println (name);
17      System.out.println (major);
18      System.out.println (gpa);


   // another way of display using an escape character tab, "\t" REMOVE THIS
19      System.out.println (name + " in " + major + " earns " + gpa);
    }
}


Here is the output:
Enter your name:
Linda Smith
Enter your major:
math
Enter your gpa:
3.9
Linda Smith
math
3.9
Linda Smith in math earns 3.9
```

Example 4: Here is the program which tests the concepts discussed above on arithmetic operations:

Coding List 2.4: Operators.java

```java
/* Author:
 * Date:
 * Input: none
 * Output: This program tests the use of ++ operator. -- will be similar
 * It also shows how combining string and numbers with concatenation works.
 */

public class Operators
{
  public static void main(String args[]){
    int a = 5;
    System.out.println("a++ is "+ a++);
    System.out.println("a after a++ is "+ a);
    System.out.println("++a is "+ ++a);
    System.out.println("a after ++a is "+ a);
    int b = a++ +5;
    System.out.println(" b="+b);
    System.out.println(a);

    b = ++a +5;
    System.out.println(" b="+b);
    System.out.println(a);

    String name="Mercy", major = "CS";
    double gpa=3.75, bonus=0.2;

    System.out.println(name +major+gpa);
    System.out.println(name +bonus+gpa);
    System.out.println(name + (bonus+gpa));

  }
}
```

```
Here is the output:
a++ is 5
a after a++ is 6
++a is 7
a after ++a is 7
b=12
8
b=14
9
MercyCS3.75
Mercy0.23.75
Mercy3.95
```

Example 5: Here is an example of graphics. Here we will draw a square. We will read the coordinates of the left-top corner of the square (rectangle) and the length (length and width are the same for a square) of the side of the square. This part of getting the values from the keyboard is additional to what we did in Chapter 1. So, the steps that we need to add new are:

1. Include `import java.util.Scanner;` statement to the import statements.
2. Create the Scanner object to access the keyboard by adding `Scanner kb = new Scanner(System.in);` to the class variable block just below the class line as shown below.
3. Define all variables (`int x1, y1, len;`) that need to be used in the program in this class variables block.
4. Include the reading statements in the class constructor. We had not touched this until now. We are going to add all the statements needed to read the values from the keyboard. Here is the constructor:

```
public SquareGraphics()
   { System.out.println("Enter x1,y1,length, and width. press enter
after each value:");
     x1 = kb.nextInt();
     y1 = kb.nextInt();
     len = kb.nextInt();

     setTitle("Introduction to Graphics");
     setSize(1800,1200);
     setVisible(true);
     setDefaultCloseOperation(EXIT_ON_CLOSE);
   }
```

Here is the program with that constructor:

Coding List 2.5: SquareGraphics.java

```
/* Author:
 * Date:
 * Input: Receives the coordinates of the top-left
 * corner and the length=width values from the keyboard
 * Output: Will draw a square with the input data.
 */
import java.awt.Graphics;
import java.awt.Color;
import javax.swing.JFrame;
import java.util.Scanner;

public class SquareGraphics extends JFrame
{ Scanner kb = new Scanner(System.in);
  int x1, y1, len;

  public SquareGraphics()
  { System.out.println("Enter x1,y1,and side length. Press enter after each
value:");
    x1 = kb.nextInt();
    y1 = kb.nextInt();
    len = kb.nextInt();

    setTitle("Introduction to Graphics");
    setSize(1800,1200);
```

```
    setVisible(true);
    setDefaultCloseOperation(EXIT_ON_CLOSE);
  }

  public void paint(Graphics g)
  { g.setColor(new Color(234,231,231)); //234, 231, 231
    g.fillRect(0,0,1800,1200);

    g.setColor(Color.RED);
    g.fillRect(x1,y1,len,len);

  }

  public static void main(String args[])
  {
      SquareGraphics sg = new SquareGraphics(); }
}
```

```
Here is the output:
Enter x1,y1,and side length. Press enter after each value:
100
100
500
```

What did you learn?

- What data types can you use?

- What is the implication of declaring a type for a variable?

- If primitive data types are provided, what other types would be available or definable?

- Is there any complex data type provided by jdk, although not defined by you? What is it? How can you learn about it?

- Is the precedence of arithmetic operations in Java programming the same as the one in mathematics?

Type Conversion As Value Assignment		
	Question: Can any value be assignment to a variable of any type? Remember that data type will determine the size of the memory allocated to that variable. For example, can an integer be assigned to a double type variable? Can a double value be assigned to an integer variable? If not, explain why not? If it is possible, how?	

More to Know	Answer	There are three ways of converting data from one type to another. Those three ways take place when (1) an assignment is made, (2) a computation is preformed, (3) a data type is casted:
		
		 • When a value is assigned, for example
		
		 `int homework1 = 4;`
		
		 `double homework;`
		
		 `homework = homework1;`
		
		 In this case, the variable `homework` holds 4.0.
		
		 A double requires more space than an int. So we can assign an integer value (4) to a double variable and the value becomes double indicated by 4.0. On the other hand, if a double value is assigned to an int variable (with not enough space), "loss of precision" error will be generated.
		
		 • When a computation is performed, for example
		 `int homework1 = 4;`
		
		 `int homework2 = 3;`
		
		 `double average;`
		
		 `average = (homework1 + homework2) / 2;`
		
		 `homework = homework1;`
		
		 In this case, the variable `average` holds 3.0 as the right is an integer division (all the quantities are integers). However, if the variable average is declared as int, what will average hold?
		
		 • When a value is casted, for example

```
        average = (double) (homework1 + homework2) / 2;
```

In this case, the variable average holds 3.5 as the numerator will be a double.

- We can make an expression double by making one of the numbers double: we can change 2 in the denominator to 2.0, for example. Or we can cast one of them or the expression as above.

Challenge

Consider the following two cases:

Widening Conversion	Narrowing Conversion

`int homework1 = 4;`
 `double homework;`
 `homework = homework1;`
	`double homework1 = 4.0;`
	 `int homework;`
	 `homework = homework1;`

- Is a widening conversion valid?
- Is a narrowing conversion invalid? If so, why?

2.5 Exercises

Concept Understanding

1.   Consider the following code segment.

```
System.out.println("11+3= " + 11 + 3);

System.out.println("11+3= " + (11 + 3));

System.out.println("11/3= " + 11/3);

System.out.println("11%3= " + 11%3);

total++;

System.out.println("total++ =" + total);

total += ++total;

System.out.println("total += ++total => " + total);

total += another++;

System.out.println("total += another++ = " + total +
                            "\t\t another = " + another);
```

What is the output for each print statement? Explain why and how the output is obtained for each line of the coding list.

2.   Consider an integer variable called pi.

   a.   What is the range of integer values for the size of memory allocated for pi.

b. Suppose that a statement assigns the value 21475000000 to pi. Verify this by printing pi value.

c. Suppose you assign 2147483647 to pi. What happens if you keep increasing pi value?

3. Check out the web page https://en.wikipedia.org/wiki/Buffer_overflow and understand the concept of buffer overflow.

a. Does it occur in Java? Explain.

b. Suppose there is a programming language that does not allow to restrict the size of variable values. Is buffer overflow possible? Explain.

Programming

4. Recall Q1 in Concept Understanding above. Verify the following in a Java program:
   a. Define two integers pip and pin.
   b. Assign 2147483647 to pip and -22147483648 to pin
   c. Increase pip by 1 and decrease pin by 1
   d. Print pip and pin

5. Recall Q2 above. Write Pi.java code to verify the concepts. However, Java Native Interface (JNI) is not safe. Read the webpage http://seclists.org/vuln-dev/2002/jun/357. Therefore, is Java safe because the language restricts the size of the variables or because JVM manages Java?

6. Write a Java program that will calculate the sum and average of input numbers. The program should ask a user to enter the scores of 3 tests. Then, it should return the sum and the average of those input scores. A sample run in command-line is as follows:

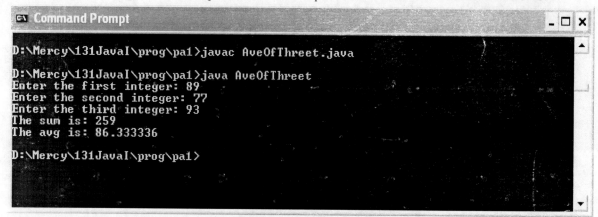

You could also use an IDE for any of these problems.

7. Write a program to calculate the batting average (number of hits / number at bat) of a baseball player. You should read the name of the player, number at bat, and the number of hits from the keyboard. You should prompt the user to enter the data at the keyboard. Print all the data in a sentence as below:

XXX had XXX hits in XXX at-bats for an average of XXX.

8. John has four $10 bills, three $5 bills, three quarters, seven dimes, 13 nickels, and 17 pennies. Write a program to calculate the total value of his amount in pennies. Print all the denominations and the total number of pennies.

9. Rewrite #4 to receive all the denomination values from the keyboard.

10. Write a program to read integer values into the variables x and y. Print x and y. Now, switch the values of x and y: now x must have the previous y value and y must have the previous x value. Print x and y.

11. Sometimes planes face head winds (wind blowing against the plane) which will slow them down and sometimes they face tail winds (wind blowing in the direction of the plane) which speed up the planes. Winds could change the speeds of automobiles, boats, and planes. If the real ground speed of a plane is rSpeed (in the absence of any wind), wind speed is wSpeed, time of travel is tTravel, and distance travelled is dTravel, the formula connecting them is

    dTravel = (rSpeed ± wSpeed)*tTravel.

    We can calculate any of these quantities given the values of the others. Generally our interest will be how much time it takes to reach the destination. So, write a program to calculate the tTravel give the values of dTravel, rSpeed, and wSpeed. Read the values from the keyboard.

12. Maggi buys two pants for $37.50 each and three blouses for $21.50 each. Calculate the subtotal and then add 7.5% sales tax. Print the details with the total purchase cost.

13. Rewrite #7 to read all the values from the keyboard.`

14. The area of a right triangle is (1/2)*base*height. Read the base and the height in inches from the keyboard. Print the base, height, and area of the triangle with proper labels and units.

15. Body Mass Index (BMI) is a number calculated from a person's weight and height. BMI is a fairly reliable indicator of body fatness for most people. The formula for calculating BMI is BMI= (weight in pounds * 703)/(height in inches)^2. Write a program to accept the weight and height of a user, calculate his/her BMI and output all the results to the monitor.

16. Write a program to accept the slope and y-intercept of a straight line and print the equation of the straight line in y=mx+b format.

17. Do you know what mileage (miles per gallon, mpg) your car gives? Write a program that gives the user the mileage of a car given the distance travelled and number of gallons used. (mpg = distance in miles/number of gallons).

18. Write a program to draw Olympic rings. This time the program should ask for the radius of the rings and draw the rings of that size. Note: you could check the colors of the rings on the Web.

19. Write a program to draw a triangle. It should ask for the coordinates of three points and draw the lines to form the triangle.

20. Consider bank accounts in a banking system. Each bank account has a balance at certain point in time. The balance can increase as more money is deposited, or decrease if money is withdrawn. Write a program to accept a deposit (positive number) amount or a withdrawal (negative number) amount. Read the amount from the keyboard by prompting appropriately. Assume that the initial balance in the account is $250.39.

21. We all know Eistein's equation $E = mc^2$. It is one of the most simple and most famous equations. It is simply amazing that this equation links three disparate entities: energy (in Joules J), mass (in kilograms kg), and speed of light (in meters per sec m/s, 3×10^8 m/s)! It tells how mass is converted to energy by a factor of the square of the speed of light. For example, you will spend about 1 J of energy to lift a cantaloupe above your head. 1 kg of mass will produce 9×10^{16} J of energy. Can you imagine how enormous this energy is? Now think of all the bombs. Write a program to receive mass from the keyboard and print the value of E. Let us not be very scientific about the units. You can enter any numbers to test the program. Print the units with the values.

22. Assume that you are carpeting your living room. Write a program to calculate the cost of carpeting a living room. The program should receive the length and width of a rectangular living room, the price per square foot of the carpet you selected. Also read the installation charge and the sales tax rate from the keyboard. Calculate the total cost for carpeting the living room. Print all the information with proper labels and units. (Example: L=25 ft, W=40 ft, price/sq ft = $3.50, installation charge = $100, sales tax rate = 7.5%. Area = 25x40=1000 sq ft. cost of carpet = 3.50x1000 = $3500. Sales tax = 3500x0.075 = $262.50, total cost = $3500+262.50+100=$3862.50).

23. Assume you bought a laptop based on monthly payments and a down payment. Write a program to calculate (a) interest paid at the end of the payment period, (b) annual percent rate (APR) that this interest amount will result in, and (c) the total finance charges. The program should read from the keyboard the price of the laptop (p), the down payment (d), monthly payment (m), and the number of months (n) of the loan period. (Example: Let p=$1285, d=$60, m=$55, n=24. (a) Amount of loan over 24 months = price – down payment = 1285-60 = $1225. Interest paid = amount paid – the loan amount = (24*55) – 1225 = 1320-1225=$95. (b) interest/price =95/1285=0.074, APR=7.4%. (c) Finance charge = price + interest = 1285+95=$1380)

Conditional Statements

3.1 Introduction

We make decisions everyday – whether to take an umbrella or not depending on whether it will rain or not; whether to fly or drive depending on the distance; whether to give an 'A' grade or not depending the average grade. When we write programs to solve problems like this where decisions have to be made depending on a condition or a combination of conditions, we need Java instructions that will help us solve such problems. Java provides two instructions to solve such problems.

This chapter will describe how data (values) are computed and compared. The values, either read from user or given in code, can be computed and its result will then be stored or involved in a decision making process.

For example, students are evaluated by one or more scores with different weights. Suppose that there are midterm and final exams and 2 homework assignments. Two exams weigh 60% (30% each) and two homework assignments weigh 40% (20% each). Each number can be either stored in a memory variable or it can be computed directly without having to store. The advantage of storing in variables is that they can be reused later in the program. But, if no additional use is expected, it can be directly computed.

We will explain the following two cases: one with variables that can hold values, and another without.

3.1.1 Case for variables:

Consider the following statements:

```
System.out.print ("The scaled score is ");
System.out.println ((mid + finl)*0.3 + (hw1 + hw2)*0.2);
```

The second statement computes the scaled scores (30% is 0.3 and 20% is 0.2), and the result is not stored but displayed only. If we need the average grade later for either printing or for statistical analysis of the class performance, we need to recalculate with the same formula. By assigning the formula to a variable will save the average grade in the variable that can be accessed later. So, it is a good practice to assign formulas to variables.

Can we combine these two statements in one? The answer is in the coding list 3.1.

Another question: what about this?

```
System.out.println ("The scaled score is " + (mid + finl)*0.3 +
(hw1 + hw2)*0.2);
```

Explain what is displayed by the statement above.

Example 1:

Coding List 3.1: ComputeScores.java

```
/* Author:
 * Date:
 * Input: none
 * Output: This program illustrates the behavior of print statements
 * in calculating and printing in a print statement. Arithmetic
 * expressions have to be in parentheses for the calculation to happen.
 */

public class ComputeScores
{
    public static void main (String[] args) {
      // variables declared
      int mid, finl, hw1, hw2;

       // value assignment
       mid = 75;
       finl = 89;
       hw1 = 100; hw2 = 90;

       // compute and display without having to store
    System.out.println("Midterm ="+mid+"\tFinal ="+finl+"\tHW1=" +hw1+
"\tHW2=" +hw2+"\n");
7   System.out.print ("The scaled score is ");
8   System.out.println ((mid + finl)*0.3 + (hw1 + hw2)*0.2);

    }
}
```

Here is the output:

```
Midterm =75      Final =89         HW1=100 HW2=90

The scaled score is 87.19999999999999
```

The print statements in lines 7 and 8 can be rewritten in one statement as follows:

```
System.out.println ("The scaled score is " + ((mid + finl)*0.3 +
(hw1 + hw2)*0.2));
```

Now, let's convert the average grade (scaled score) to a letter grade. The conversion is made as follows:

A   for higher than or equal to 90

B   for higher than or equal to 80 and lower than 90

C   for higher than or equal to 70 and lower than 80

D   for higher than or equal to 60

F   otherwise

How can we express the F grade in English? We would say

If the average is less than 60 the letter grade is F.

Here, "If" is a condition. Some condition has to be satisfied to determine the letter grades. A condition is expressed over a relational operator (e.g., ==, !=, >, <, >=, <=) which can be evaluated to return a Boolean value (true or false). Conditional expressions can be connected among themselves by logical connectives (negation, conjunction, disjunction, etc.) and its evaluation returns a Boolean value. Examples are illustrated below.

Condition Statement			
	Relational Operator	**Example of a simple condition**	**Assuming that gpa is 3.5, the evaluation is**
	Equals == Not equal != Less than < Greater than > Greater than or equal >= less than or equal <=	(gpa == 3.5) (gpa != 3.5) (gpa < 3.5) (gpa > 3.5) (gpa >= 3.5) (gpa <= 3.5)	true false false false true true
	Logical Connector	**Example of 2 conditions connected by "AND"**	**assuming that gpa is 3.5 the evaluation is**
Example	Conjunction symbol: && is a logical AND like in grade >=80 && grade <90 for a B grade	(gpa > 3.5) && (gpa < 3.7)	false (The evaluation does not necessarily continue to the second condition since the first condition already becomes false and so without having to evaluate the second condition, the overall returning value is false.) For AND, both the conditions have to be true.

Disjunction symbol: || is a logical OR like in gpa >= 3.5 || income < 25000 for eligibility for a grant	(gpa >= 3.5) || (income <= 25000)	true (The evaluation does not necessarily continue to the second condition since the first condition already becomes true and so without having to evaluate the second condition, the overall returning value is true. For OR, the expression will be true if even one of the conditions is true. For AND, the expression is false if even one of the conditions is false. So, for AND, both the conditions must be true. For example for grade B, the average grade must be >=80 AND the average grade must be <90.)
Negation symbol: ! is a logical NOT like in !(gpa>3.5) to mean gpa is NOT greater than 3.5, it is actually equal to 3.5	!(gpa > 3.5)	true (Since the condition (gpa > 3.5) is false, its negation is gpa<=3.5. this is true)

Two values (in more general, two objects) can be checked for equality. It can be done by using the comparison operator == or by the methods equals() and compareTo(). The symbol == is an equality operator, which returns true if two numbers are identical (when values are objects, their references i.e. addresses must be pointing to the same object. This will be clearer when classes and objects are introduced.) String values should be compared with the method equals(). It returns "true" if the String values are identical. These methods will be introduced in Chapter 4. For more detailed explanation of the two comparison methods, equals() and compareTo() can be found at
http://docs.oracle.com/javase/tutorial/java/IandI/objectclass.html and
http://docs.oracle.com/javase/7/docs/api/java/lang/Comparable.html.

3.2 if...else Statement

Let us consider assigning 'A' grade. Let avgGrade be the variable holding the average grade of a student. Let letterGrade be the variable to hold the letter grade. So, we should assign 'A' grade to letterGrade if the avgGrade is 90.0 or above. This is a statement to make a decision. In a speaking language we would say "if the average grade is >=90.0, the letter grade is 'A'". The statement in Java is almost the same:

```
if (aveGrade >=90.0) letterGrade = 'A';
```

Observe that the condition goes inside the parentheses immediately after the word '*if*' and the action to be taken when the condition is *true* follows the closing parentheses. The above statement does not have the 'else' part of the `if...else` statement. 'else' part is optional. If we need it, we will use it. In the statement above, `avgGrade>=90.0` is the 'condition' and `letterGrade= 'A';` is the 'true block'.

Let us consider another example where we can use 'else' part: We want to determine the sales tax in two areas, Manhattan and Dobbs Ferry. The sales tax in Manhattan (assume Manhattan is `area =1`) is 8.875% and it is 7.675% in Dobbs Ferry (`area = 2`). If we use `salesTax` as the variable name for sales tax and `area` to determine the city, we can write the if...else statement as

```
if(area == 1)
    salesTax=0.0875;
else
  salesTax = 0.0765;
```

Here the condition is `area == 1`. Observe two = signs in the condition. So, we need to use == in a condition and = in an assignment statement. If the condition is true, it means area is Manhattan. So, the true block is `salesTax = 0.0875;`. Notice a single = sign in the assignment statement `salesTax=0.0875;`. Notice the semicolon to end just that statement. Observe also that there is no semicolon at the end of `if(area == 1)`. The reason is that the 'if' statement does not end there. It continues to the 'true block', 'else' part, and the 'false block'. If *area == 1* is not true, it is the 'else' part. In that case it will be Dobbs Ferry area ('else' just means that the area is not 1, so could be anything else, including 2) and the sales tax is 0.0765.

Now the question is the evaluation flow of `if ... else` code sequence.

Evaluation of { Block } Segment	

Challenge	Consider the following where areas 1 and 2 are explicitly checked:
	
	``
	if (area == 1)
	    salesTax = 0.0875;
	else if (area == 2)
	    salesTax = 0.0765;
	``
	
	Only one block will be executed: either the true block or the false block. One of the two blocks will be skipped.

	We could also have written two separate 'if' statements without the 'else' part:
	
	``
	if (area == 1)
	    salesTax = 0.0875;
	if (area == 2)
	    salesTax = 0.0765;
	``
	
	In this format, two conditions <u>have to be checked</u> whatever the condition is instead of only one when we use the 'else' part. Both the 'if' statements have to be executed in this format.

Let us now consider a statement which contains two conditions. Assume that we have to assign the letter grade 'B' if 80.0 <= average grade <90.0. This has two conditions combined in one Boolean expression. The first condition is 80.0 <= letter grade and the second condition is letter grade <90.0. In Java we need to spell them out separately. Also, both the conditions have to be satisfied. For example if the average grade is 83.5, then 80.0<=83.5 is true and 83.5<90.0 is also true. So this student will get the 'B' grade. If the average grade is 95.5, then 80.0<=95.5 is true but 95.5<90.0 is not true (it is false). This student's grade should not be 'B'. Such conditions where both conditions have to be true are connected by the logical operator && (AND). Hence the statement is

```
if (80.0 <= aveGrade && aveGrade <90.0)
    letterGrade = 'B';
```

Challenge	Question	
	What does 'else' mean for this condition?	
	Answer	It means that average grade is NOT between 80.0 and 90.0. It means that average grade is either <80.0 or >=90.0
	What is the statement for grade 'C'?	

Using 'else' parts will generally make statements more efficient. Look at the following program which calculates the letter grade of a student. Letter grades are found in two different ways: one with 'else' parts and another set with independent 'if' statements for each grade. You should count how many conditions will be checked for each format.

Example 2:

Coding List 3.2: Grades.java

```
/* Author:
 * Date:
 * Input: none
 * Output: This program illustrates the behavior of print statements
 * in calculating and printing in a print statement. Arithmetic
 * expressions have to be in parentheses for the calculation to happen.
 */

public class Grades {
  public static void main(String args[]){
      double aveGrade = 83.5;
      char letterGrade;

// first with if...else. We do not have compound Boolean expressions here
      System.out.println("Using if...else statements");
```

```
    System.out.println("--------------------------");
    if (aveGrade >= 90.0)
        letterGrade = 'A';
    else if(aveGrade >= 80.0) // else means aveGrade is less than 90
            letterGrade = 'B'; //so have to check if aveGrade is>=80
        else if (aveGrade >= 70.0)
                letterGrade = 'C';
            else if (aveGrade >= 60.0)
                    letterGrade = 'D';
                else
                    letterGrade = 'F';
// Observe, condition is checked only once if the avgrade is 'A', everything
// else is skipped.
// Now print the information - average grade and letter grade

    System.out.println("Average Grade = "+ aveGrade +"\tLetter Grade =
"+letterGrade);

// now with only if statements. Most of them need compound Boolean
// statements // Also, all the if statements will be checked even if
// avgGrade is >=90.0
    System.out.println("\n\nUsing only if statements");
    System.out.println("----------------------");
    if (aveGrade >=90.0)
        letterGrade = 'A';
    if ( aveGrade >= 80.0 && aveGrade < 90.0)
        letterGrade = 'B';
    if (aveGrade >=70.0 && aveGrade <80.0)
        letterGrade = 'C';
    if (aveGrade >=60.0 && aveGrade < 70.0)
        letterGrade = 'D';
    if (aveGrade < 60.0)
        letterGrade = 'F';
//How many conditions will be checked if the grade is 'A'?

// Now print the information - average grade and letter grade

    System.out.println("Average Grade = "+ aveGrade +"\tLetter Grade =
"+letterGrade);
    }
}
```

```
Here is the output. The outputs are the same for both the formats.

Using if...else statements
--------------------------
Average Grade = 83.5    Letter Grade = B


Using only if statements
----------------------
Average Grade = 83.5    Letter Grade = B
```

There are many applications where we need to check two conditions AND both the conditions have to be true for the compound expression to be true. We use the symbol '&&' (logical AND symbol) with two ampersands. But there are also several applications where one condition OR the other is to be true to make the compound expression true. Assume that military enlists soldiers who are older than 18 years and younger than 40 years. Another way of saying this is that the candidates younger than 18 OR older than 40 years are not eligible. So, we have to use a 'if' statement to check if age is less than 18 OR if age is greater than 40. Here is the statement:

```
if (age < 18 || age>40)
    System.out.println("You are not eligible to be enlisted.");
```

Here two conditions are combined by '||' (logical OR symbol). So, we have now added two new operators (&&, ||). These two are called Boolean operators. Now we have nine operators in all (+, ++, -, --, *, /, %, &&, ||). We need to pay attention to their priorities in evaluating expressions. The table below, borrowed from Chapter 2, shows the operators in Java in the order of precedence – from highest to lowest.

Priority	Operators	Operation	Association
1	[ ]	Array index	left
	( )	Method call	
	.	(dot notation) member access	
2	++	Pre- or post increment	right
	--	Pre- or post decrement	
	+ -	Unary plus, minus	
	~	Bitwise NOT	
	!	Boolean (logical) NOT	
	(type)	Type case	
	new	Object creation	
3	* / %	Multiplication, division, remainder	left
4	+ -	Addition, subtraction	left
	+	String concatenation	
5	<<	Signed bit shift left	
	>>	Signed bit shift right	
	>>>	Unsigned bit shift right	
6	< <=	Less than, less than or equal to	left
	<= >=	Greater than, greater than or equal to	
	instanceof	Reference test	
7	==	Equal to	left
	!=	Not equal to	
8	&	Bitwise AND	left
	&	Boolean (logical) AND	
9	^	Bitwise XOR	left
	^	Boolean (logical) XOR	
10	|	Bitwise OR	
	|	Boolean (logical) OR	
11	&&	Boolean (logical) AND	left
12	||	Boolean (logical) OR	left
13	? :	Conditional	right

	=	Assignment	
14	*= /= += -= %= <<= >>= >>>= &= ^= !=	Combined assignment (operation and assignment)	right

Example 4: One of the conditional operators is '?' operator which can be used when we compare exactly two values and choose one of the results. It is like if...else but only for two values.

5a. Consider finding the larger of two integer values in the variables num1 and num2. Let the variable to hold the larger number of the two numbers be max. The if...else statement will be

```
if(num1 >= num2)
    max = num1;
else
    max = num2;
```

Let us now use the ? operator:

```
max = (num1 >= num2 ? num1 : num2); // max=num1 if num1 is larger, else
max=num2
```

5b. Consider you are taking a course for pass or fail. You will receive the pass grade if the average >= 65 and fail grade otherwise. Study the following code:

```
String grade;
double ave = 70;
grade = (ave >= 65 ? "pass" : "fail");
System.out.println("Your grade is "+ grade);
```

What do you think will be printed?

3.3   switch...case Statement

Whenever we have multiple choices to make, we could use *switch* Java instruction, which is described in the following section. Of course, we could also use if...else statements. In some cases, using switch ... case will be more convenient. Is also limited to only certain values (we mostly use int and char).

We were discussing sales tax in different areas. Let us write a statement that will assign the appropriate sales tax rate depending on the area. Assume that area 1 has 8.675% sales tax, area 2 has 7.765%, area 3 is 4%, and all the other areas is 0%. Assume that you are writing an application that has to calculate sales tax at these areas.

We can use the `switch` ... `case` statement as area values are integers. This statement is used in the following format:

```
switch (variable) {
    case (value1) : {action1; action2; break; }
    case (value2) : {action3; ...; break: }
    ...
    default : action_n;
    }
```

NOTE:

1. 'variable' in the switch statement cannot be a decimal (float or double). Some of the types that can be used are byte, short, int, and char. String can also be used in versions 7E or later. We will mostly use int type.

2. If we have several values having the same action, we need to list each case separately. For example, if we number the months, 1 for January and 12 for December, then months 1, 3, 5, 7, 8, 10, and 12 have 31 days. Months 4, 6, 9, and 11 have 30 days. Month 2 could be either 28 days or 29 days depending on whether it is or is not a leap year. If the month variable is `month` and the number of days is `numDays` then the switch statement can be written as

Code for the switch statement

```
switch(month){
    case 1: case 3: case 5: case 7: case 8: case 10: case 12:
        System.out.println("There are 31 days in the month."); break;

    case 2: System.out.println("February has either 28 or 29 days depending on
whether it's a leap year or not"); break;

    case 4: case 6: case 9: case 11: System.out.println("The month has 30
days."); break;

    default: System.out.println("invalid month number!");
}
```

Example 3:
Here is the code in which this switch statement is used:

Coding List 3.3: SwitchMonths.java

```
/* Author:
 * Date:
 * Input: User enters the number of the month 1 - 12 from the keyboard.
 * Output: a message with the number of days of the month. If the user
 * number is <1 or >12, execution of the program will stop with an error
 * message. We have used a combination of if..else and switch..case.
```

```
*/
import java.util.Scanner;

public class SwitchMonths
{ public static void main(String args[])
  { int month;
    Scanner kb = new Scanner(System.in);

    System.out.print("Enter the number of the month for its days:");
    month = kb.nextInt();
  // check for the invalid entry
    if(month < 1 || month > 12)
      System.out.println("Invalid month number - execution terminated");
    else
  // if the entered number is valid, process for the number of days
      switch(month)
        { case 1: case 3: case 5: case 7: case 8: case 10: case 12:
            System.out.println("There are 31 days in the month."); break;

          case 2: System.out.println("February has either 28 or 29 days
depending on whether it's a leap year or not"); break;

          case 4: case 6: case 9: case 11: System.out.println("The month has 30
days."); break;

          default: System.out.println("invalid month number!");

        }
    }
}
```

Here is the output. We have tested all the four cases by executing the program four times.


```
Enter the number of the month for its days:5
There are 31 days in the month.
```


```
Enter the number of the month for its days:4
The month has 30 days.
```


```
Enter the number of the month for its days:2
February has either 28 or 29 days depending on whether it's a leap year or
not
```


```
Enter the number of the month for its days:20
Invalid month number - execution terminated
```

Quiz: Do we need this default case in the code above???

3.4 Comparison between `if...else` and `switch...case` statements

The conditional statements primarily available in Java programming language and discussed in this chapter are 1) if...else and 2) switch...case statements. Both statements can express conditions to make a decision in programming.

The structures of the two conditional statements are illustrated in the following table. if...else statement can be used to convert the scaled score into a letter grade. The conversion is made by checking the scaled value.

if ... else statement	switch ... case statement
```if(condition) {true block} else {false block}```	```switch (variable) { case value1: { block1 } case value2: { block2 } ... default: { default block } }```

Although both statements can express conditional statements, they can be used interchangeably, but not for all the cases of decision making. If the conditional variables are bound to discrete values, switch...case statements will be better than if...else statements. If the conditional variables are bound to a value range, if...else statements is better than switch...case statements. The efficiency of those two statements is different depending on conditional expressions. If a conditional expression requires overwhelmingly many steps of evaluation due to ample discrete values to consider, its switch...case statement may be so expensive. On the other hand, if the values to consider are very limited and discrete, a switch...case statement may run more efficiently than if...else statements which compare a value range.

With this in mind, consider an advanced utilization of the two conditional statements. The following challenges with a few special cases that may lead to advanced expression.

Utilizing Conditional Statement		
	If...then statement	Switch...case statement
Example	```// Segment (a) if (grade == 'A') System.out.println("Excelle nt"); else if (grade == 'B') System.out.println("Good"); else if (grade == 'C') System.out.println("Fair"); else System.out.println("Done");```	```// Segment (b) switch (grade) { case 'A': System.out.println("Excellent"); case 'B': System.out.println("Good"); case 'C': System.out.println("Fair"); default: System.out.println("Done"); }```

Challenge		```// Segment (c)```
		 ```if (java > 85) || (gpa >=```
		 ```3.5)```
		 ```System.out.println("Recomme```
		 ```nd");```
		 ```else```
		 ```System.out.println("Done");```
			```// Segment (d)```
			 ```System.out.print("Since you know " +```
			 ```language);```
			 ```switch (language) {```
			 ``` case "Prolog":```
			 ``` System.out.print(", so Artificial```
			 ```Intelligence");```
			 ``` case "C":```
			 ``` System.out.print(", so Deep System```
			 ```Controlling");```
			 ``` case "Java":```
			 ``` System.out.print(", so Object```
			 ```Oriented");```
			 ``` default: System.out.println(" and, so```
			 ```Done.");```
			 ```}```

Challenge	Question 1	Compare the segments (a) and (b) above. How are they similar and how are they different? Note that the conditional variable used in the example is finite and discrete. With that note, which one segment is more reasonable in terms of conditional variables? More precisely, which one segment is correct? Explain why?
	Question 2	Consider the segment (b) above. Note that for a specific grade value, e.g., grade is 'B', the statement returns not only 'Good' but also 'Fair' and 'Done', which is inaccurate. Fix it and explain how.
	Question 3	Consider the segment (c) above. Assume that the conditional variable gpa is already loaded in memory while java is not yet fetched. Is there any better expression if the if...else statement can be revised?

	Question 4	Assume that the segment (d) above wants to apply all cases. For example, the segment returns
		
		     Since you know C, so Deep System Controlling, so Object-Oriented and, so Done.
		
		 Compare the segments (b) and (d) above. Recall Question 2 can be fixed by adding the statement
		
		     ```break;```
		
		 Should this statement be applicable to the segment (d)? Explain why not if not.

Example 4:

Let us draw directional arrows in graphics. They could be pointing to east, west, north, and south. The user of the application will be able to choose one of these directions and the arrow will be drawn appropriately. Here is the program:

Coding List 3.4: DrawArrows.java

```
/* Author:
 * Date:
 * Input: User enters direction of the arrow from keyboard
 * Output: This program draws the appropriate arrow. The arrow is
 * is built with a rectangle and a triangle. It is easy to draw
 * the rectangle with drawRect() method. There is no such method
 * to draw a triangle. So, drawPolygon() method is used with two
 * arrays of x- and y- coordinates of the polygon. For a triangle,
 * we need 3 sides (3 points with coordinates). Some calculations
 * to place the two figures appropriately is needed.
 */

import java.awt.Graphics; // needed to draw graphics
import java.awt.Color;    // needed to use different colors
import javax.swing.JFrame;// needed to create the window
import java.util.Scanner; // to read user selection from keyboard

public class DrawArrows extends JFrame  // create your class
{ String response;
  public DrawArrows()          // set up the window in the constructo
  { Scanner kb = new Scanner(System.in);
    System.out.println("An arrow will be drawn. Which direction do you want
the arrow to point to: East, West, South, or North?");
    response = kb.next();

    setTitle("Directional Arrows");
    setSize(1800,1800);
    setVisible(true);
    setDefaultCloseOperation(EXIT_ON_CLOSE);
  }
  // THE paint() METHOD IS NEEDED TO DRAW GRAPHICS
    public void paint(Graphics g)
    {
      if(response.equals("east"))
      { g.setColor(Color.RED);
        g.drawRect(200,400, 500,100); // rectangle for the arrow
        // draw arrow tip - east, a triangle
        g.drawPolygon(new int[] {700,900,700}, new int[] {350,450,550}, 3);
      }
      else if(response.equals("south"))
      { g.setColor(Color.BLUE);
        g.drawRect(400,100, 100,500); // rectangle for the arrow
        //draw arrow tip - south
        g.drawPolygon(new int[] {350,450,550}, new int[] {600,800,600}, 3);
      }
      else if(response.equals("west"))
      { g.setColor(Color.GREEN);
        g.drawRect(400,400, 500,100); // rectangle for the arrow
        // draw arrow tip - west
```

```
        g.drawPolygon(new int[] {400,200,400}, new int[] {350,450,550}, 3);
      }
    else if(response.equals("north"))
    { g.setColor(Color.MAGENTA);
      g.drawRect(400,200, 100,500); // rectangle for the arrow
      // draw arrow tip - north
      g.drawPolygon(new int[] {350,450,550}, new int[] {200,100,200}, 3);
      }
  }
// main() method to execute. JUST CREATE AN OBJECT OF THE CLASS
  public static void main(String args[])
  {
    DrawArrows da = new DrawArrows();
  }
}
```

Here is the output. We have tested all the four cases by executing the
program four times.

An arrow will be drawn. Which direction do you want the arrow to point to:
East, West, South, or North?
east

Directional Arrows

Exercises

Concept Understanding

1. An application program may require the use of several predicates. Consider the following
    predicates that an application needs to use:

    (a==b)
    (b>c)
    (d<=5)

a. Form a condition of these three predicates in a conjunctive (connected in one condition) form.

b. Form a condition of the predicates in a disjunctive (separate conditions) form.

2. Consider a bank account. Write independent `if` statements to increase the interest rate by 1% if the balance is $1000 or more and by 0.05% otherwise. Assume that there are already values in the `balance` and `interestRate` variables.

3. Based on the precedence of operations, show the order of the following expression

```
if (total != top + bottom) inventoryError = true;
```

and explain each step in the order.

4. Write independent if statements for each of 'C', 'D, and 'F' grades.

5. Rewrite #2 by using 'if-else' statement as a single instruction.

6. Many stores display several racks of clothes, each rack of clothes having a fixed price. Assume rack 1 clothes are $16.75, rack 2 is $19.95, rack 3 is $45.95. If rack number is not 1, 2, or 3, you should print an error message. Use a `switch` statement.

7. Rewrite the month switch statement (Note #2 on page 40) using if-else combination.

8. Consider a code segment that returns the bonus commission. Assume that the variables `bonus`, and `sales` are declared as double type.

```
bonus = ((sales > 50000) ? sales*0.1 : sales*0.05);
```

Rewrite the above using if-else statement.

9. Consider the following code segments that determine whether a student is classified as "honors", "good", or "failed" based on the student's letter grade. Assume a simple letter grading system: A, B, and F only.

Rewrite each of the following two switch statements using if-else statements.

a. Switch statement with break

```
switch (grade) {
    case 'A': {
        category = "Honors";
        break;
    }
    case 'B': {
        category = "Good";
        break;
    }
    case 'F': {
        category = "Failed";
```

```
                break;
            }
        }
```

   b. Switch statement without Break

```
switch (grade) {
        case 'A': category = "Honors";
        case 'B': category = "Good";
        case 'F': category = "Failed";
    }
```

Discuss those two cases for a student whose grade is B. What category is the student classified?

Programming

10. Write a program to accept one of the characters 'm', 't', 'w', 'f', or 's' and print the weekday(s) that starts with that character.

11. As you know, some stores give 5% discount to senior citizens. If the customer is 65 years or older, that customer should receive a 5% discount. Write a program to receive the purchase price and age from the keyboard and print net purchase price.

12. The speed limit on many highways is 60 mph. Many GPS devices show the speed in red if we exceed the speed limit. Simulate it by a java program. Write a program to receive the speed from the keyboard and print "You have exceeded the speed limit of 60 mph by xxx miles." if the speed exceeds 60mph and "Your speed is within the speed limit" otherwise.

13. Some employers pay 1.5 times the hourly rate for overtime. For example, if an employee worked for 50 hours in a week and is paid at $20 an hour, he/she will be paid $20/hr for the first 40 hours and 20+10=$30 /hr for the overtime of 10 hours. Choose variable names for hours worked, hourly rate, and weekly salary. Write a program to calculate the correct weekly salary and print all the information. Read the values from the keyboard with appropriate prompts.

14. If the length and the width of a rectangle are equal, the figure is a square. Otherwise, it is a rectangle. Read length and width and check if it is a rectangle or a square. Print the type of the appropriate figure. Read the data from the keyboard with appropriate prompts. Draw the figure in graphics (assume the top left corner of the figure is (100,100)).

15. Write a program to prompt the user to choose a circle, a square, an oval, or a rectangle. Depending on the choice of the user, draw the appropriate figure. Also ask if the figure should be filled with a particular color and do so when chosen. Note: Circle and square require only one side length whereas rectangle and oval require both the length and the width.

16. Write a program to draw a triangle. The program should read the coordinates of three points. It is should then calculate the lengths of the three sides. Not all three sides will make a triangle (for example 2, 1, and 4 will not for a triangle as 2+1 = 3 < 4, the two sides will collapse into the third side). The program should check if the sides form a triangle (sum of any two sides must be greater than the third side) and then draw the triangle if they do. Also state whether the triangle is a right triangle, an isosceles triangle, an equilateral triangle, or none of them.

17. Chapter 2 problem 8 was on calculating BMI. Go back to that program and add the following: Underweight if below 18.5, normal weight in 18.5 – 25 range, overweight in 25.1 – 30 range, and obese if BMI is over 30. Print a message stating what category a person belongs to.

18. One must be 21 years or older to purchase alcohol in New York state. Write a program to accept the date of birth of a customer and print a message stating if the customer is eligible to buy alcohol or not. You may have seen a sign in liquor stores which says: If you are born after today's date in 1994, you cannot buy alcohol. If today's date is June 14, 2017, a person can buy alcohol if he/she is born on or before June 14, 1996. Hint: Read the year, month, and day separately from the keyboard.

19. Write a conversion program which converts from one unit of measurement to another. The user should be able to choose any of several conversions like yard to inches and miles to kilometers. Use a switch statement to select different conversions. Here are some of the conversions:

Length: 12 in = 1 ft; 1000 mm = 1 m; 1 yd = 3 ft; 10 mm = 1 cm; 1 yd = 36 in; 100 cm = 1 m; 1 mi = 5280 ft; 10 dm = 1 m; 1 km = 1000 m; 2.54 cm = 1 in; 1 m = 3.28 ft; 1.61 km = 1 mi

Volume: 1 mL = 1 cc = 1 cm3; 1 pt = 16 oz; 1 L = 1000 mL; 1 qt = 2 pt; 1 L = 100 cL; 1 gal = 4 qt; 1000 L = 1 kL; 3 1.06 qt = 1 L; 3.79 L = 1gal

Area: $1 ft^2 = 144 in^2$; 1 a = 100 m^2; 1 yd^2 = 9 ft^2; 1 ha = 100 a; 1 acre = 43,560 ft^2; 640 acres = 1 mi^2; 1 ha = 2.47 acres

Weight (Mass): 1 lb = 16 oz; 1 g = 1000 mg; 1 T = 2000 lb; 1 g = 100 cg; 1000 g = 1 kg; 1000 kg = 1 t; 28.3 g = 1 oz; 2.2 lb = 1 kg

Time: 60 sec = 1 min; 60 min = 1 hr; 3600 sec = 1 hr; 24 hr = 1 day

20. Consider bank accounts in a banking system. Each bank account has a balance at certain point in time. The balance increases as more money is deposited, and decreases if money is withdrawn. The bank pays interest on the balance amount based on how many days that balance was in the account. For example, if the annual rate is 5%, this is for 365 days. If the balance amount is in the account for 80 days, then the rate should be adjusted to 80 days. So the rate will be 80*0.05/365. An annual interest rate is proportionally applied to an interest computation. If x days passed, the interest rate would be $x*rate/365$. The bank also pays cash bonus depending on the deposit amount. The bonus is 10% of the deposit amount if the deposit is $10,000 or higher, the bonus will be 5% if the deposit is $1,000 or more but less than $10,000. No bonus will be added for deposits less than $1,000. Write a program to perform the above specifications. You should read (1) current balance, (2) number of days the balance was in the account, (3) the annual interest rate, and (4) the deposit amount. Note that the bonus cash addition will be made only after the interest computation. Your program should display all the information including the final balance which should include both interest and bonus. Do not try to create a class and construct an object at this stage.

21. A wireless telephone company has some options for new customers. Three of them are the following: (1) Buy the phone for $200 and sign a contract for two years with a monthly charge of $96, (2) Lease the phone for $600 by paying $144 per month with an option to buy the phone. The $144 will include the lease amount and monthly phone charges. The purchase price after two years is $100. (3) Buy the phone for $600 and pay $60 per month without a two-year contract. Write a program to implement it with proper messages. The program should educate the user by showing the total cost at the end of two years, for comparison. The user should be able to choose one of the options and based on that, the program should print the total cost for two years.

22. Write a program to calculate the target training heart rate. The target training heart rate is a useful measure of exercise intensity, which is used by everyone from athletes to patients recovering from heart attacks. The Karvonen formula is commonly used to determine a target training heart rate when exercising. This formula takes into consideration both the age of the person training as well as their resting heart rate. Using this formula, the maximum heart rate ($HR_{max - most}$ of the cardio machines will show what the maximum heart rate is appropriate) is computed as,

$$HR_{max} = 220 - A,$$

where A represents the age of the person training. The reserve heart rate (HR_{rsv}) is computed as,

$$HR_{rsv} = HR_{max} - HR_{rest},$$

where HR_{rest} is the resting heart rate in beats per minute (bpm – you can easily find this by putting two fingers just below the thumb and counting the pulses for 30 secs and doubling it). Using these measures, the target heart rate (HR_{targ}) is computed as,

$$HR_{targ} = p \cdot HR_{rsv} + HR_{rest},$$

where p is the training percentage (Fitness is 21-24% for women and 14-17% for men, though we all have our own goals). Depending on the specific training goals, p is commonly between 50% and 85% (0.50 - 0.85) when exercising. In practice, lower values of p correspond to an intensity of exercise consistent with health maintenance and weight loss while higher values of p correspond to an exercise intensity compatible with intense fitness training.

Calculate the target heart rate given the resting heart rate and training goal.

23. Relative risk (RR) is a statistical term used to describe the risk of a certain event happening in one group versus another. It is commonly used in epidemiology and evidenced based medicine. For example, smoking is found to be a cause for cancer. The formula for calculating the risk of cancer for smoking cigarettes is RR= $(\frac{A}{A+B})/(\frac{C}{C+D})$ where (a) A=number of people who smoke and also have cancer, (b) B=number of smokers not having cancer, (c) number of people who did not smoke but still have cancer, and (d) D=number of people who neither smoked nor have cancer.

If RR>1, smokers are at higher risk than non-smokers. If RR=1, the risk could go either way and if RR<1, the risk of smoking does not have any impact on cancer. This test can be used for any pair of exposure and cause (drinking and driving accidents,...). Write a program to receive the four quantities from the keyboard, calculate RR, and print the appropriate remark.

Answer

Concept Understanding:

1) joint && (balance > 1000)

2) if (joint && (balance > 1000)) interestRate = interestRate * 1.01; else interestRate = interestRate * 1.005

3) if (total != top + bottom) inventoryError = true;

In the if condition, the arithmetic expression (addition +) should be evaluated before the logical comparison (inequality !=). If the condition is true, then the inventoryError is set to true, otherwise do nothing.

Repetition Statements

4.1 Introduction

So far we have learned how to create and access a few field values for a record. There was no repetition of statements. Many applications require repetition. For example, if there are 30 students in a class and the professor needs to calculate their average grades, whatever the professor does for the first student has to be repeated 29 more times. Repeating the same steps for several students requires repetition of the same statements.

Such a repetition can be found in many examples: If you enter a word in Google, it will have to repeatedly search a huge database to list all the sites which are related to that word. When you click on a folder, the application has to repeat the task of finding a file and listing it until all the files are listed. Java provides three statements to loop around the tasks to be repeated. These repetitions are called iterations. This chapter describes how the java programming language handles iterations of reading, processing, and writing data.

The three iteration statements are:

1. `for` loop

2. `while` loop

3. `do-while` loop

Back to the example illustrated in the previous chapters, consider the repetition of reading a number of student records and group them based on school name. The repetition of reading data of several students can be written using one of the three statements as listed above.

This chapter will describe how data (values) are processed (computed, compared, output – for example). The values, either read from the user, from a database, or given in code, can be processed and required results can be generated for output.

In what follows, those three repetition statements are explained.

4.1.1 `for` Loop

Consider calculating the average grades of 30 students. Assume that students took three tests and the three variables of `double` type are `test1`, `test2`, and `test3`. Let the average value be defined by the variable *aveGrade*. The java statement for calculating the average grade of each student is:

```
avgGrade = (test1+test2+test3)/3;
```

But, before we calculate the aveGrade, we need to read the grades into the test variables. The statements for this are, assuming keyboard object is already created:

```
test1=keyboard.nextDouble();   //read test 1 grade

test2=keyboard.nextDouble();   //read test 2 grade

test3=keyboard.nextDouble();   //read test 3 grade
```

We have to repeat these statements thirty times, once for each student. This can be achieved very easily surrounding this block of statements with a for statement. The general format of the for statement is

Format of a for loop with one action statement	Format of a for loop with a block of action statements

`for (init_val; cond; upd_val)`
`{ for block  }`
	`for(init_val; cond; upd_val)`
	`{ statement 1;`
	`   statement 2;`
	`    ...`
	`}`

Note that init_val; cond; upd_val denote respectively initial value, condition, update value.	

The use of for loop is illustrated with the following examples:

Example 1: In the test grade problem above, we need to start with student one. So, the **initial value** is 1. We need to have a variable to keep track of the count. Let us call it count. So, the 'initial value' in the 'for' statement will be

```
int count = 1;
```

Since count is a counter, it takes the values 1, 2, 3, ... So, its type is int . We need to repeat it until count becomes 30. So, the **condition** is

```
count<= 30;
```

We started the count value at 1. After we process the first student, count should become 2 for the second student, then 3 for the third student, and so on. This is what **updating value** is. The statement is

```
count = count +1;            or
```

```
        count++;
```

Assume *test1, test2, test3,* and avgGrade are all of type double. Let us put all of them together in a for statement:

```
        for(int count=1; count<= 30;count++)

        { test1=keyboard.nextDouble();   //read test 1 grade
            test2=keyboard.nextDouble();   //read test 2 grade
            test3=keyboard.nextDouble();   //read test 3 grade


            avgGrade = (test1 + test2 + test3)/3;

        // calculate average grade for this student


            System.out.println("test 1 = "+test1+"\ttest 2 = "+test2+"\ttest 3 =
        "+test3);
            System.out.println ("Average grade = "+avgGrade);
          }
```

where count is an index which iterates 30 times. This for loop initializes the index count to 1, and repeats a series of actions by increasing count by 1 in he subsequent iteration. count++ is identical to count = count + 1 in java, resulting in incrementing by one. This iteration continues until the index reaches 30 and exits the loop when count becomes 31.

Generally, we start the index count at zero as in count=0, and stop one before the size of the number of times the block has to be repeated as in count< 30. If size is the number of times 'for' block has to be repeated, then count<size will make the loop repeat from 0 to size-1, resulting in size number of repetitions. For example, let the size be defined as int size = 5;. The number of repetitions from the *for* loop statement for (int count = 0; count<size; count++) will be 5, count going from 0 to 4. In each iteration, three values are entered in response to the prompt questions about three test scores, average is calculated, and results are printed.

Here is the full program that uses this block:

Coding List 4.1: ComputeAverage.java

```
/**
 * Author:
 * Date:
 *
 * INPUT: 3 test grades of each student. We have limited
 * loop to repeat only 3 times to avoid the monotony of
 * entering 30*3=90 values from the keyboard. It will be
 * much easier to read such data from a database or a
 * text file.
 * OUTPUT: The test grades and the average grade of each student
 */
```

```java
import java.util.Scanner;

public class ComputeAverage
    {
        public static void main (String[] args)
        {   // variables declared
            double test1, test2, test3, aveGrade ;
            Scanner keyboard = new Scanner(System.in);

            for(int count=1; count<= 3;count++)
            {   System.out.println("\nEnter 3 test grades, one at a time:");
                test1=keyboard.nextDouble();   //read test 1 grade
                test2=keyboard.nextDouble();   //read test 2 grade
                test3=keyboard.nextDouble();   //read test 3 grade

            // calculate average grade for this student
                aveGrade = (test1 + test2 + test3)/3;

                System.out.println("test 1 = "+test1+"\ttest 2 = "+test2+"\ttest
3 = "+test3);
                System.out.println ("Average grade = "+aveGrade);
            }


        }
}
```

```
Here is the output:

Enter 3 test grades, one at a time:
78.5
89.75
69.25
test 1 = 78.5    test 2 = 89.75   test 3 = 69.25
Average grade = 79.16666666666667

Enter 3 test grades, one at a time:
90
80
70
test 1 = 90.0    test 2 = 80.0    test 3 = 70.0
Average grade = 80.0

Enter 3 test grades, one at a time:
57.5
67.4
73.7
test 1 = 57.5    test 2 = 67.4    test 3 = 73.7
Average grade = 66.2
```

Example 2: Let us use for loops to print a rectangular box made up of # symbol. Let us have 20 # symbols for the horizontal sides and 15 # symbols for the vertical lines. The 20 # symbols have to be printed on the same line, so we need to print one # symbol, stay on the same line and print the second # symbol, then the third and so on until all the 20 # symbols are printed. We have used `System.out.print` to print and stay on the same line to print the next one. We will use this in a *for* loop which repeats 20 times:

```
for(int n=0; n<20; n++)  System.out.print("#");    // loop 1
```

The *for* loop above will print 20 symbols on one line. Notice that we started the counter n at zero and ended the last value at 19 as in n<20. Now, we need to go to the next line and start printing one # symbol on column one and another on column 20. We need to repeat this 15 times for the two vertical sides (Observe that if we print 15 # symbols, we will have 17 # symbols in each of the two vertical sides, when you include the two horizontal lines. So, the next loop will repeat only 13 times.). So, we will use the "`println`" method:

```
System.out.println(); // to go to the next line

for (int m=0; m<13; m++)      // loop 2
    System.out.println("#                    #");
```

Now, print the lower horizontal line: we need to just repeat loop 1. Let us put all these ideas into a complete program, called *Rectangle*:

Coding List 4.2: Rectangle.java

```
/* Author:
 * Date:
   Input: none
   Output: We are drawing a rectangle using 'for' loop.
   The rectangle will have 20 # symbols in the horizontal sides.
   It will have 16 # symbols in the vertical sides, including two
   from the horizontal sides. So, we use 3 for loops, 2 for
   horizontal sides and one for the vertical sides.
*/
public class Rectangle
{ public static void main(String args[])
  { System.out.println("\n\n\n"); // insert three blank lines

    for(int n=1; n<=20; n++)                          //loop 1
    { System.out.print("#");

    }

    System.out.println();    // to go to the next line    loop 2
    for ( int m=1; m<=13; m++)
    { System.out.println("#                    #");

    }

    for(int n=1; n<=20; n++)                          //loop 3
    { System.out.print("#");
    }
  }
}
```
ï

```
Here is the output.

####################
#                  #
#                  #
#                  #
#                  #
#                  #
#                  #
#                  #
#                  #
#                  #
#                  #
#                  #
#                  #
#                  #
####################
```

Example 3: Example 2 showed three independent loops, looping separately. This example will show how nested loops work. It is a simple program with two loops, one inside another. As you know, once the control enters a loop, it will be stuck in that loop until the condition becomes false. Only after the loop completes, the control will go to the next instruction that follows the end of the for block in the program. Once the control enters the inner loop, it will not loop back to the outer loop until the inner loop completes. Now study the following program:

Coding List 4.3: NestedLoops.java

```java
/* Author:
 * Date:
 *
 * Input: none
 * Output: This program shows how NESTED (one loop inside another loop)
 * loops work. Compare this to an hour hand and a minute hand in a clock.
 * The hour hand moves very slowly, one hour at a time. During this one
 * hour, the minute hand ticks 60 times. The minute hand moves fast and
 * only after it completes 60 minutes, does the hour changes to the next
 * hour. The outer loop is like the hour hand and the inner loop is like
 * the minute hand. Only after the inner loop completes, the outer loop
 * moves to the next step. Here the m-loop is the outer loop and n-loop
 * is the inner loop. Study the output.
 */

public class NestedLoops
{ public static void main(String args[])
  { System.out.println("\n\n\nm\t\tn"); //headers for m and n columns
    System.out.println("==\t\t==");

    for(int m=0; m<5; m++)
```

```
    {   System.out.println(m);

        for(int n=5; n<=20; n=n+4)
            System.out.println("\t\t"+n);
    }
}
}
```

Here is the output:

```
m                   n
==                  ==
0
                    5
                    10
                    15
                    20
1
                    5
                    10
                    15
                    20
2
                    5
                    10
                    15
                    20
3
                    5
                    10
                    15
                    20
4
                    5
                    10
                    15
                    20
```

Example 4: This is a simple example to add integers 1 – n. User will enter any integer value for n and the program will add the integers and prints the sum. Remember the variable that accumulates, sum, must be first initialized to zero when you are adding the integers (if you were multiplying the integers, you would initialize the product variable to 1) inside a loop. Here is the program:

Coding List 4.4: Summing.java
```
/**
 * Author:
 * Date:
 * Input: an integer n to print the sum of all integers
 * 1 - n.
 * Output: sum in a sentence.
 */
```

```
import java.util.Scanner;

public class Summing
{ public static void main(String args[])
  { int sum=0, n; // sum to add all the integers, must be
                  // initialized to zero outside the loop
    Scanner kb = new Scanner(System.in); // to read from kb

    System.out.println("Enter the integer you want the sum for:");
    n=kb.nextInt();

    for (int i=1; i<=n; i++) // i loops through 1 - n
      sum = sum+i;     // adds all the integer values taken by i

    System.out.println("Sum of integers 1 - "+n+" is "+sum);
  }
}
```

```
Here is the output:

Enter the integer you want the sum for:
10
Sum of integers 1 - 10 is 55
```

Example 5: The problem is to find the averages of math and java grades. The program should read from the keyboard the student name, java grade, and math grade for each student. The goal is to calculate the average java grade and average math grade. All this will be done repeatedly, one student at a time. When the control comes out of the loop, average grades should be calculated and data printed. Here is the program:

Coding List 4.5: MoreScores.java

```
/**
 * Author:
 * Date:
 * Input: Name and grades of java & math courses for
 * each student
 * Output: display the grades of the students and the
 * class averages of the java and math courses. We are
 * printing name, java grade, and math grade of each
 * student inside the loop. The class averages are
 * printed outside the loop. Averages have to be
 * calculated after adding all the grades inside the
 * loop. Since we are reading and immediately printing
 * the data, we cannot present the data in a table. When
 * we learn arrays, we will be able to print them in a
 * proper table.
 */

import java.util.Scanner;

class MoreScores
{
```

```java
        // no variables for the class
    public static void main (String[] args) {
            // object to read user input
        Scanner scn = new Scanner (System.in);

        // variables to hold user inputs
        String name;
        int java, math;
// variables to accumulate scores, must be initialized to 0
        int javaSum = 0, mathSum = 0;
        double avgJ = 0.0, avgM = 0.0;

        // assume there are 5 students
        int stdNo = 5;

        for (int i = 0; i < stdNo; i++)
        {   System.out.print("Enter student name: ");
            name = scn.next();

            System.out.print("Enter the score of Java Programming Language: ");
            java = scn.nextInt();

            System.out.print("Enter the score of Mathematics: ");
            math = scn.nextInt();

            System.out.println(name+"\t"+java+"\t"+math);

            javaSum += java; // add java grades
            mathSum += math; // add math grades
        }

        avgJ = (double) javaSum / stdNo;
        avgM = (double) mathSum / stdNo;

        System.out.println("Math Average = "+avgM);
        System.out.println("Java Average = "+ avgJ);
    }
}
```

```
Here is the output:

Enter student name: john
Enter the score of Java Programming Language: 80
Enter the score of Mathematics: 80
john    80        80
Enter student name: lisa
Enter the score of Java Programming Language: 90
Enter the score of Mathematics: 90
lisa    90        90
Enter student name: maria
Enter the score of Java Programming Language: 70
Enter the score of Mathematics: 70
maria   70        70
Enter student name: david
Enter the score of Java Programming Language: 60
Enter the score of Mathematics: 60
david   60        60
```

```
Enter student name: nancy
Enter the score of Java Programming Language: 100
Enter the score of Mathematics: 100
nancy    100      100
Math Average = 80.0
Java Average = 80.0
```

Parameterizing a value makes the program more efficient and adoptable. For example, we know there are 5 students. But, instead of hard coding 5 in the loop, we use the variable stdNo in the loop, for (int i=0; i<5; i++). Although they are the same computations, the parameterized variable stdNo can be reused multiple times as needed (as in avgJ computation in the program above) and it can be simply updated if needed (if we want to increase the number of students to 10, we need to make the change in one place only, in int stdNo = 5;. Updating parameterized variables is better than changing hard-coded numbers. Also, if a professor is teaching several courses and each course has a different number of students, he/she can read the number of students in a particular course into stdNo and enter the data. He/she can repeat it to each of the courses by running the program several times.

The second loop statement is the while loop, which is described in the following section.

4.2. while **Loop**

The for loop has three segments: *initial value; condition; update value.* These three segments are needed in all the three loop statements, but will be at different locations in the loops. The general structure of the while loop is

Format of a while Loop

```
initial value;// before the loop
while (condition)  // in the loop statement
{ statement 1;
  statement 2;
   …..
  update value;    // updating at the end of the loop
//before going back to the loop and checking the condition
}
```

Let us print "Hello" ten times using the for loop and write the same using the while loop. Let index be the variable used to count the repetitions. Then, the initial value is int index =0; The condition will be index < 10; The update value will be index++. Hence the for loop is

```
for (int index = 0; index < 10; index++)
{ System.out.println("Hello"); }
```

The same action with the while loop is

```
int index = 0;                  // initial value
while (index < 10)              // condition
{    System.out.println("Hello");
     index++;                   // update value
}
```

Example 6: We could apply this structure of while loop in the three examples listed above by changing the for loop to while loop. Here is the RectangleWhile program which is the same as the Rectangle program except that all the for loops are replaced with while loops:

Coding List 4.6: RectangleWhile.java

```
/* Author:
 * Date:

   Input: none
   Output: This is the same as the Rectangle program where we used 'for'
   loop. Here we are replacing all the 'for' loops with 'while' loops.
   Observe how the three segments of the 'for' loop fit into the 'while'
   loops.
*/
public class RectangleWhile
{ public static void main(String args[])
  {   System.out.println("\n\n\n");

     // Replacing for(int n=1; n<=20; n++)
     int n=1;
     while (n<=20)                              //loop 1
     { System.out.print("#");
       n++;
     }

     // Replacing for(int m=1; m<=13; m++)
     int m=1;
     System.out.println();   // to go to the next line     loop 2
     while (m<=13)
     { System.out.println("#                    #");
       m++;
     }

 // Replacing for(int n=1; n<=20; n++). We could have used n=1 instead of p
     int p=1;
     while (p<=20)                              //loop 3
     { System.out.print("#");
       p++;
     }

  }
}
```

Example 7: In the following java class, MoreScores2.java, we will use a `while` loop which will use non-numerical condition. Here we will check the value of each name entered and continue the loop reading student data until "end" word is entered to end the loop. You cannot do this using a for loop. The while loop has the expression `(!name.equals(""))` in line (2). The variable name holds the value given by user as shown in line (1) and (3). Note that there is a negation, the ! symbol, in the expression `name.equals("")`. It means that the `while` block continues until a user enters the word "end".

Coding List 4.7: MoreScores2.java

```
/**
 * Author:
 * Date:
 *
 * If we do not know the number of records, we could use a while
 * loop with an end condition. "end" is used to end the loop. We
 * could have used a counter as in MoreScores program. But, we
 * decided to add more functionality that a "while" loop is
 * capable of.
 * Input: name, java, and math scores for unknown number of students
 *          number of repetitions will end by entering "end" word
 * Output: display the statistics of students
 */

import java.util.Scanner;

class MoreScores2
{ // no variables for the class
   public static void main (String[] args) {
           // object to read user input
       Scanner scn = new Scanner (System.in);

       // variables to hold user inputs
       String name;
       int java=0, math=0;

       // variables to accumulate scores
       int javaSum = 0, mathSum = 0;
       int stdNo=0;  // initialize student count, no student yet
                     // will be used as a counter
       double avgJ = 0.0, avgM = 0.0;

       // use while loop
       // iterate as long as non-null student names are read

       System.out.print("Enter student name, \"end\" to end: ");
1      name = scn.next();  // <--

2      while (!name.equals("end")) { //enter "end" to end the loop
          System.out.print("Enter the score of Java Programming Language: ");
          java = scn.nextInt();
          System.out.print("Enter the score of Mathematics: ");
          math = scn.nextInt();

          stdNo++;
```

```
            javaSum += java;
            mathSum += math;

            System.out.print("Enter student name, \"end\" to end: ");
3            name = scn.next(); // update condition // <--
        }
        System.out.println("end has ended the while loop\n");

        if (stdNo == 0)
            System.out.println("No data entered!");
        else {
          avgJ = (double) javaSum / stdNo;
          avgM = (double) mathSum / stdNo;
          System.out.println("Number of Students = " + stdNo+"\t Msum
="+mathSum +"\tJavaSum="+javaSum);
          System.out.println("Math Average = "+avgM);
          System.out.println("Java Average = " + avgJ + "\n\n\n");
        }
    }
}
```

```
Here is the output:

Enter student name, "end" to end: john
Enter the score of Java Programming Language: 80
Enter the score of Mathematics: 80
Enter student name, "end" to end: lisa
Enter the score of Java Programming Language: 90
Enter the score of Mathematics: 90
Enter student name, "end" to end: mary
Enter the score of Java Programming Language: 70
Enter the score of Mathematics: 70
Enter student name, "end" to end: david
Enter the score of Java Programming Language: 87
Enter the score of Mathematics: 78
Enter student name, "end" to end: nancy
Enter the score of Java Programming Language: 100
Enter the score of Mathematics: 100
Enter student name, "end" to end: end
Number of Students = 5    Msum =418       JavaSum=427
Math Average = 83.6
Java Average = 85.4
Enter student name, "end" to end: end
end has ended the while loop
```

The condition part in a while loop can be an expression or a boolean variable. A while loop is interpreted in two ways: while an expression returns true; or while a boolean variable becomes true, as illustrated below.

While average is greater than 95, take actions, value of average>95 is true or false	With the expression of a Boolean variable yes, whose values could be true or false

Compute average;
while (average > 95)
{ action1;
  action2;
  ... ;
  Action to change average;
}
	Initialize yes;
	while (yes) {
	{ action1;
	  action2;
	  ... ;
	  Action to change the Boolean value yes if needed }

The `while` statement continually executes a block of statements which may contain a sequence of actions as shown above as long as the condition is true and exits the loop when the condition becomes false.

The former evaluates the expression by comparing the value bound to the variable average with the value 95. The average for each repetition can be compared with 95 and the expression will return true or false. As long as the expression returns true, the block of action statements will be executed.

The latter evaluates the variable `yes`, which is a Boolean variable. This `while` statement continues testing the value bound to the variable `yes` and executing its block until the variable `yes` evaluates to false. It means that if the variable `yes` is not changed to false, the while loop runs indefinitely.

NOTE: The 'for' loop cannot run on a Boolean variable like 'yes' where as a 'while' can not only do all that a 'for' loop does but also can work for problems where you need to use Boolean variables to control the loop.

4.3   do-while **Loop**

The Java programming language also provides a `do-while` statement. The `do-while` statement is similar to the other loops and uses *initial value; condition; update value* segments. But do-while loop <u>does not check the condition before entering the loop</u> as the other two repetition loops do. Here is the structure of the do...while loop:

Format of a do-while Loop

```
initial value;
do {
    statement 1;
    statement 2;
    ....
    update;
} while (condition);
```

<u>Example 8:</u> Here is the RectangleDo program, similar to the Rectangle program except that 'for' statements are replaced by 'do...while' statements:

Coding List 4.8: RectangleDo.java

```java
/**
 * Author:
 * Date:
 * Input: none
 * Output: display a rectangle formed with the symbol #
 * using do - while loop.
 */

public class RectangleDo
{
 public static void main(String args[])
  { //for(int n=0; n<20; n++)                         loop 1
    int n=0;
    do {
        System.out.print("#");
        n++;
      } while (n<20);

     System.out.println(); // to go to the next line  loop 2
    //for ( int m=0; m<15; m++)
     int m=0;
     do {
        System.out.println("#                        #");
        m++;
       }while(m<13);

    //for(int n=0; n<20; n++)                         loop 3
     int p=0;
     do {
        System.out.print("#");
        p++;
       }while (p<20);
  }
}
```

It will print the same rectangle as in Rectangle.java

The difference between do-while and while is that do-while evaluates its expression at the bottom of the loop instead of the top as in while statement. Therefore, the statements within the do block are always executed at least once.

4.4 Formatting Output Data

We receive lots of bills which we expect them to be very clear with money clearly expressed as dollars with dollar sign ($), commas in bigger numbers, and amount with two decimal digits. Rate of taxes must be presented as a percentage (%) and numbers with decimal digits (to two decimal places or whatever is needed). Our programs accept inputs and produce outputs. These outputs (like bills) must be formatted to present in a meaningful format. We will introduce some of these packages in this section.

Formatting Numbers		
Challenge	Some numbers have a special meaning, and the numbers should then be formatted in a certain way. A number in currency should be formatted as a floating point with two decimal digits. Another number may be formatted as a percentage. The statements shown in the steps below can format such numbers.	
	Class to be imported	`import java.text.NumberFormat;`

	An object of NumberFormat to be constructed.	`NumberFormat fmtDollar =`
		`    NumberFormat.getCurrencyInstance();`
		
		`NumberFormat fmtPerc =`
		`    NumberFormat.getPercentInstance();`

	Printing	`System.out.println("The amount is " +`
		`    fmtDollar.format(balance));`
		
		`System.out.println("The interest rate is " +`
		`    fmtPerc.format(intRate));`

Example 9: We have been printing numbers without formatting them. If a bank prints a customer balance, the money should be formatted to have $ sign and commas at appropriate positions. For example if the balance is 7890567.123456, it should be printed as Balance=$7,890,567.12. When we print interest rates, we print them with % sign as a postscript. If the interest rate is 7.5, we print it as 7.5%. Java provides NumberFormat class to output values in the money format and percent format.

We have used `println()` and `print()` methods from the `System.out` class. `System.out` class also provides `printf` method to format values in a specified format using format specifiers. The structure of `printf` is

```
System.out.printf("format string", argument list separated by commas);
```

The format string will include texts and format specifiers. For example, %20s is a string specifier which will output a string in 20 character spaces. If the length of the string is bigger than the specified 20 character spaces, the string will be printed using exactly the length of the string. You could use just %s without specifying any length, in which case, the string will printed without any extra spaces. If the length of specifier is bigger than the length of the string, the string will be printed left justified leaving blank spaces on the right. %10.3f is used to print decimals in 10 spaces with 3 decimal places. %10d is used for integers. If the argument list has 4 values separated by commas, there must be corresponding 4 format specifiers matching the types of respective arguments. The following code shows how the NumberFormat and printf are used.

Coding List 4.9: Formatting.java

```
/* Author:
   Date:
   Input: none
   Output: This program illustrates formatted output. Java provides classes
   to format money with $ symbol and commas at appropriate positions in a
   double type number and also to express interest rates with % symbol.
   Notice that the interest rate must be in the decimal format: if the
   interest rate is 15%, we need to enter it as 0.15 to use the percent
   format. Also notice what happened to 7.5 for intRate!

   Using NumberFormat class will give professional looking output for
   money and percents when compared to using printf.
*/

import java.text.NumberFormat;

public class Formatting
{ public static void main(String args[])
  { NumberFormat fmtDollar = NumberFormat.getCurrencyInstance();
    NumberFormat fmtPerc = NumberFormat.getPercentInstance();

    double balance = 7890567.123456;
    double intRate = 7.5;
    String name = "Washington";
    System.out.println("NumberFormat output");
    System.out.println("--------------------");
    System.out.println("The amount is " + fmtDollar.format(balance));
    System.out.println("The interest rate is " + fmtPerc.format(intRate));

    System.out.println("\n\n\nprintf format output");
    System.out.println("--------------------");
    System.out.printf("Name:%1s\tBalance =$%1.2f\tInterest Rate =
%1.2f",name, balance,intRate);
  // observe that strings and numbers are printed right justified
  // when more space than required is specified. We may want to
  // print names right-justified. If so, you can use minus sign
  // in the specifier as in %-25s.
    System.out.printf("\n\n%25s",name);
    System.out.printf("\n\n%-25s",name);
    System.out.printf("\n\n%25.2f",balance);
    System.out.printf("\n\n%25d",5);
  }
}
```

```
NumberFormat output
--------------------
The amount is $7,890,567.12
The interest rate is 750%



printf format output
--------------------
Name:Washington Balance =$7890567.12      Interest Rate = 7.50

                 Washington

Washington

             7890567.12

                    5
```

4.5   Reading from a Text File

So far, multiple records are given in user-active manner, and they are read by a java program. A simple text scanner can parse primitive types and strings. A Scanner breaks its input into tokens using a delimiter pattern, which by default matches whitespace. The resulting tokens may then be converted into values of different types using the various next methods.

For example, the following code segment allows a user to read one integer from System.in (which is keyboard):

```
Scanner scan = new Scanner(System.in);
int num = scan.nextInt();
```

Remember Example 5 (MoreScores.java) in which we read name and two test grades for several students. We mentioned that reading 90 data values from the keyboard would be monotonous and a better method would be to read from a text file. Here is how we can do that. First we will give a simple example of reading just the names of students from a text file. After that we will provide modified MoreScores.java.

Reading from text files

File Introduction System.in is to read from the keyboard. We System.in to create Scanner object kb (or scan or whatever you want to call). Hence
 	
`Scanner scan = new Scanner(System.in);`
 	
Will connect scanner to the keyboard. If we want to connect (or point to) a text file, we need to provide an object of File pointing to the file. If we want to connect to fileExample.txt, we need to use
 	
`Scanner f1 = new Scanner(new File("fileExample.txt"));`

	Here new File("fileExample.txt") is an object of File, which could have been created separately. Here are the steps:	
	Classes to be imported	```import java.util.Scanner; import java.io.*; // #1```

	An object of Scanner included in which is the object of File	Observe that many things can go wrong when we read from a text file: file may not exist, there may not be valid data, could be trying read a number where there is a string, and so on. So, we need to check for IO exceptions. That is done in the main() definition line.
		
		```public static void main (String args[]) throws IOException // #2```
		
		Now create the Scanner object:
		```Scanner file = new Scanner(new File("fileExample.txt"));// #3```

	Reading	Reading from a text file is exactly the same as reading from the keyboard. When we read from the keyboard, we enter the data in the order that we have the 'next' statements – a name for a string, a grade for a nextDouble(). So, we need to read the text file data in the order the data is entered. Since we are reading from a text file, we may not always know the number of records in the file. So, a while loop which will check for the end of the file will be used as in ```while (file.hasNext()) // #4 if there is data available in the next line { name = scn.next(); System.out.println(name); }```

We have read values from the keyboard. We import the Scanner class. We have used next() to read one word, nextLine() to read several words in a string, nextInt() to read an integer, and nextDouble() to read a decimal number. These are the same to read from a text file that could be on a hard disk or a flash drive. Here is a program that illustrates how to read from a text file:

Example 10: In this example we will create fileExample.txt first. Each record will have a name, number of students served, and the income of the professor. We will read these data until the end of the file. We have four records in the file and hence reaches the end of file after four records. We will print them.

Coding List 4.10: FileExample.java

```java
/* Author:
 * Date:

   Input: This program illustrates how to read data from a text file. Data
   are read from a previously created text file called fileExample.txt.

   Output: It also illustrates how printf() can be used to format output.
   Bear in mind that you need 4 items to be included in the program to read
   From a file: (1) import both Scanner class and also java.io.*, (2)
   include throws IOException on the line with the main() method, (3) create
   the object 'file' to point to the designated file, (4) use next methods
   to read the data in the order the data is entered in the text file.
*/

import java.util.Scanner;
import java.io.*;                        //  #1

public class FileExample
{  public static void main (String args[]) throws IOException      // #2
     {  double decimal;
        int integer;
        String name;

        Scanner file  = new Scanner(new File("fileExample.txt"));   // #3

        while (file.hasNext())                                       // #4
        { name = file.next();
          integer = file.nextInt();
          decimal = file.nextDouble();

          System.out.printf ("%1s has taught %1d students and has earned $%1.2f
dollars.\n\n",name, integer,decimal);
        }
     }
}
```

Here is the output:

```
Washington has taught 12345 students and has earned $12345.68 dollars.

Adams has taught 1111 students and has earned $1111111.11 dollars.

Jefferson has taught 2222 students and has earned $2222222.22 dollars.

Roosevelt has taught 3333 students and has earned $3333333.33 dollars.
```

First create your text file. In the program above, we are reading from the text file fileExample.txt. This is created using Notepad. Do not enter blank space or return immediately after the last data value. Save the file in the same folder as the program that reads it. If the text file is in a different folder, you have to provide the full path. Here is what we have in fileExample.txt:

```
Washington 12345 12345.6789
Adams 1111 1111111.11
Jefferson 2222 2222222.22
Roosevelt 3333 3333333.33
```

<u>Example 11</u>: Here is the modified MoreScores program. Here we are reading name, java grade, and math grade from `myFile.txt`. `myFile.txt` is already created. We can print them in a table format as we are not entering from the keyboard. We will print the averages at the end. Here is the program:

Coding List 4.11: MoreScores4.java

```java
/**
 * Author:
 * Date:
 * Input: scores of java and math for students from different schools
 *
 * Output: display the statistics of students for each school.
 * #1, #2, #3, and #4 below identify the steps needed to read from a
 * text file. Note that the file must be created before reading it.
 */

import java.util.Scanner;  // #1
import java.io.*;          // #2

public class MoreScores4
{
// Observe the following main line, #3
    public static void main (String[] args) throws    FileNotFoundException
    {
// scanner object to read from user given file name
        Scanner scn = new Scanner (new File("myFile.txt")); // #4

// variables to hold user inputs
        String name;
        int java, math;

// variables to accumulate scores by school
        int javaSum = 0, mathSum = 0;
        int stdNo = 0;
        double avgJ = 0.0, avgM = 0.0;

System.out.println("\n==============================================\n");
        System.out.println("NAME \t JAVA \t MATH");
        System.out.println("---- \t ---- \t ----");

        while (scn.hasNext())  // if there is data available in the next line
        { name = scn.next();
            java = scn.nextInt();
            math = scn.nextInt();

// The scanner object should move to the next line and read next students
            stdNo++;
            javaSum += java;
            mathSum += math;

            System.out.println(name + "\t " + java + "\t " + math);

        }

System.out.println("\n==============================================\n");
```

```
        if (stdNo == 0)
        System.out.println("No data entered!");
        else
        { avgJ = javaSum / stdNo;
          avgM = mathSum / stdNo;
          System.out.println("Number of Students =" + stdNo);
          System.out.println("Math Average = " + avgM);
          System.out.println("Java Average = " + avgJ+"\n\n");
        }
    }
}
```

Here is the output:

```
================================================
NAME    JAVA    MATH
----    ----    ----
Lisa    98      78
John    99      77
Chris   88      66
Maria   55      99
================================================
Number of Students =4
Math Average = 80.0
Java Average = 85.0
```

In iterations, one of the most important elements to specify is an end (or so-called terminal) condition. The following blue box changes some for that.

End (Terminal) Condition		
Challenge	Question 1	Suppose that a program runs endlessly. What problems would it cause if the program uses memory space, if the program communicates in the Internet, and the program accesses external devices (e.g., storages, printers, etc)?
	Question 2	There are some situations or applications that need to run infinitely. Please list any example application domains that need an endless program.

4.6 Exercises

Concept Understanding

1. Consider the following code segment:

```
    int cnt1 = 1;
    while (cnt1 <= 10) {  // outer loop
      System.out.print(cnt1);
      int cnt2 =1;
```

```
    while (cnt2 <= 20) {      // inner loop
          System.out.print("\t" + cnt2);
          System.out.println("\tHere -- ");
          cnt2++;      // increasing the inner loop
    }
    cnt1++;          // increasing outer loop
    }
```

a) How many of the word "Here" will be displayed?

b) Rewrite the above **while** statement usig **for** loop statements.

c) The above code segment can be extended to a certain point that the following output is displayed. To that end, complete and extend the above code segment.

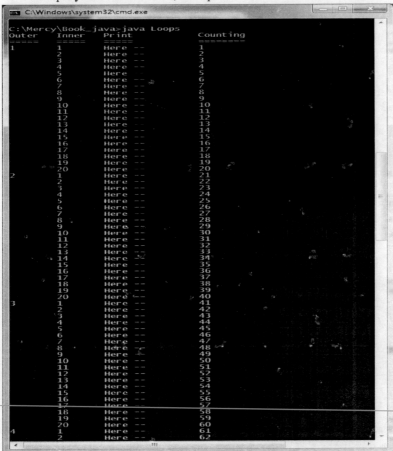

The above screen capture shows the first few lines of the output.

2. Fill in the blank below so that the two code segments are equivalent.
    a) for (int i = 0; i < 10; i = _____)
    b) for (int i = 0; i <= _____ ; i++)

3. Consider the following code segments together with a screen capture of their execution.

a) While loop	b) Do-while loop	Execution them together

int cnt = 1;
while (cnt >= 5) {
  System.out.println(cnt);
  cnt++;
}
	int cnt = 1;
	do {
	  System.out.println(cnt);
	  cnt++;
	}
	while (cnt >= 5);
		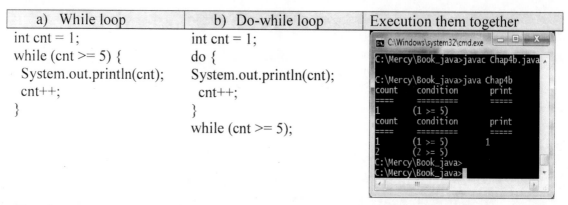

The above two code segments are extended and so the head line appears. In the third column above, two executions, upper output and lower output, are shown. Which execution might be the while loop and so the other the do-while loop. Explain why.

4. Rewrite the following segment using a do-while loop:

```
int a = 3;
boolean truu = true;
while (truu) {
   System.out.print("*");
   a += 2;
   if (a > 2) truu = false;
}
```

Programming:

5. Write a program to print ten asterisks each using 'for', 'while', and 'do…while' loops in the same program so that the output will be three lines of asterisks.

6. Write a program to print 1 through 100. Modify it so that you print 20 numbers per line.

7. Searching for items/information is extremely common: browsing websites, looking for your grades in the college system, when you use a variable name in a program the compiler has to search for that identifier in a table of identifiers, and so on. Create a text file of integers in the range 1 - 100. Prompt the user to enter an integer. Print an error message if the number is out of this range and then prompt to enter a valid number. Search the text file for the user number. Print a message stating whether the user number is in the database or not.

8. Write a program to accept a total amount in the pocket and print the maximum of each of the denominations in that amount. For example, if the amount entered is $345.78, it should print

$100 – 3

$50 – 0

$20 – 2

$10 – 0

$5 – 1

$1 – 0

Quarters – 3

Dimes – 0

Nickels – 0

Cents - 3

9. Write a program to search a text file of last names for a user entered last name and print an appropriate message.

10. Write a program to read an integer from the keyboard and print all the divisors of that integer. For example, if the user enters 85, print all the integers that divide 85. So, the program should print 1, 5, 17, and 85; if the user enters 110, the program should print 1, 2, 5, 10, 11, 22, 55, and 110.

11. Write a program to prompt the user to guess a computer generated two-digit integer. The computer should generate a random integer between 10 and 99, both inclusive. The program should give not more than three guesses for each integer. After each guess, the computer should say whether the target integer is higher or lower. The user should be allowed to continue the guesses until the user enters "no" to the question "Do you want to continue guessing?". Print the percent of correct answers.

12. Write a program to print Fibonacci numbers. The program should ask how many Fibonacci numbers to be printed and print that many integers. The Fibonacci numbers are 1, 1, 2, 3, 5, 8, 13,…The first two are 1 and 1. Each integer after these is the sum of the previous two integers: 2 is the sum of 1 and 1; 8 is the sum of 5 and 3; 13 is the sum of 8 and 5.

13. Write a program to calculate your GPA of one semester. Read the letter grade of each course you have completed and their corresponding numerical values from the keyboard (from a text file). Refer to the catalogue to find numerical value of each of these grades (for example, A is 4, A- is 3.67, and F is 0). You have to multiply each of these numerical values by the number of credits of the course. The GPA is the average of all these products (sum of the products divided by the total number of credits). For example, let a student have grades A, C, B-, and C+ (numerical values are 4, 2, 2.67, and 2.33) in four courses. Assume each of these courses is 3 credits (total 12 credits). Then the GPA = (3x4+3x2+3x2.67+3x2.33)/12 = 2.75. If you have taken five courses, your loop should repeat five times, for example. Add all the products inside the loop and calculate the GPA outside the loop. Print a table of letter grades and their corresponding numerical values and then print the GPA.

14. Write a program to simulate the purchases in a grocery store. One customer may buy only one item and another could buy 50 items. So, you should use either a 'while' or a 'do-while' loop. You should read price of each item and number of that item until you enter a terminal value to end the loop. You should add all the prices inside the loop. Add a sales tax of 7.5% to the total price (after coming out of the loop). Print a receipt to indicate all the details of the purchase. All numbers must be appropriately formatted. You could use a text file.

15. You may have learned multiplication tables to memory in primary school. Write a program to print multiplication table for 1 – 13. Hint: first print a table for one integer, say 7. This needs one 'for' loop going 1 – 10. Repeat this loop 13 times for the 13 integers. This will be another 'for' loop containing the first loop inside it. Observe that the 7 you had before should keep changing each iteration starting at 1 and running until 13.

16. Write a program to draw a braid made of squares as shown below. You should read a user entered integer (n=7 for example). You should draw that many squares (length=width=100, for example) using a loop. NOTE: You need to move the coordinates of the left-top corner of the square inside the loop. Maybe use a graph paper to understand it.

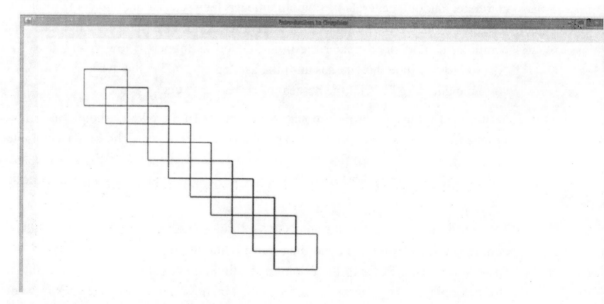

17. Draw several concentric squares as shown below (7 concentric circles). You should prompt the user to enter the number of circles to be drawn and then draw that many concentric circles. NOTE: Circles are inscribed in rectangles/squares. Drawing circles and squares are similar.

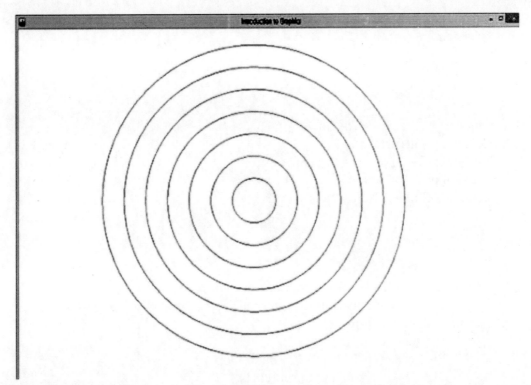

18. Consider bank accounts in a banking system. Each bank account has numerous transactions: deposits, withdrawals, interest calculations, balance check, etc. These transactions are performed repeatedly. The amount of deposit will be added to an account balance, the amount of withdrawal will be subtracted from the balance, and an interest amount will be added to the balance. Assume that the interest rate is 5% annually, and an interest calculation is performed once a month with the $1/12^{th}$ the annual interest. It means that interest is calculated every month and added to the balance. Format the numbers (Refer to Coding List 4.9). A sample run at the command line is shown below:

```
C:\Windows\system32\cmd.exe

C:\Mercy\Book_java>java BankAcctLoop
** Welcome Mercy Bank **
--------------------------------------------------------------
Choose a Number (1) Deposit; (2) Withdrawal; (3) Interest Calc; (4) Display; (0)
 Exit
1
Enter the Deposit Amount:
450
--------------------------------------------------------------
Choose a Number (1) Deposit; (2) Withdrawal; (3) Interest Calc; (4) Display; (0)
 Exit
2
Enter the Amount to Withdraw:
34.21
--------------------------------------------------------------
Choose a Number (1) Deposit; (2) Withdrawal; (3) Interest Calc; (4) Display; (0)
 Exit
3
The Balance before Interest is $415.79
The Interest for this Month is $1.7324583333333334
The Balance after Interest Calculation is $417.52245833333336
--------------------------------------------------------------
Choose a Number (1) Deposit; (2) Withdrawal; (3) Interest Calc; (4) Display; (0)
 Exit
1
Enter the Deposit Amount:
99.99
--------------------------------------------------------------
Choose a Number (1) Deposit; (2) Withdrawal; (3) Interest Calc; (4) Display; (0)
 Exit
4
The Balance is $517.5124583333334
--------------------------------------------------------------
Choose a Number (1) Deposit; (2) Withdrawal; (3) Interest Calc; (4) Display; (0)
 Exit
0
Thanks for Using Mercy Bank...

C:\Mercy\Book_java>
```

Answer

Concept Understanding

1. a) 200 times

   b)
   ```
   for (int cnt1 = 1; cnt1 <=10; cnt1++) {
   System.out.print(cnt1);
      For (int cnt2 = 1; cnt2 <= 20; cnt2++) {
   System.out.print("\t" + cnt2);
   System.out.println("\tHere –");
      }
   }
   ```

   c)
   ```
   System.out.println("Outer \tInner \tPrint \t\tCounting");
                   System.out.println("===== \t===== \t===== \t\t========");
                   int counting =1;
                   int cnt1 = 1;
                   while (cnt1 <= 10) {  // outer loop
                           System.out.print(cnt1);
                           int cnt2 =1;
                           while (cnt2 <= 20) {   // inner loop
                                   System.out.print("\t" + cnt2);
                                   System.out.println("\tHere -- \t" + counting);
                                   cnt2++;   // increasing the inner loop
                                   counting++;  // counting the word HERE
                           }
                           cnt1++;    // increasing outer loop
                   }
   ```

2. for (int i = 0; i < 10; i =**i+1**_____)
   for (int i = 1; i <= 10 _____; i++)

Java Application Programming Interfaces (API)

5.1 Introduction

All programming languages provide libraries. These libraries will include several code packages written by somebody else and which are available to users of the language. Most of the commonly needed features are generally provided by these libraries. For example, square roots are very common in mathematics. So, Java provides the code to find the square roots of numbers. This is a small segment of code called a "**method**". Its name is "sqrt()". First, we need to give a number to "sqrt()" to find its square root. If we want to find the square root of 64.0, we need to put 64.0 in the parentheses. So, to invoke (or call), we need to use sqrt(64.0). 64.0 is the 'input'. The method sqrt(64.0) will 'return' 8.0 as the square root of 64. 8.0 is the 'output'. Again, sqrt() receives a double number as input and returns a double number as output. The inputs are listed inside the parentheses as parameters. Some methods like sqrt() will return a value to the location that is invoked and some may not return any value but may do some other tasks inside them. When a method returns a value, we need to use the output value in some way – maybe in some other instruction, print the value, or use it in an expression. For example, we could print the value of sqrt(64.0) with the statement

```
System.out.println("Square root of 64 is +Math.sqrt(64.0));
```

We just have to know how to use them and what features are available. The general structure of any method in a class will be

static *type name (parameter list separated by commas)*

Return type   Name of the method   List of parameters as input

The square root method will be

static double *sqrt* **(double** *x)*

Return type   Name of the method   List of one parameter

Similarly, there is a method to find the larger of two integer numbers. The name of this method is 'max'. It takes two integer inputs and returns the larger of the two integers as output. Observe how it is defined

$$\textit{static int max (int a, int b)}$$

Return type   Name of the method   List of parameters as input

Observe that when there is more than one parameter, <u>each of them must have its type</u>.

Java has several library packages – Application Programming Interfaces (API). Some of the classes are:

- Math class (java.lang.Math)
- String class (java.lang.String)
- Graphics package (java.awt.* and javax.swing.*)
- Networking package (java.net.*)

We will use only the Math and the String classes in this chapter. We have been using the graphics packages already.

5.2   Math Class

Math methods are in the Math class. It provides many methods and also the constants PI and E (exponential constant e=2.71…). We can invoke the Math methods by Math.x or Math.m() where x is a constant (like PI) and m() is a method like sqrt(). Let us print these two values:

```
System.out.println("e="+Math.E+"\tsquare root of 81 is  "+Math.sqrt(81.0));
```

The following table will include some of the common math methods:

Modifier and Type	Methods and Description
static double	<u>abs</u>(double a) Returns the absolute value of a double value.
static double	<u>floor</u>(double a) Returns the largest (closest to positive infinity) double value that is less than or equal to the argument and is equal to a mathematical integer.
static double	<u>log</u>(double a) Returns the natural logarithm (base e) of a double value.
static int	<u>max</u>(int a, int b) Returns the greater of two int values.

static float	min(float a, float b)
	Returns the smaller of two float values.
static double	pow(double a, double b)
	Returns the value of the first argument raised to the power of the second argument.
static double	random()
	Returns a double value with a positive sign, greater than or equal to 0.0 and less than 1.0.
static double	sin(double a)
	Returns the trigonometric sine of an angle.
static double	toRadians(double angdeg)
	Converts an angle measured in degrees to an approximately equivalent angle measured in radians.

Example 1: Write a program to simulate tossing of a coin. The program should print whether it is a king (aka head) or a queen (aka tail).

We will simulate this by generating a zero or a one randomly. We know that coin tossing is random. If the number generated is zero, it is a king. Otherwise, it is a queen. We can generate random numbers in two different ways:

1. `static double random()` method in the Math class will generate a pseudorandom number between 0.0 (inclusive) and 1.0 (exclusive). It is invoked by `Math.random()`.
2. `import java.util.Random` – generates an object and then calls different `Random()` methods which generate pseudorandom integers.

The following code will introduce both the generators but will use Random generator for the coin toss application. This is more convenient to generate 0 and 1.

Here is the program

Coding List 5.1: RandomGenerators.java

```
/**
 * Author:
 * Date:
 * Input: Introducing random generators. Simulating coin toss. Observe how
   the Random class is imported, how a Random object (gen) is created, and
   how this object is used to invoke gen.nextInt(2) method. Also observe
   that Math.random() method does not require an object to generate random
   decimal numbers.
   Output: Generates 0 or 1 randomly with 0 being King and 1 Queen. It
   also shows the random generator Math.random() method.
```

```
*/

import java.util.Random; // needed to generate random integers #1

public class RandomGenerators
{ public static void  main (String args[])
  { int coin; // to hold 0 or 1 for king or queen
    double randomNum; // for the decimal random number [0,1)
    Random gen = new Random(); // needed to create the object gen to use
                              // with nextInt(2) #2
    coin = gen.nextInt(2);  // nextInt(2) will generate either 0 or 1,
                            // integers less than 2, nextInt(51)
                            // will generate random integers 0-50.
    System.out.println("coin="+ coin);
    if(coin == 0)
        System.out.println("It is a King");
    else    // if not 0, it should be 1
        System.out.println("It is a Queen");

// second way of generating random numbers is to use Math.random()
    randomNum = Math.random();// random number in [0,1)
    System.out.println("Decimal random number = "+ randomNum);


    }
}
```

Here is the output:
iiii
coin=0
It is a King
Decimal random number = 0.7512613029079557

Example 2: This example is to write a program which will accept two decimal values from the keyboard as the two sides of a right triangle and find the hypotenuse side. We will use the Pythagorean Theorem. If a and b are the two sides of a right triangle then the hypotenuse c is

$$c = \sqrt{(a^2 + b^2)}.$$

Here is the program

Coding List 5.2: Pythagorean.java

```
/**
 * Author:
 * Date:
 * INPUT: Two sides a and b of a right triangle entered from keyboard
 * OUTPUT: Length of the hypotenuse using Pythagorean Theorem.
 * Math methods sqrt() is used. Program will check for invalid data entry.
 */

import java.util.Scanner;  // needed to generate path to keyboard

public class Pythagorean {
```

```
public static void main (String args[]) {
    double a, b, c; // sides of a right triangle
    Scanner  keyboard = new Scanner(System.in);    // keyboard object

    System.out.print("Enter the first side: ");
    a=keyboard.nextDouble();
    if(a <= 0)
      System.out.println(a + " is an invalid side. Program ends.");
    else
    { System.out.print("Enter the second side: ");
      b=keyboard.nextDouble();
        if (b <= 0)
            System.out.println(b + " is an invalid side. Program ends.");
        else
          { c = Math.sqrt(a*a+b*b);
            System.out.println("\nside a = "+a);
            System.out.println("side b = "+b);
            System.out.println("hypotenuse = "+ c);
          }
      }
    }
}
```

Here is the output of all the three cases, including invalid entrees:

```
Enter the first side: -1
-1.0 is an invalid side. Program ends.


Enter the first side: 5
Enter the second side: -2
-2.0 is an invalid side. Program ends.


Enter the first side: 3
Enter the second side: 4

side a = 3.0
side b = 4.0
hypotenuse = 5.0
```

5.3 String Class

We routinely do several string manipulations. We search strings for specific words (like to find/search words in Word or PDF documents), we find the number of characters in a string document, we want to change all the characters to uppercase or lowercase, and so on. Java provides several methods in `java.lang.String` class. Here is the table of some of the commonly used string methods:

Modifier and Type	Methods and Description
char	**charAt**(int index) Returns the char value at the specified index.
int	**compareTo**(String another String) Compares two strings lexicographically.
boolean	**contains**(CharSequence s) Returns true if and only if this string contains the specified sequence of char values.
boolean	**equals**(Object an Object) Compares this string to the specified object.
static String	**format**(String format, Object... args) Returns a formatted string using the specified format string and arguments.
int	**indexOf**(int ch) Returns the index within this string of the first occurrence of the specified character.
int	**length**() Returns the length of this string.
String	**replace**(char oldChar, char newChar) Returns a new string resulting from replacing all occurrences of oldChar in this string with newChar.
String[]	**split**(String regex) Splits this string around matches of the given regular expression.
String	**substring**(int beginIndex) Returns the substring of this string starting at beginIndex until the end
String	**substring**(int beginIndex, int endIndex) Returns the substring of this string starting at beginIndex and ending at endIndex-1
String	**toString**() This object (which is already a string!) is itself returned.
String	**toUpperCase**() Converts all of the characters in this String to upper case using the rules of the default locale.
String	**trim**() Returns a copy of the string, with leading and trailing whitespace omitted.
static String	**valueOf**(float f) Returns the string representation of the float argument.

0	1	2	3	4	5	6	7	8	9	10	11	12	13	14	15	16
	E	O	R	G	E		W	A	S	H	I	N	G	T	O	N

Example 3: Let us write a program to read a full name of a person and separate the first name and last name. As you would notice, a blank space separates the first name from the last name. Consider "George Washington" as shown in the table above. The letter 'G' is at index zero and 'W' is at index 7. The first name "George" starts at index 0 and ends at index 5 (letter 'e'). So, "George" is a sub-string (a part of the name) from index 0 to index 5. Java has the method substring(0,6) which will return the substring starting at index 0 and ending at index 6-1=5 of any string referenced to. The number of letters in the full name is 17. Java has the method length() to find the length (number of characters in the string) of any referenced string. The index of the letter 'n' at the end is 16 as we start the indices at 0. What is the index of the blank space? So, the last name is returned by substring(7,17). The numbers in the example given here are very specific to "George Washington". So, we need to first find the position (called the index) of the blank space in the name. Java has the method indexOf(' ') that returns the index of any character in the referenced string. If we number the characters in the name, java always starts at zero. But what if you enter "John Adams"? All the numbers will change. So, when we write a program, we should make the program find all these numbers for any input we provide. Note that we do not have to import the String class, compared to importing the Random class. Here is the program to separate the first and last name of any name entered at the keyboard:

Coding List 5.3: FirstLastName.java

```
/* Author:
 * Date:

   This program introduces several String methods.
   This program separates first and last names from a full name.
   length() is a string method that returns the number of
   characters in the string specified. We need to specify which
   string we are trying to find. we do that by referring to the
   string fist followed by the method length(). If we want the length
   of name1, we will invoke name1.length(). If we want the length
   of name2, we will say name2.length(). If we want the length of
   "Mississippi", we will invoke "Mississippi".length().


   INPUT: Full name of a person from the keyboard read into one variable
```

```
     OUTPUT: First and second names are separated and assigned to
     To two different variables. Then they are printed.
*/


import java.util.Scanner;  // needed to generate path to keyboard


public class FirstLastName
{ public static void main (String args[]) {
   { int length, index; // for indices of letters
     Scanner  keyboard = new Scanner(System.in);    // keyboard object
     String name, firstName, lastName;


     System.out.print("Enter the full name: ");
     name=keyboard.nextLine();//Use nextLine for strings with more than one
word
     length = name.length(); // number of characters in name
     System.out.println("Full name: "+name+"\tNumber of letters = "+length);
     index = name.indexOf(' '); // index of the blank space
     firstName = name.substring(0,index); // index is one before blank space
     lastName = name.substring(index+1,length);
     System.out.print("First Name: "+firstName+"\tLast Name = "+lastName);
     System.out.println("\nIndex of blank space = "+index);
     System.out.println("\nNumber of chars in Missippi is
"."Missippi".length());

   }

}
```

Here is the output:

```
Enter the full name: George Washington
Full name: George Washington    Number of letters = 17
First Name: George       Last Name = Washington
Index of blank space = 6

Number of chars in Missippi is 8
```

5.4   Reading from and Writing to a Text File

It is very common to read from text files (databases) and write into text files. Java allows us to read from and write into databases in a similar way. We will focus on reading from and writing to text files. If we are reading from a file, that file needs to be already created. On the other hand, we could write into an existing file or could write into an empty file. For reading from a file, we use the Scanner class and we use PrintWriter class for writing into files. The import statements will be the same as above. Here are the instructions to create the two objects for reading from jobs.txt file and writing into jobs2.txt:

```
Scanner flIn = new Scanner(new File("jobs.txt"));

PrintWriter flOut = new PrintWriter("jobs2.txt");
```

Example 4: Here is a program which illustrates how to read from and write to text files. The jobs.txt is already created with each record having a name, salary, and job title. Here is the data:

```
nagaraj          23000.00            professor
bhanu            49999.00            engineer
smith            22222.00            manager
einstein         1111111.00          commissioner
smith            83000.00            manager
jones            120000.0            ceo
brown            27800.00            Assistant
jefferson        125000.00           teacher
gandhi           63000.00            principal
```

We will read this data into three variables: name, salary, and title. We will write them into jobs2.txt file. Here is the program:

Coding List 5.4: ReadWriteFiles.java

```
/* Author:
 * Date:

 * Input:
 * This program illustrates I/O from text files. Pay attention to how the
 * print statements are written. It is very critical for the formatting to
 * be correct for all the instructions to work properly. We are closing the
 * text files every time we are done using the file. Observe the format
 * specifiers so as to print in a table. Jobs2.txt will be created when
 * the object is created (#3).
 * Output:
 * Prints the records of jobs.txt and jobs2.txt.
 */

import java.io.*;                          // #1
import java.util.Scanner;


public class ReadWriteFiles
{ public static void main(String args[]) throws IOException        // #2
  { Scanner fl = new Scanner(new File("jobs.txt"));                // #3
    PrintWriter flOut = new PrintWriter("jobs2.txt");             // #4

    String name;
    String title;
    double salary;
```

```
    System.out.println("\n\nData from jobs.txt - read file");
    while (fl.hasNextLine())                                          // #5
    { name= fl.next();
      salary = fl.nextDouble();
      title = fl.nextLine();
      System.out.printf("%-15s\t%10.2f\t%-15s\n", name, salary, title);
//monitor
      flOut.printf("%-1s\t%.2f\t%1s\n", name, salary, title); // jobs2.txt

    }
    fl.close();        // close open files                            // #6
    flOut.close();

    System.out.println("\n\n\n Data from written file - jobs2.txt");

    Scanner fl2 = new Scanner(new File("jobs2.txt")); // open jobs2.txt for
reading

    while (fl2.hasNext())
    { System.out.printf("%-15s\t%10.2f\t%-15s\n", fl2.next(),
fl2.nextDouble(), fl2.nextLine());

    }

  fl2.close();
  }
}
```

Here is the output, first from jobs.txt and the second from jobs2.txt after
writing into it:

```
Data from jobs.txt - read file
nagaraj          23000.00               professor
bhanu            49999.00               engineer
smith            22222.00               manager

einstein       1111111.00               commissioner
smith            83000.00               manager
jones           120000.00               ceo
brown            27800.00               Assistant
jefferson       125000.00               teacher
gandhi           63000.00               principal

M

Data from written file - jobs2.txt
nagaraj          23000.00               professor
bhanu            49999.00               engineer
smith            22222.00               manager
einstein       1111111.00               commissioner
smith            83000.00               manager
jones           120000.00               ceo
brown            27800.00               Assistant
jefferson       125000.00               teacher
gandhi           63000.00               principal
```

5.5   What did you learn?

1. Math class and several math methods. Know the input and output types of each method. Know how to invoke them. No need to import Math class.
2. String class and its several methods. No need to import the String class.
3. Print formatted output using `printf()` method. Know format specifiers and using the `printf()` statement.
4. Create a text file using Notepad. Import Scanner class and `java.io.*`. Create a Scanner object to point to the text file. Read different types of data from the text file.

Note: We are using 'keyboard' identifier as the Scanner object to read from the keyboard and 'file' identifier as the Scanner object to point to a text file. Different authors use different identifier names.

5. Write to text files using `PrintWriter`.

5.5 Exercises

Concept Understanding

1. Consider a programming manual in general and API in particular for object-oriented programming (OOP).

   a. Why API is more appropriate to OOP?

   b. Visit the website https://docs.oracle.com/7/docs/api. There are packages and classes on the upper left box. Are the classes you code the subclasses to the classes you import from these packages and classes?

   c. In the website above, packages in the java language begin with java or javax. List some of the sub-categories of java packages. For example, javax.security.auth and javax.security.cert are in the sub-category of javax.security.

2. In the java API, e.g., https://docs.oracle.com/javase/7/docs/api, there are two identical class names in the lower left box.
   a. Explain the similarity and difference between them.
   b. Show how differently they are used.

Programming

3. Write a program to generate and print 1000 random integers in the range 1 – 100. Also, count how many of them are in the range 1-10, 11-20, 21-30, ..., 91-100. Print the counts.
4. Simulate flipping a coin 1000 times. This can be done by 0's and 1's randomly and counting them. What are the counts?

5. Write a program to verify if an email address is valid or not. Receive the email address from the keyboard. Print a message stating whether the entered address is valid or not. There must be a '@' symbol and there must be one extension like .edu or .com, etc.

6. Write a program to read a last name. Print the number of characters in the name and also the number of ovals (a, e, I, o, and u) in the name.

7. Write a program to read a quote from the keyboard. Print the sentence and the number of words in the sentence.

8. Write a program for the user to guess an integer in the range 5-10, randomly generated by the computer. Repeat this until a terminal value is entered. Count the number of correct answers and number of incorrect answers. BONUS: Give 3 chances for each random number.

9. Write a program to accept a radius of a sphere from the keyboard and print its volume and surface area. The formulas are

$$\text{Surface area} = 4\pi r^2$$
$$\text{Volume} = (4/3)\pi r^3$$

Note: Be careful with integer division.

10. Write a program to read the coordinates of two points and print the distance between them. The distance formula is

$$\text{Distance} = \sqrt{((x1-x2)^2 + (y1 - y2)^2)}$$

11. Find the area of a triangle using two different methods. Print the information in both the cases. The formulas are

(a) Heron method: area = $\sqrt{(s(s-a)(s-b)(s-c))}$ where s = (a+b+c)/2, a,b,c are sides of the triangle.
Note: Accept the lengths of the 3 sides of a triangle, calculate s and then the area. Be careful with integer division.

(b) SAS method: area = (1/2)bc sin(A)
Side Angle Side (SAS) is side b, angle A, and side c.
Note: Accept two sides of a triangle and the angle, in radians, of the included angle A.

12. Write a program to find and print the initials of a three-word name. For example, if the name is John Quincy Adams, the program should concatenate the initials J, Q, and A and print JQA.

13. Create a text file of three employees. Each employee should have a name, an annual income, and number of deductions. The program should read each of these employee data and print their income taxes. If the net income is less than $50,000, the tax rate should be 20% and it should be 35% otherwise. Let the dependent deduction be $3000 per dependent (children and spouse for example). Do not use a loop. For example, assume the employee is "Jefferson" with an annual income of $83,500 per year and has three deductions for his two children and wife. Then the net income = 83500 – 3*3000 =

$74,500. Since this is greater than $50,000, the tax rate is 35%. Hence, tax = 0.35*77500 = $27,125. The program should print

> *Name: Jefferson*
> *Income: $83,500*
> *Tax Rate: 35%*
> *Tax: $27,125*

14. Write a program to find the index of a character in a sentence. Let the sentence be

    "Our greatest weakness lies in giving up. The most certain way to succeed is always to try just one more time." **Thomas A. Edison**

    If the user enters the character 'p' to be found, the program should return the index of the letter 'p' which is 38. 'p' is actually the 39th character, but its index is 38.

    Hint: Look up the API for String class and use the method, indexOf().

15. Write a program, Reverse.java, that can read a word from the keyboard and return the word that reads backwards of the given word. For example, if "Mercy" is entered, then Reverse.java returns "ycreM". Scrambling characters of a word will make it difficult to understand. Scramble letters of a word randomly and assign it to the variable `scrambled`.

16. Read a sentence from the keyboard and print whether it is a palindrome or not. (A **palindrome** is a word, phrase, <u>number</u>, or other sequence of <u>characters</u> which reads the same backward or forward. Allowances may be made for adjustments to capital letters, punctuation, and word dividers. Famous examples include "A man, a plan, a canal, Panama!", "Amor, Roma", "race car", "stack cats", "step on no pets", "taco cat", "put it up", "Was it a car or a cat I saw?" and "No 'x' in Nixon". Wikipedia.org)

17. Extend #13 to write a program, ReverseSentence.java, that can read a sentence and return the reverse of the given sentence. For example, if "Mercy is great." is entered, then ReverseSentence.java returns "taerg si ycreM".

18. Consider bank accounts in a banking system. Each bank account will have numerous transactions: Deposits, withdrawals, interest calculations, balance check, etc., are performed repeatedly. The amount of deposit will be added to an account balance, the amount of withdrawal will be subtracted from the balance, and an interest amount will be added to the balance. Assume that the interest rate is 5% annually, and an interest calculation is performed once a month with the 1/12 the annual interest. It means that each time of the Interest Calculation choice is a new month. Do not worry about the float point numbers at this point. For those who want to challenge, the box below explains how to format numbers in US dollar.

A sample run is shown below:

```
C:\Windows\system32\cmd.exe

C:\Mercy\Book_java>java BankAcctLoop
** Welcome Mercy Bank **
------------------------------------------------------
Choose a Number (1) Deposit; (2) Withdrawal; (3) Interest Calc; (4) Display; (0)
 Exit
1
Enter the Deposit Amount:
450
------------------------------------------------------
Choose a Number (1) Deposit; (2) Withdrawal; (3) Interest Calc; (4) Display; (0)
 Exit
2
Enter the Amount to Withdraw:
34.21
------------------------------------------------------
Choose a Number (1) Deposit; (2) Withdrawal; (3) Interest Calc; (4) Display; (0)
 Exit
3
The Balance before Interest is $415.79
The Interest for this Month is $1.7324583333333334
The Balance after Interest Calculation is $417.52245833333336
------------------------------------------------------
Choose a Number (1) Deposit; (2) Withdrawal; (3) Interest Calc; (4) Display; (0)
 Exit
1
Enter the Deposit Amount:
99.99
------------------------------------------------------
Choose a Number (1) Deposit; (2) Withdrawal; (3) Interest Calc; (4) Display; (0)
 Exit
4
The Balance is $517.5124583333334
------------------------------------------------------
Choose a Number (1) Deposit; (2) Withdrawal; (3) Interest Calc; (4) Display; (0)
 Exit
0
Thanks for Using Mercy Bank...

C:\Mercy\Book_java>
```

Classes and Objects

6.1 Introduction

The real-world consists of numerous objects, visible and invisible objects, tangible and intangible objects, existing and non-existing objects, etc. Each object consists of two aspects of information: common-value information and behavioral information.

Recall the student example. There are a number of students. A student object could have attributes such as student name, college ID, and grades. These attributes are common to all students. In addition to attributes to be defined, a student object may have behavioral components such as the calculation of GPA and management of tuition. Behavioral components of an object are defined as methods.

We have created several identifiers of different types. For example, the identifier *name* was of type String. The identifier gpa was of type 'double'. Similarly, every object we create must have a type. For example, Scanner is a class. We have created objects of type Scanner. The two objects that we have created in the past are *keyboard* and *file,* both of Scanner type. In Java programming, to represent and handle an object, e.g. students, we need to first define the type of student object. We call it a **class**. A class can be compared to a mold from which you make several toy cars. The shape of the mold is the same for all the cars but you create several different toy cars which all have same characteristics. Similarly you can create several different students with different values (like John and Mary for the name attribute) but all of them will have the same attributes (like name, gpa, and tuition).

We have been using predefined classes so far. For example, Scanner and Random are predefined classes (that can be used as types). We have used them as types to create objects. Part of those pre-defined classes come with JDK and some are available in Java Virtual Machine (JVM) by default (String and Math, for example) or some others are also available when imported. As opposed to these pre-defined classes, we can also define our own classes. These are called user-defined classes.

Class names are similar to variable and method names except that we start class names with capital letters, like in Scanner and Random. It is not required but is a good habit to recognize classes and also to reduce errors.

A way that such a class is used is to

1)   import it in the form of jar file,

2)   create an object of that class, and

3)   invoke methods of that object.

For example, assume that Student is defined as a class called Student.java.

6.1.1 Importation of Class

If a jar file, say edu.mercy.OurStud.jar, is created by including Student.class and if it is stored in a computer, then it can be imported:

```
import edu.mercy.OurStud.Student;
```

Compare this import statement with the import statement for Scanner:
```
import java.util.Scanner;
```

6.1.2 Construction of an Object

The class Student can be instantiated by

```
Student john = new Student();
```

This will create the object john, assuming that there is a Student() constructor in the Student class. Student() constructor takes no input argument unlike Scanner(System.in) which takes "System.in" as an argument. The constructor with no arguments is called the default constructor.

6.1.3 Invocation of a Method

Going back to Student class and its object john, assume we want to calculate the financial support of john. The Student class must have a method to calculate this. Let us call it financialSupport(). The john object needs to execute the method financialSupport(). The following statement can do that:

```
john.financialSupport();
```

Assume that we created another object called mary. Let us create the mary object

```
Student mary = new Student();
```

Now if we want to calculate mary's financial support, we have to invoke financialSupport() for mary. Here is the statement for mary:

```
mary.financialSupport();
```

If financialSupport() returns the financial amount for mary or john, that value has to be utilized in some other statement like printing, in a conditional, or in an expression. This chapter describes how to create user-defined classes and their objects.

Some of the information pieces are variable or constant fields, while some are methods.
Access to any of these can be restricted. For example, consider your grades in the college system. If the system did not have restriction to modify your grades, most of the students would change all their grades to A! So, students should not be given access to change the grades, but

only to view them. Java has features to restrict access to data and methods. Also, John's data should be protected from others. Some should be available to any object in JVM, while others must be restricted to the objects of the class which they are defined in. For example, sqrt() method is accessible to any class object whereas John's grade should be accessible to only John object. Analogously, in our world, some information can be viewed by anyone in the world, some can be viewed by anyone in their family, for example, brother, mother, grandparents, etc, and some can be viewed only by the individual.

This chapter also shows the definition of constructors. Constructors of a class are a special case of methods. These will have the <u>same name as the class</u> and will be used to CONSTRUCT objects of that class. For example, Student() is a constructor in the Student class to construct Student objects like `john` and `mary`. Similarly, `Scanner()` is a constructor in which we can pass `System.in` or a file object.

6.2   User-Defined Classes

As an example, consider the class of students. Let each student be defined by name, major, schoolCode, math and java. As illustrated above, we should be able to calculate financial aid and gpa. Those are defined as methods, say `financialSupport()` and `gpaCalculation()`.

Consider the following statement:
```
    public double java;
```
All the students in this example takes the java course and will have a grade. So, java attribute (variable) is the same for all the students but will take different values for different students. Now consider the statement:

```
    public static int schoolCode;
```

All the students are in the same school and hence the value of the variable `schoolCode`, which is static, is the same to all the students of the class Student, and its value can be viewed by all objects. Every student will have the same school code and hence is the same for all the students. This variable is called a *class variable* and has the static modifier. Another example of class variable is a bank routing number, which is the same to all accounts in the bank. In a bank, each bank account is unique and different from others, but its routing number is common to all accounts in the bank. To make variables class variables, the modifier `static` is used as above.

As opposed to a class variable, in the code segment below, there are four object variables, name, major, math and java. An *object variable* is the variable which belongs to a particular object (or an instance of an object) and it has a different value according to instance.

With this, the class is created as follows:

public class Student

{   // class variables are defined, instance variables

    public static int schoolCode; // class variable common to all objects

```java
    public String name; // any object can access public fields
    public String major;
    private double java; // only specific objects can access these, private to the object
    private double math;

    /* one or more constructors can be defined in this way, constructors are overloaded
       From the overloaded constructors, each object can be constructed based on one
       definition of the overloaded constructors depending on arguments specified. Overloaded
       is when we have more than one method with the same method name, but will receive different
       parameter lists default constructor will not have any parameters
    */
    public Student() {
      name = null;
      major = null;
    }
    // constructor that can enter two fields only
    public Student (String name, String major) {
      this.name = name;
      this.major = major;
    }
    /* Student() is a default constructor. Student(String name, String major) is an overloaded
    constructor. We will use one of these to construct a Student object, like john and mary objects.
    This is a segment of the full Student class.
    */
}
```

The class `Student` defined above can be represented in Unified Model Language (UML) as described below.

UML: Class Diagram
Challenge — This diagram follows the features of Unified Modeling Language (UML, www.uml.org). UML represents both structural and behavioral information. Writing this diagram before coding will help in understanding the structure of the class as well as will make it easier to write the code. The structural information of objects is depicted in class diagram as shown

below:

```
 Student
 schoolCode: int
 name: String
 major: String
 java: double
 math: double
 financialSupport()
 financialSupport(rea: String)
 avgCalculation(): double
```

The UML representation of a class is a rectangle containing three compartments stacked vertically, as shown above. The top compartment shows the class's name, the middle compartment lists the field attributes, and the bottom the operations. The top compartment is mandatory, while the bottom optional.

Class fields	Field attributes are listed in the format of attribute_name: attribute_type
Class operations	Operations documented in the third compartment of the class diagram's rectangle are in the following notation: name (parameter list) : type of value return

6.2.2. User-Defined Methods

A Java method is a collection of statements that are grouped together to perform an operation. When a method is called, a sequence of statements defined in the method is executed. When you call the System.out.println() method, for example, the system actually executes several statements in order to display a message on the console (which is System.out).

In addition to the methods provided by JDK, methods can be defined in a user-defined class. We can create our own methods with or without return values, invoke a method with or without parameters, overload methods using the same names (but different parameters), and etc.

Here are some examples to illustrate various types of methods. They also give you ideas of how you can create your own methods.

```
// method funcName1() does not take values (empty parameter list) nor return a value
(void type)
public void funcName1 () {
    // statements
}
```

```
// method funcName2() takes values (has parameters) but does not return a value (void
type)
public void funcName2 (int a, double b) {
    // statements
}
```

// method funcName3() does not take values but returns a value (int type)
// notice the method type (int) is the same as the type of the
// return value (int). <u>Every non-void method must have a `return` statement.</u>

```java
public int funcName3 () {
    int val;
    // statements
    // finally, at the end of the body of funcName3
    return val;
}
```

// method funcName4()takes values (has parameters) and returns a value (double type)
```java
public double funcName4 (int b, String s) {
    double val;
    // statements
    // finally, at the end of the body of funcName3
    return val;
}
```

If a method receives one or more values from the caller statement, those values should be declared in the parenthesis of a method signature, as shown in `funcName2()` and `funcName4()` above. An example of caller statements for these two methods can be:

// assume an object obj2 is constructed and ready to be invoked:
// caller statement invoking the method funcName2().
```java
obj2.funcName2 (12, 23.99);
```

// caller statement invoking the method funcName4().
```java
double d = obj2.funcName4 (11, "Mercy");
```
// since the `funcName4` returns a value `val`, the caller side
// should be ready to receive and store, or print, or do something with that value
// In this case, the `double` variable d will hold the `double` return value.

On the other hand, if no parameters are passed to a called method, as shown in methods `funcName1`and `funcName3`, the caller statement will be much simpler.

// assume an object obj3 is constructed and ready to invoke
// caller statement invoking the method `funcName1()`.
// Since it does not return a value, it stands by itself
```java
obj3.funcName1 ();
```

// caller statement invoking the method `funcName3()`.
```java
System.out.println(obj3.funcName3 ());
```
// since the funcName3 returns a value val, the caller side
// should be ready to receive and use it in some way.

```
// In this case, we are printing the return value.
```

As illustrated above, if a method returns a value, then its type should appear as modifier. If no value is returned, simply the keyword void is used. void methods will not have a return statement.

```
public void financialSupport(String reason) {
    System.out.print("Due to ");
    System.out.print(reason);
    System.out.println("financial support is requested");
}
```

Here is the method to calculate the average of math and java grades. It has to first calculate the average and then return that value. This value will come to wherever the method is invoked at.

```
public double avgCalculation() {
    return (java + math)/2;
}
```

Example 1: Together with variables and methods, here is the Student1.java class:

Coding List 6.1: Student1.java

```
/*
 * Author:
 * Date:
 * Input: Student information: java and math grades, school code
 *        and name of the student. NO VALUES WILL BE INVOLVED IN
 *        THIS CLASS AS THERE IS NO main() METHOD AND SO CANNOT BE
 *        EXECUTED.
 * Output: NONE AS THERE IS NO EXECUTION
 */
class Student1
{ // following variable fields defined here are sometimes called
  // instance variables. Every instance of this class (each object
  // of the class is an instance of the class. Each instance
  // (object) will get its own instance of these variables.

  static int schoolCode; // class variable for all object
  String name;
  String major;
  double java;
  double math;
  // one or more constructors are defined
  // in this way, constructors are overloaded
  // From the overloaded constructors,
  // each object can be constructed based on one definition of the
  // overloaded constructors depending on arguments specified.

  // default constructor
  public Student1() {
      name = null;
      major = null;
  }
```

```
   // constructor that can enter two fields only
   public Student1 (String name, String major)
   { this.name = name;
     this.major = major;
   }

   // methods are defined
   public void financialSupport(double income) {
     if (income < 50000)
       System.out.print("Financial support is requested due to low income.");
     else
       System.out.print("Financial support is not requested due to high
income.");

   }
   public double avgCalculation() {
      return (java + math)/2;
   }
}  // end of class
```

Now, we have use this class in some other class which has a man() method and hence can be executed. We will create objects of Student1 class and execute the methods through those objects. Here is the driver for Student1:

Coding List 6.2: Student1Driver.java

```
/**
 * Author:
 * Date:
 * Input:
 * Two students are created using Student1 class. Student1
 * class has two constructors: default one without any parameters and
 * the second with two parameters - name and major. Notice all the
 * class variables of Studet1 are created without any visibility
 * modifier. This means they all have public modifier. So, they can
 * be accessed/modified by any class, including outside classes.
 *
 * Output:
 * Builds the two students (objects std1 and std2). Observe
 * how they are getting the values into their variables. This is a
 * driver class (to test the class Student1) with a main() method.
 * This is executable. It will print all the information for both the
 * students. Observe how typed and un-typed (void) methods are
 * invoked.
 */

public class Student1Driver
{ public static void main(String args[])
   { Student1 std1 = new Student1(); //invoking default constructor
        // constructor with 2 parameters
     Student1 std2 = new Student1("Washington", "Math");

     //all variables in Student1 are public as no visibility modifier specified
     std1.name="Lincoln";//name is public in Student1, directly changed
     std1.major = "CS";    // major is public too.
```

```
    std1.math = 85.5;
    std1.java = 93;

    std2.math= 65;
    std2.java = 37;

    // now test the methods for the two objects, std1 and std2

    System.out.println("Student 1:");
    System.out.println("Math and java grades of "+std1.name +" are
"+std1.math+" and "+std1.java);
//avgCalculation() method returns an average value, so is in a print statement
    System.out.println("The average grade of "+std1.name+" is
"+std1.avgCalculation());
// financialSupport() is a void method. It does not return any value.
// So, it is invoked standing alone.
    std1.financialSupport(43560);

    System.out.println("\n\nStudent 2:");
    System.out.println("Math and java grades of "+std2.name +" are
"+std2.math+" and "+std2.java);

    System.out.println("The average grade of "+std2.name+" is
"+std2.avgCalculation());
    std2.financialSupport(250000);
  }
}
```

```
Here is the output. Study the output and the corresponding statements in the
class above.
Student 1:
Math and java grades of Lincoln are 85.5 and 93.0
The average grade of Lincoln is 89.25
Financial support is requested due to low income.

Student 2:
Math and java grades of Washington are 65.0 and 37.0
The average grade of Washington is 51.0
Financial support is not requested due to high income.
```

6.2.3. Scope Identifier

Recall that variables are declared for values in different memory sizes. The memory size allocated for a variable is determined by the type. In a similar manner, variables are declared for memory allocation as well as for visibility that can determine who can view directly or cannot (which class object could use it). Variables declared in a class have four levels of visibility to other classes. The modifier that can determine visibility includes `public`, `private`, `protected` and none.

For example, in the coding list of Student1.java, we could have defined variables in the following manner:

```java
// default visibility by no modifier, same as public
String name;

// public visibility – major can be viewed by any class
public String major;

// private visibility – variable, java can be viewed only within the class
private double java;

// protected visibility – math can be viewed by the only classes
// along the class hierarchy.
protected double math;
```

The visibility modifier can be summarized as follows:

- `public` modifier: visible to all classes.
- `private` modifier: visible only within the class, not by inheritors, not by other classes in the package.
- `protected` modifier: visible to classes outside the package that inherit the class, also to all classes in the package.
- Default or no modifier: visible to all classes of the package. This will be public.

The visibility modifiers can be applied to not only variables but also to classes and methods.

Example 2: For example, the class Student2.java has public and private modifiers added to its variables. Here `java` and `math` are private. Observe how they are accessed when compared to `name` and `major` which are public.

Coding List 6.3: Student2.java

```java
/**
 * Author:
 * Date:
 * Input:
 * We have made java and math variables private. name and major
 * variables will remain public. We have added schoolCode variable.
 * This is public and is static as it applies to all the students
 * in the same school. When a variable is static, it is the same for
 * all the objects of the class. If it is not static, it belongs to
 * a single object of the class.
 * Output:
 * display the statistics of students for each school
 */

public class Student2
{
    // variable fields are defined
    public static int schoolCode;
    public String name;
    public String major;
    private double java;// private, usable by objects of this class only
    private double math;
```

CLASSES AND OBJECTS   115

```
    // default constructor
    public Student2() {
        name = null;
        major = null;
    }

    // constructor that can enter two fields only
    public Student2 (String name, String major) {
        this.name = name;
        this.major = major;
    }
    // methods are defined
    private void financialSupport(double income) {
      if (income < 50000)
        System.out.print("Financial support is requested due to low income.");
      else
        System.out.print("Financial support is not requested due to high
income.");
    }

    public double avgCalculation() {
        return (java + math)/2;
    }
}
```

Here is Student2Driver:

```
Coding List 6.4: Student2Driver.java
/**
 * Author:
 * Date:
 * Input:
 * Two students are created using Student2 class. Student2 is the same
 * as Student1 except that math and java are private class variables. So they
 * cannot be accessed outside of Student2 class. They cannot be accessed in
 * this driver class which is outside of Student2 class. We have left the
 * main() method as in Student1 to observe the difference in accessing public
 * and private variables. We will have "java has private access..." error
 * message when we try to modify math and java values. We will add
 * accessor and mutator methods in Student3 class and repeat the main()
 * method using the new accessor and mutator methods.
 *
 * Output:
 * Builds the two students (objects std1 and std2). Observe how they
 * get the values into their variables. This is a driver class (to test the
 * class Student2) with a main() method. This is executable. It will give an
 * error messages when we try to access the private variables. The error
 * output is also included below.
 */

public class Student2Driver
{ public static void main(String args[])
  { Student2 std1 = new Student2();
    Student2 std2 = new Student2("Washington", "Math");
```

```
    // all variables in Student1 are public as no visibility modifier specified
    std1.name="Lincoln";  // name is public in Student1, directly changed
    std1.major = "CS";     // major is public too.
    std1.math = 85.5;
    std1.java = 93;

    std2.math= 65;
    std2.java = 37;

    // now test the methods for the two objects, std1 and std2

    System.out.println("Student 1:");
    System.out.println("Math and java grades of "+std1.name +" are
"+std1.math+" and "+std1.java);
    // avgCalculation() method returns the average value. So, it is in a print
statement
    System.out.println("The average grade of "+std1.name+" is
"+std1.avgCalculation());
    // financialSupport() is a void method. It does not return any value.
    // So, it is invoked standing alone.
    std1.financialSupport(43560);

    System.out.println("\n\nStudent 2:");
    System.out.println("Math and java grades of "+std2.name +" are
"+std2.math+" and "+std2.java);
    System.out.println("The average grade of "+std2.name+" is
"+std2.avgCalculation());
    std2.financialSupport(250000);
  }
}
```

```
Here is the output. Match the error messages with the statements above.
Student2Driver.java:29: error: math has private access in Student2
std1.math = 85.5;
       ^

Student2Driver.java:30: error: java has private access in Student2
std1.java = 93;
       ^

Student2Driver.java:32: error: math has private access in Student2
std2.math= 65;
       ^

Student2Driver.java:33: error: java has private access in Student2
std2.java = 37;
       ^

Student2Driver.java:38: error: math has private access in Student2
System.out.println("Math and java grades of "+std1.name +" are "+std1.math+"
and "+std1.java);
                                                                        ^

Student2Driver.java:38: error: java has private access in Student2
System.out.println("Math and java grades of "+std1.name +" are "+std1.math+"
and "+std1.java);

 ^

Student2Driver.java:43: error: financialSupport(double) has private access in
Student2
std1.financialSupport(43560);
       ^

Student2Driver.java:46: error: math has private access in Student2
```

```
System.out.println("Math and java grades of "+std2.name +" are "+std2.math+"
and "+std2.java);

Student2Driver.java:46: error: java has private access in Student2
System.out.println("Math and java grades of "+std2.name +" are "+std2.math+"
and "+std2.java);
                                                                    ^
Student2Driver.java:48: error: financialSupport(double) has private access in
Student2
std2.financialSupport(250000);
                     ^
10 errors
```

6.2.4   Accessing Visibility Modified Values

Consider once more Coding List 6.3, where some variables and methods are modified for their different visibility. In this section, as another class is created to drive the class Student2, we will discuss how to access each variable and method. Two ways of accessibility will be addressed: reading and writing.

The variables `math` and `java` are private in `Student2` class. But they can be accessed/modified in `Student2` (Coding List 6.3), as in its `avgCalculation()` method. `Student2Driver` class is outside `Student2` class. So, it cannot access the private variables `math` and `java`, and the private method `financialSupport()` method. When we tried to access them in `Student2Driver`, we got 10 error messages on accessibility. Let us resolve these errors by adding accessor and mutator methods. Let us create `Student3` and `Student3Driver` classes. Let us create objects `std4` and `std5` as below:

Objects in Two Different Classes		
Challenge	In Student3.java	In Student3Driver.java

	// std4 constructed in Student3 class
	// by default constructor
	
	Student3 std4 = new Student3();
		// std5 constructed in Student3Driver
		// outside of Student3 class
		
		Student3Driver std5 = new
		Student3Driver();

	Question	std4 in Student3 class and std5 in Student3Driver class, i.e., one constructed within its class and another in an outside class. How can both objects, std4 and std5 be constructed?
	Answer	The constructors defined in the Coding List 6.5 are public!! So they can be used in any class to create objects of type Student3
	Question	Do both std4 and std5 access private variables and methods?

The objects std4 and std5 have null values of all variables except the class value since they are constructed based on the default constructor without any parameters. Please note that the variables, name and major are set to null.

- Public variables can be accessed directly by any object. Both the objects std4 and std5, constructed in different classes, can read and write (change) the public variables name and major. For example, the following statements are possible:

// print the name and major of std3

```
System.out.println(std4.name + "\t" + std4.major);
```

```
// set values for std4
Std4.name = "Sam";
Std4.major = "Math";
```

The above statements can be evaluated from any objects of any classes as major and name are public fields.

- Public methods can be accessed by any object. Objects std4 and std5 can execute the method, avgCalculation(). For example, the following statements are possible:

```
// invoke and execute the method of std3
 double avg = std4.avgCalculation();
 // This method returns the average of std4's math and java
 // and the average is stored in the variable avg.
```

The above statements can be evaluated from any object.

- Private variables cannot be directly accessed but can access indirectly through methods created for that purpose. If the following is stated in a code segment, it works:

```
// print the java and math of std4, constructed in Student3
System.out.println(std4.java + "\t" + std4.math);
 // works well! You can access ANY variable (even private variables) inside the class
```
that created these variables. Private variables cannot be accessed directly outside of this class, as in Student2Driver class.

If the following is included in Student3Driver, there will be an error:

```
// print the java and math of std5, constructed in Student3Driver
System.out.println(std5.java + "\t" + std5.math);
 // this causes a visibility error!!
 // error: java has private access in Student3
```

A direct access of private variables and methods is impossible. Since private variables are invisible to other classes, there should be methods which should be public and provide indirect access to those private variables. So, this kind of public methods are called *accessor* (just accessing without changing private values) or *mutator* (changing private values) methods depending on whether they are accessing to read or write the private variables.

6.3   Accessors and Mutators

Accessors and Mutators	
Accessors are public methods that can read private variables or private methods on behalf of a caller object. Accessors allow to read only, cannot change them. Mutators are public methods that can write private variables or private methods on behalf of a caller object. Mutators change values. One of the ways we can enforce data encapsulation is through the use of accessors and mutators.	

Implementation	Consider the following accessor method that we will be included in Student3 class:
	
	``java
	public double getJava() {
	    return java;
	}
	``

Discussion	Although the variable `java` is invisible to an outside object, since the object can access the method `getJava()` (being public), and since `getJava()` is in Student3 and returns the private value of `java`, it turns out that the object can eventually access the private value. This is read only, can access the value but not change it. You could compare this with accessing your grades, without being able to change them. You could access these values and use them in calculations, for example. All accessibility is up to the implementation of `getJava()` method, or similar methods. If the method does not show, the private variable is invisible. If the method encrypts the private value, the object needs to decrypt it to read, etc.
Question	Any other benefits from accessors and mutators?
Discussion	Encapsulation of information – encapsulaltion is to hide the private data from outside the class (protecting private data). So all these variables and methods are invisible and hidden in a black box but public variables and methods are accessible in any class, including outside classes.

Challenge

Example 3: Private methods cannot be directly accessed but can be accessed indirectly. Assuming getJava() and getMath() methods are available, observe how the following errors can be eliminated:

```
// print the java and math of std5, constructed in Faculty
System.out.println(std5.java + "\t" + std5.math);
  // this causes a visibility error!!
  // we will now replace direct access of math and java with indirect access methods:
System.out.println(std5.getJava()+"\t"+std5.getMath());
```

We will now present Student3 and Student3Driver classes:

Coding List 6.5: Student3.java

```java
/**
 * Author:
 * Date:
 * Input:
 * We have made java and math variables private. name and major
 * variables will remain public. We have added schoolCode variable.
 * This is public and is static as it applies to all the students
 * in the same school. When a variable is static, it is the same for
 * all the objects of the class. If it is not static, it belongs to
 * a single object of the class.
 * Output: display the statistics of students for each school.
 */

public class Student3
{
    // variable fields are defined
    public static int schoolCode;
    public String name;
    public String major;
    private double java;// private, usable by objects of this class only
    private double math;
    // one or more constructors are defined
    // in this way, constructors are overloaded
    // From the overloaded constructors,
    // each object can be constructed based on one definition of the
overloaded
    // constructors depending on arguments specified.

    // default constructor
    public Student3() {
        name = null;
        major = null;
    }

    // constructor that can enter two fields only
    public Student3 (String name, String major) {
        this.name = name;
        this.major = major;
    }

    // WE WILL NOW ADD ACCESSOR/MUTATOR METHODS
    public double getMath() // accessor method, no change to math value
```

```
    { return math; }   // will return the value of private math

    public double getJava()
    { return java; }

    public void setMath(double mth) //mutator method, changes value of math
    { math = mth;    } // does not return any value, void type method

    public void setJava(double jva)
    { java = jva; }
    // methods are defined
    public void financialSupport(double income) {
      if (income < 50000)
        System.out.print("Financial support is requested due to low income.");
      else
        System.out.print("Financial support is not requested due to high
income.");
    }

    public double avgCalculation() {
        return (java + math)/2;
    }
}
```

Coding List 6.6: Student3Driver.java

```
/**
 * Author:
 * Date:
 * Input:
 * Two students are created using Student3 class. Student3 is the same
 * as Student2 except that we have added accessor/mutator methods. So they
 * math and java private variables can be accessed/modified outside of
Student3
 * class in Student3Driver class. Observe how the main() method is modified.
 *
 * Output:
 * Builds the two students (objects std4 and std5). Observe how they
 * getting the values into their variables. This is a driver class (to test
the
 * class Student3) with a main() method. This is executable. It will print
all
 * the information for both the students using accessor/mutator methods.
 */

public class Student3Driver
{ public static void main(String args[])
  { Student3 std4 = new Student3();
    Student3 std5 = new Student3("Washington", "Math");

    // all variables in Student1 are public as no visibility modifier
specified
    std4.name="Lincoln";   // name is public in Student3, directly changed
    std4.major = "CS";     // major is public too.
    std4.setMath(85.5);    // math is private, needs mutator method to change
    std4.setJava(93);
```

```
    std5.setMath(65);   // its constructor does not have math and java
    std5.setJava(37);   // as parameters

    // now test the methods for the two objects, std4 and std5

    System.out.println("Student 4:");
    System.out.print("Math and java grades of "+std4.name +" are
"+std4.getMath());
    System.out.println(" and "+std4.getJava());
    // avgCalculation() method returns the average value. So, it is in a
print statement
    System.out.println("The average grade of "+std4.name+" is
"+std4.avgCalculation());
    // financialSupport() is a void method. It does not return any value.
    // So, it is invoked standing alone.
    std4.financialSupport(43560);   // changed financialSupport() to public

    System.out.println("\n\nStudent 5:");
    System.out.print("Math and java grades of "+std5.name +" are
"+std5.getMath());
    System.out.println(" and "+std5.getJava());
    System.out.println("The average grade of "+std5.name+" is
"+std5.avgCalculation());
    std5.financialSupport(250000);
  }
}
```

```
Here is the output of Student3Driver, which is exactly the same
Student1Driver, even though Student3 has private variables.
Student 4:
Math and java grades of Lincoln are 85.5 and 93.0
The average grade of Lincoln is 89.25
Financial support is requested due to low income.
M
Student 5:
Math and java grades of Washington are 65.0 and 37.0
The average grade of Washington is 51.0
Financial support is not requested due to high income.
```

6.3.2 Class with the main() method

We know that we cannot execute a class without the `main()` method in it. We have been creating classes (like Student1, Student2,...) and then creating their corresponding drivers (Student1Driver, Student2Driver,...) to test out the classes. The rationale in this organization is that methods in classes could be used in any class or application that imports that class. In our set up, we need to alternate between the class (Student3 for example) and its driver (Student3Driver) in order to develop Student3 class. If the application is very big, this arrangement will become cumbersome, to say the least. For developing tasks, we could include the main method inside the class (as the last method of the class) and execute the class without the need to go to its driver. When we include the `main()` method in a class (say Student3), the main() method becomes a part of the class and hence all private units become accessible to the main() method, unlike in their drivers.

Example 4: Here is Student3M (Student3 with M-main() method) with the main method in it, becoming executable:

```
Coding List 6.7: Student3M.java
/**
 * Author:
 * Date:
 * Input:
 * We have made java and math variables private. name and major
 * variables will remain public. We have added schoolCode variable.
 * This is public and is static as it applies to all the students
 * in the same school. When a variable is static, it is the same for
 * all the objects of the class. If it is not static, it belongs to
 * a single object of the class.
 * Output:
 * display the statistics of students for each school. This includes
 * the main() method. Hence this class is EXECUTABLE.
 */

public class Student3M
{
    // variable fields are defined
    public static int schoolCode;
    public String name;
    public String major;
    private double java;// private, usable by objects of this class only
    private double math;

    // default constructor
    public Student3M() {
        name = null;
        major = null;
    }

    // constructor that can enter two fields only
    public Student3M (String name, String major) {
        this.name = name;
        this.major = major;
    }

    // WE WILL NOW ADD ACCESSOR/MUTATOR METHODS
    public double getMath() // accessor method, no change to math value
    { return math; }  // will return the value of private math

    public double getJava()
    { return java; }

    public void setMath(double mth) //mutator method, changes value of math
    { math = mth;  } // does not return any value, void type method

    public void setJava(double jva)
    { java = jva; }
    // methods are defined
    public void financialSupport(double income) {
```

```
      if (income < 50000)
         System.out.print("Financial support is requested due to low
income.");
       else
         System.out.print("Financial support is not requested due to high
income.");
     }

     public double avgCalculation() {
         return (java + math)/2;
     }

     /* main() METHOD INSIDE THIS CLASS */
   public static void main(String args[])
   { Student3M std4 = new Student3M();
     Student3M std5 = new Student3M("Washington", "Math");

     // all variables in Student1 are public as no visibility modifier
specified
     std4.name="Lincoln";  // name is public in Student3, directly changed
     std4.major = "CS";     // major is public too.
*    std4.math=85.5;    // math is private, needs mutator method to change
     std4.setJava(93);

     std5.setMath(65);  // its constructor does not have math and java
     std5.setJava(37);  // as parameters

     // now test the methods for the two objects, std4 and std5

     System.out.println("Student 4:");
*    System.out.print("Math and java grades of "+std4.name +" are
"+std4.math);
     System.out.println(" and "+std4.java);
     // avgCalculation() method returns the average value. So, it is in a
print statement
     System.out.println("The average grade of "+std4.name+" is
"+std4.avgCalculation());
     // financialSupport() is a void method. It does not return any value.
     // So, it is invoked standing alone.
     std4.financialSupport(43560);  // changed financialSupport() to public

     System.out.println("\n\nStudent 5:");
     System.out.print("Math and java grades of "+std5.name +" are
"+std5.getMath());
     System.out.println(" and "+std5.getJava());
     System.out.println("The average grade of "+std5.name+" is
"+std5.avgCalculation());
     std5.financialSupport(250000);
   }

}
```

Here is the output of Student3M, which is exactly the same as Student3 with main() method. Observe the statements with *: we have replaced accessor/mutator methods by directly accessing the private variables. This is possible as main() is a method in the class. The output is exactly the same as for Student3Driver.

```
Student 4:
Math and java grades of Lincoln are 85.5 and 93.0
The average grade of Lincoln is 89.25
Financial support is requested due to low income.
M
Student 5:
Math and java grades of Washington are 65.0 and 37.0
The average grade of Washington is 51.0
Financial support is not requested due to high income.
```

6.3.3   Overloaded Methods

<u>Example 5:</u> Here are the complete codes for Student.java and StudentDriver.java. It has two overloaded constructors and three overloaded financialSupport() methods. Overloaded methods will have the same name but must have different parameter lists.

Coding List 6.8: Student.java

```java
/*
 * Author:
 * Date:
 * This class consists of three overloaded constructors, three
 * overloaded financialSupport() methods, has accessor/mutator
 * methods for the private variables, and toString() method which
 * is capable of printing the class information with object as
 * argument.
 */

public class Student
{
   // variable fields are defined
    public static int schoolCode;
    public String name;
    public String major;
    private double java;
    private double math;

    // one or more constructors are defined
    // in this way, constructors are overloaded
    // From the overloaded constructors,
    // each object can be constructed based on one definition of the
    // overloaded constructors depending on arguments specified.

    // default constructor #1
    public Student() {
        name = null;
        major = null;
    }

    // constructor that can enter two fields only #2
    public Student (String name, String major) {
        this.name = name;
        this.major = major;
    }
```

```java
      // constructor that can accept four fields    #3
      // in part by invoking a constructor, #2, which already defined.
      public Student (String name, String major, double myJava, double myMath)
{
        this(name, major);
        java = myJava;
        math = myMath;
      }

      // methods are defined
      public double getMath() // accessor method, no change to math value
      { return math; }  // will return the value of private math

      public double getJava()
      { return java; }

      public void setMath(double mth) //mutator method, changes value of math
      { math = mth;   } // does not return any value, void type method

      public void setJava(double jva)
      { java = jva; }
      // the following three methods are overloaded,
      // they have the same name financialSupport but with different parameters
in ()
      public void financialSupport() {
         System.out.println(this + ": Insufficient message!");
      }

      public void financialSupport(String reason) {
         System.out.print("Due to ");
         System.out.print(reason);
         System.out.println("financial support is requested by " + this);
      }

      public void financialSupport(double income) {
       if (income < 50000)
         System.out.print("Financial support is requested due to low income.");
       else
         System.out.print("Financial support is not requested due to high
income.");
      }
   public double avgCalculation() {
        return (java + math)/2;
      }

      // method "toString()" is automatically invoked in response to
      // the access to an object reference. It returns a String type value.
      public String toString() {
        return name + " in " + major;
      }
}
```

Here is the driver for Student.java:

Coding List 6.9: StudentDriver.java

```java
/**
 * Author:
 * Date:
 * Input:
 * Create Student objects corresponding to each of the three
 * constructors. Print their information using toString() method to
 * print objects.
 * Output: display student information
 */

public class StudentDriver
{
    public static void main(String[] args) {
        Student john = new Student();  // object #1
        Student sam = new Student("Samuel", "Computer Science");   // #2
        Student brown = new Student("Bob", "Computer Science", 90, 80);   //#3
        sam.financialSupport(); // overloaded method #1
        sam.financialSupport(" no reason "); // overloaded method #2
        sam.financialSupport(100000);   // overloaded method #3
        System.out.println(brown + " earns the average " +
brown.avgCalculation());
        System.out.println(john);
        john.setMath(99.9);//Observe this mutator gives math grade to john
        System.out.println("\n\nJohn's math grade is "+john.getMath());
    }
}
```

```
Here is the output:

Samuel in Computer Science: Insufficient message!
Due to  no reason financial support is requested by Samuel in Computer
Science
Financial support is not requested due to high income.Bob in Computer Science
earns the average 85.0
null in null


John's math grade is 99.9
```

Example 6: Here is a very simple Animal class. We will have one constructor, the accessor and mutator methods, and toString method. We will write the driver in two different ways: one as a separate driver class and another inside the Animal class itself. Create a class of Animals. Each animal must have a species name (elephant for example), a weight (an elephant weighs in the range 650 pounds to 20000 lbs), and a breed (African and Asian). The class must have one constructor, get and set methods and a toString method. Write a driver to create at least two objects and print their information.

Here is the code with the main method in the Animals class at the end:

```
Coding List 6.10: Animals.java
/**
 * Author
 * Date:
 * Input:
 * Each animal's name, breed, and weight as constructor parameters.
 * We have made weight private just to illustrate how public and private
 * variables are handled. We have included the main() method in this
 * class and hence both public and private variables are directly
 * accessible. But when we create an independent driver - a different class
 * public and private variables behave differently: public variables can
 * directly accessed where as a private variable needs accessor/mutator
 * method to access by an outside class.
 * Output:
 * Three Animals objects will be created in a driver to display
 * their information.
 */


public class Animals
{ // instance object variables, no static modifier
  private String name, breed;
  public double weight; // we have made weight public intentionally

  public Animals(String nm, String brd, double wt)
  { name = nm;
    breed= brd;
    weight = wt;
  }

  public String getName()
  { return name; }

  public String getBreed()
  { return breed; }

  public double getWeight()
  { return weight; }

  public void setName(String nm)
  { name = nm; }

  public void setBreed(String brd)
  { breed = brd; }

  public void setWeight (double wt)
  { weight = wt; }

  public String toString() {
        return " This "+name + "'s breed is " + breed +" and weighs "+weight;
    }


  public static void main(String args[])
  { Animals a1 = new Animals("elephant", "Asian", 2.5);
```

```
    Animals a2 = new Animals("dog", "Labrador", 25);
    Animals a3 = new Animals("hippo", "African", 3.5);

    System.out.println(a1); // cannot print whole object a1 without
toString() method
    System.out.println(a2);
    System.out.println(a3);

    System.out.println("\nName: "+a1.name); //public name printed directly
    System.out.println("\nWeight: "+a1.weight); //private weight printed
directly
    System.out.println("\nBreed: "+a1.getName()); // using an accessor method


    }
}
```

Here is the output:

```
This elephant's breed is Asian and weighs 2.5
This dog's breed is Labrador and weighs 25.0
This hippo's breed is African and weighs 3.5

Name: elephant

Weight: 2.5

Breed: elephant
```

Here is the Animals class without the main() method but followed by `AnimalsDriver`:

Coding List 6.11: Animals.java

```
/**
 * Author:
 * Date:
 * Input:
 * Each animals name, breed, and weight as constructor parameters.
 * We have made weight private just to illustrate how public and private
 * variables are handled. We have included the main() method in this
 * class and hence both public and private variables are directly
 * accessible. But when we create an independent driver - a different class
 * - public and private variables behave differently: public variables can
 * directly accessed where as a private variable needs accessor/mutator
 * method to access by an outside class.
 * Output:
 * Three Animals objects will be created in a driver to display
 * their information.
 */


public class Animals
{ // instance object variables, no static modifier
  private String name, breed;
  public double weight; // we have made weight public intentionally

  public Animals(String nm, String brd, double wt)
```

```
    { name = nm;
      breed= brd;
      weight = wt;
    }

    public String getName()
    { return name; }

    public String getBreed()
    { return breed; }

    public double getWeight()
    { return weight; }

    public void setName(String nm)
    { name = nm; }

    public void setBreed(String brd)
    { breed = brd; }

    public void setWeight (double wt)
    { weight = wt; }

    public String toString() {
        return " This "+name + "'s breed is " + breed +" and weighs "+weight;
    }
}
```

Here is the driver and its output:

Coding List 6.12: AnimalsDriver.java

```
/**
 * Author:
 * Date:
 * Input:
 * Create three Animals objects. Print their information using toString()
 * method to print objects.
 * Output:
 * display Animals information and study how private and
 * public instance variables are handled. We will try to print
 * a1.weight where weight is private. We cannot print it in a
 * different class. An error message is printed. We will then
 * run by replacing it with a1.getWeight() accessor method.
 */


public class AnimalsDriver
{ public static void main(String args[])
    { Animals a1 = new Animals("elephant", "Asian", 2.5);
      Animals a2 = new Animals("dog", "Labrador", 25);
      Animals a3 = new Animals("hippo", "African", 3.5);

      System.out.println(a1); // cannot print whole object a1 without
                              // toString() method
      System.out.println(a2);
      System.out.println(a3);
```

```
        System.out.println("\nName: "+a1.name); //public name printed directly
        System.out.println("\nWeight: "+a1.weight); // private weight printed
                                              // directly
        System.out.println("\nBreed: "+a1.getName()); // using an accessor method


    }
}
```

```
Here is the output with a1.name in the print statement:

AnimalsDriver.java:25: error: name has private access in Animals
System.out.println("\nName: "+a1.name); //private name printed directly
                                  ^
1 error

Here is the output with a1.getName() in the print statement:

This elephant's breed is Asian and weighs 2.5
This dog's breed is Labrador and weighs 25.0
This hippo's breed is African and weighs 3.5

Name: elephant

Weight: 2.5

Breed: elephant
```

Example 7: We are going to give one more example. This will be a Family class. Each family has a father, mother, number of children, and annual income. The class will have two constructors, accessor/mutator methods, method to calculate taxes, a method to check if a family falls into poor category, and toString() method to print the objects. We have created three objects just to illustrate the class structure. Here is Family class with the main() method in it:

Coding List 6.13: Family.java

```
/**
 * Author:
 * Date:
 * Input:
 * All the values are entered in the creation of objects.
 * Output:
 * This class will create several objects of families. It will
   add all the incomes with a static class variable totalIncome.
   It uses a boolean variable to check if a family is a "poor"
   family or not. We could add several more features to this
   class.
*/

public class Family {

    private double income;
    private String fName, mName, lName;
    private int nChildren;
```

```java
    private boolean isPoor;
    private static double totalIncome=0;

    public Family()
    {
    }

    public Family(String f, String m,  int ch,   double in)
    {   fName = f;
        mName = m;
        nChildren = ch;
        income = in;
        totalIncome +=income;
    }

    public String getFname()
    {   return fName; }

    public void setFname(String f )
    { fName = f; }

    public String getMname()
    { return mName; }

    public void setMname(String m )
    {   mName = m; }

    public String getLname()
    { return lName; }

    public void setLname(String l )
    {   lName = l; }

    public int getNumChild()
    { return nChildren; }

    public void setNumChild(int ch )
    { nChildren = ch; }

    public double getIncome()
    { return income;   }

    public double getTotalIncome()
    { return totalIncome;   }

    public void setIncome(double in )
    { income = in; }

    public boolean isPoor()
    {   if ((income - (nChildren * 3000)) < (15000))
            isPoor = true;
        else
            isPoor = false;

        return isPoor;
    }
```

```
    public double taxAmount()
    { double tax=0;
      double netIncome = income - nChildren * 3000;
      if (isPoor)
        tax = -1000*nChildren;
      else if (netIncome >= 250000)
            tax =netIncome*0.4;
          else if (netIncome >= 150000)
                  tax = netIncome*0.3;
              else if (netIncome >= 50000)
                      tax = netIncome*0.1;
     return tax;
    }

    public String toString()
    {  return "Father: "+fName+"\tMother: "+mName; }

    public static void main(String args[])
    { Family f1 = new Family("John", "Mary", 3, 89567.89);
      Family f2 = new Family("Bill", "Nancy", 1, 100000);
      Family f3 = new Family("David", "Liz", 4, 200000);
      System.out.println(f1); // can print an object - toString method
      System.out.println("All families' total income is $"+
f3.getTotalIncome());
      System.out.println(f2.getFname()+"'s taxes are $"+f2.taxAmount());
      if(f1.isPoor())
        System.out.println(f1.getFname()+" is poor ");
      else
        System.out.println(f1.getFname()+" is not poor ");
    }

}
```

```
Here is the output:

Father: John    Mother: Mary
All families' total income is $389567.89
Bill's taxes are $9700.0
John is not poor
```

Example 8: We will now add some more features:
- Read from a text file
- Print data in a table
- Print tax/credit depending on the net income, using toString() method
- Format amounts

Coding List 6.14: Family_File.java

```
/*
 * Author:
 * Date:
 * Input:
 * A text file of a families is created and data are read from this text file
 * Output:
 * This class will create several objects of families. It will
```

```
    add all the incomes with a static class variable totalIncome.
    It uses a boolean variable to check if a family is a "poor"
    family or not. We could add several more features to this
    class. This program includes:
    - accessor/mutator methods
    - uses toString() method to print family records
    - observe how toString() is coded to take care of credit/taxes
    - calculates taxes
    - reads data from text file
    - formats dollars
    - prints data in a table
    - adds all the incomes and prints after the table of records
*/

import java.util.Scanner;
import java.io.*;
import java.text.NumberFormat;

public class Family_File {

    NumberFormat fmtDollar =  NumberFormat.getCurrencyInstance();
    private double income;
    private String fName, mName, lName;
    private int nChildren;
    private boolean isPoor;
    private static double totalIncome=0;

    public Family_File(){

    }

    public Family_File(String f, String m,  int ch,    double in)
    {   fName = f;
        mName = m;
        nChildren = ch;
        income = in;
        totalIncome +=income;
    }

    public String getFname()
    {   return fName; }

    public void setFname(String f )
    { fName = f; }

    public String getMname()
    { return mName; }

    public void setMname(String m )
    {   mName = m; }

    public String getLname()
    { return lName; }

    public void setLname(String l )
    {   lName = l; }
```

```java
   public int getNumChild()
   { return nChildren; }

   public void setNumChild(int ch )
   { nChildren = ch; }

   public double getIncome()
   { return income;  }

   public double getTotalIncome()
   { return totalIncome;   }

   public void setIncome(double in )
   { income = in; }

   public boolean isPoor()
   {   if ((income - (nChildren * 3000)) < (15000))
         isPoor = true;
      else
         isPoor = false;

      return isPoor;
   }

   public double taxAmount()
   { double tax=0;
     double netIncome = income - nChildren * 3000;
     if (isPoor)
        tax = -1000*nChildren;
     else if (netIncome >= 250000)
             tax =netIncome*0.4;
          else if (netIncome >= 150000)
                  tax = netIncome*0.3;
               else if (netIncome >= 50000)
                       tax = netIncome*0.1;
    return tax;
   }

   public String toString()
   {
      if (this.isPoor())
         return fName+"\t\t"+mName+"\t\t"+nChildren+"\t\t"+
fmtDollar.format(income)+"\t "\t($"+taxAmount()+")**";
      else
         return Name+"\t\t"+mName+"\t\t"+nChildren+"\t\t"+
fmtDollar.format(income) +"\t"+ fmtDollar.format(taxAmount());

   }

   public static void main(String args[]) throws IOException
   { Scanner fl = new Scanner(new File("families.txt"));
     NumberFormat dollar = NumberFormat.getCurrencyInstance();
     Family_File fam=new Family_File();
     String father, mother;
     int numChildren;
     double income;
```

```
System.out.println("\n\n\nFather\t\tMother\t\tChildren\tIncome\t\tTaxes");
    System.out.println("------\t\t------\t\t--------\t------\t\t-----");

    while (fl.hasNext())
    { father = fl.next();
      mother = fl.next();
      numChildren = fl.nextInt();
      income = fl.nextDouble();
      fam = new Family_File(father, mother, numChildren,income);
      System.out.println(fam); // can print an object - toString method
    }
    System.out.println("\nTotal income of all the families="
+dollar.format(fam.getTotalIncome()));
    System.out.println("\n\n\n");
  }

}
```

```
Here is the output with a1.name in the print statement:

Father          Mother          Children        Income          Taxes
------          ------          --------        ------          -----
John            Mary            3               $89,567.89      $8,056.79
Bill            Nancy           1               $100,000.00     $9,700.00
David           Liz             4               $200,000.00     $56,400.00
Jose            Maria           2               $97,000.00      $9,100.00
Bhanu           Lakshmi         2               $110,000.00     $10,400.00
Ahmad           Jesna           5               $85,000.00      $7,000.00
Charles         Angela          0               $30,000.00      $0.00
John            Abigail         6               $20,000.00      (-$6000.0)**

Total income of all the families=$731,567.89
MM
```

Exercise 9: Here is an example on combining graphics and textual content. This Shapes class will print information about shapes of circles and rectangles, and also draw those shapes. We have included two constructors: one for the circle with shape and radius as parameters; the second constructor for the rectangle with shape, length, and the width. In addition to get, set, and toString methods, we have included methods to return the areas and the perimeters of the shapes. For drawing the shapes, we have included the paint() method. Each constructor has the graphics frame set up instructions. Test the class with at least one object for each type. The main method is included in the class. Once the class is developed, it is good to test it in a separate driver.

Here is the program:

Coding List 6.15: Shapes.java

```
/**
 * Author:
 * Date:
 * Input:
 * We have created a class to draw shapes. We have written
 * several graphics problems before. We are doing it in an
 * user-defined class. We have introduced drawing strings,
 * setting font style and size. There are 4 constructors:
 * for circle, rectangle, line, and error. For a shape error,
```

```
 *  the program draws a message and !.
 *  Input:
 *  User will be prompted with what shape user wants to be drawn.
 *  User can enter one of three choices: circle, rectangle, line
 *  We need to import Font package for drawing the message.
 *  We have to import Scanner to get the selection. Depending on
 *  the selection, user will be prompted for appropriate data.
 *  Shapes will be drawn when the object is created. So, each
 *  if selection will receive the data and then creates corresponding
 *  shape. Observe how graphic and non-graphic parts fit together.

 *  Output:
 *  The selected shape, its data: area and perimeter for circle and
 *  rectangle, length of the line for the line, and error message
 *  with "!" symbol for invalid data entry.
*/

import java.awt.Graphics;
import java.awt.Color;
import javax.swing.JFrame;
import java.util.Scanner;
import java.awt.Font;

public class Shapes extends JFrame
{ String shape;
  static int length, width, height, radius, area, perimeter;
  static int x1,y1,x2, y2, len;

  public Shapes(String sp, int r)
  { shape = sp;
    radius= r;
    setTitle("Circle");
    setSize(1800,1800);
    setVisible(true);
    setDefaultCloseOperation(EXIT_ON_CLOSE);
  }

  public Shapes(String sp, int l, int w)
  { setTitle("Rectangle");
   setSize(1800,1800);
    setVisible(true);
    setDefaultCloseOperation(EXIT_ON_CLOSE);

    shape = sp;
    length = l;
    width = w;
  }

  public Shapes(String sp, int a1, int b1, int a2, int b2)
  { setTitle("Line");
    setSize(1800,1800);
    setVisible(true);
   setDefaultCloseOperation(EXIT_ON_CLOSE);

    shape = sp;
    x1 = a1;
    y1 = b1;
```

```java
    x2 = a2;
    y2 = b2;
  }

  public Shapes(String sp)
  { setTitle("Question");
    setSize(1800,1800);
    setVisible(true);
    setDefaultCloseOperation(EXIT_ON_CLOSE);

    shape = sp;
  }
  public void paint(Graphics g)
  { if (shape.compareToIgnoreCase("circle") == 0)
      drawCircle(g);    //using a method
    else if (shape.compareToIgnoreCase("rectangle") == 0)
        drawRectangle(g); // using a method, they are below
        else if (shape.compareToIgnoreCase("line") == 0)
            drawStLine(g);
          else
            drawError(g);
  }
  // you just have to replace these methods with your methods
  public void drawCircle(Graphics g)
  { g.setColor(Color.RED);
    g.fillOval(300,300,radius,radius);
  }

  public void drawRectangle(Graphics g)
  { g.setColor(Color.BLUE);
    g.fillRect(300,300,length,width); // x, y, width, height
  }

  public void drawStLine(Graphics g)
  { g.setColor(Color.GREEN);
    g.drawLine(x1,y1,x2,y2); // x, y, width, height
  }

  public void drawError(Graphics g)
  { g.setColor(Color.MAGENTA);
    g.fillRect(500,300,40,100); // x, y, width, height
    g.fillOval(500,400,40,40);
    Font f = new Font("Serif", Font.BOLD, 40);
    g.setFont(f);
    g.drawString("Invalid Selection",150,350);
  }
  public String getName()
  { return shape; }

  public double getLength()
  {  return length;  }

  public double getWide()
  {  return width;  }

  public void setLength(int l)
  {  length=l;  }
```

```
   public void setWidth(int w)
   {   width = w;   }

   public double areaCircle()
   { return Math.PI*radius*radius; }

   public double perimeterCircle()
   { return 2*Math.PI*radius;   }

   public double areaRectangle()
   { return length*width;   }

   public double perimeterRect()
   { return 2*(length+width);   }

   public double lengthLine()
   { return Math.sqrt((x1-x2)*(x1-x2)+(y1-y2)*(y1-y2));   }

   public String toString()
   { if (shape.compareToIgnoreCase("circle") == 0)
       return shape+"\t"+radius+"\t"+areaCircle()+"\t"+perimeterCircle();
     else if (shape.compareToIgnoreCase("rectangle") == 0)
       return
shape+"\t"+length+"\t"+width+"\t"+areaRectangle()+"\t"+perimeterRect();
     else if (shape.compareToIgnoreCase("Line") == 0)
       return shape+" from ("+x1+","+y1+") to ("+x2+","+y2+")
length="+lengthLine();
         else return "-1";

   }

   public static void main(String args[])
   { Scanner kb = new Scanner(System.in);
     double len, wid, rad;
     System.out.print("Enter circle, rectangle, or straight line: ");
     String shape = kb.next();
     if (shape.compareToIgnoreCase("circle") == 0)
     {   System.out.print("Enter radius: ");
       radius = kb.nextInt();
       Shapes s1 = new Shapes(shape, radius);
       System.out.println(s1);
     }
     else if (shape.compareToIgnoreCase("rectangle") == 0)
           {  System.out.print("Enter length: ");
               length = kb.nextInt();
               System.out.print("Enter width: ");
               width = kb.nextInt();
               Shapes s2 = new Shapes("Rectangle", length, width);
               System.out.println(s2);
           }
         else   if (shape.compareToIgnoreCase("line") == 0)
               {  System.out.print("Enter x1: ");
                   x1 = kb.nextInt();
                   System.out.print("Enter y1: ");
                   y1 = kb.nextInt();
                   System.out.print("Enter x2: ");
```

```
                    x2 = kb.nextInt();
                    System.out.print("Enter y2: ");
                    y2 = kb.nextInt();
                    Shapes s3 = new Shapes("line", x1,y1,x2,y2);
                    System.out.println(s3);
                }
                else
                { Shapes s4= new Shapes("Error");   }

        }
}
```

```
Here is the text output using toString() method:

Enter circle, rectangle, or straight line: erro

Enter circle, rectangle, or straight line: circle
Enter radius: 100
circle    100       31415.926535897932      628.3185307179587

Enter circle, rectangle, or straight line: rectangle
Enter length: 100
Enter width: 200
Rectangle         100      200      20000.0 600.0

Here is the graphics, three objects:
```

6.4 Exercises

Concept Understanding

1. Suppose there is a class called TwoInteger.java, which has two integer variables and constructs objects with two integers. This class has methods called max(), min() and average(), which return respectively the maximum, minimum and average of those two integers which are available for an object. To illustrate this, try the steps below:

   a) Create a class, TwoInteger, with two instance variables, v1 and v2.

   b) Create a constructor, TwoInteger (int v1, int v2), in the class TwoInteger.

   c) Create those three methods, each of which takes no input parameter, but uses the instance variables to return a value.

d) Create another class called TwoIntegerDriver.java, which takes two integers from user to construct an object. Then the minimum, maximum and average will be computed by invoking those methods. For example, suppose obj1 is constructed using the constructor. Then the invocation of the method min() will be obj1.min() which should be displayed.

e) Modify those variables private. Fix all the visibility issues by creating and invoking those methods, getV1() and getV2(), for those private variables v1 and v2.

f) In the scenario described above, getV1() is needed but setV1() is unnecessary. Explain why.

2. Consider real-world "things" (like a refrigerator, for example) and "objects" (like in Java) in the object-oriented paradigm. Both "things" and "objects) represent instances (a refrigerator in a house is an instance of all refrigerators, std1 was an instance of Students).

a. Explain the concept of "generalization" and "instantiation" using the relations between instances and things & objects.

b. Is it possible to create instances first and then define a class based on the instances already created?

3. An object can be specified over its behavioral aspects. A behavioral aspect can be a method or a constructor.

a. Explain a method and a constructor

b. Explain similarities and differences between methods and constructors

c. Both methods and constructors can defined multiple times but with different arguments. It is called "overloading". Explain the benefits of overloading.

d. Which is the method that does not allow overloading?

Programming

1. Write a class of Sales. Each Sales object must have a merchandize name (sweater for example), number of items bought (3 sweaters bought for example), and price per item ($30 per sweater, for example). Include get, set, and toString methods. Also, include a bill() method which will calculate the total bill for the purchase. The total bill should include a 7.5% sales tax. For the sweater sale in the problem, price for the 3 sweaters = 3*30= 90. The sales tax = 90*0.075 = 6.75. The total bill = 90+6.75 = $96.75.

2. Java graphics provides methods to draw standard shapes like circles, rectangles, etc. There is no method to draw a face or a robot. This problem is to create a class which let the user select one of three special images: a face, a robot, or a house, or any images that you wish. It should draw whichever object the user selects. Drawing each object must be a method. Depending on the selection, it should execute the corresponding method. Maybe it is possible to include the areas, surface areas, and/or volumes for bonus points.

3. Assume that you are hired to code a real application that helps the agents manage real-estate transactions. As a small part of that application code, write a class called Houses. Each house must have a style (bungalow, ranch, colonial, split, capecod), square footage (size of living area like 2000 sq. ft.), price per sq. ft. (like $100 per sq. ft. The price of the house will be 2000*100=200000), and sales tax (sales taxes differ from town to town. If the sales tax

rate is 8%, the sales tax is 200000*0.08=16000). Include set, get, and toString methods. Also include a method that will return the total cost of the house for a purchaser (For the numbers used in this problem, the total cost for purchase will be 200000+16000 = $216000). Include a driver with at least five houses of different styles. All the data must be read from a text file and objects are created.

4. Create an application for a restaurant. Each restaurant should have a name, number of employees, annual revenue, annual overhead (we will use the total of rents, phone, utility, salaries, and food for overhead), and sales tax paid. It should have constructor(s), toString() method, netRevenue() method which should calculate and return the net revenue (=annual revenue – annual overhead – sales tax). Assume each object created is one of several restaurants that an owner owns. The owner wants to know the annual revenues and net revenues but also the total revenues from all the restaurants together. This must be a static variable in the class. Print all the details. Read the data from a text file.

5. Create an application for a real estate company. A company may have several offices at different places. Each office will have its own monthly sales and corresponding commissions. This application is to read all the sales and commissions from several offices. It should print a table of all the sales and commissions and then finally should print the total sales and the total commission for each month. Each office is an object with sale and commission as the parameters for the constructor.

6. Create an ExtendedMath class that will include following methods which are not available in the Math class:
   averageGrade() method which will return the average of three decimal numbers
   areaRectangle() method which will return the area of a rectangle
   areaCircle() method which will return the area of a circle
   volumeSphere() method which will return the volume of a sphere
   surfaceAreaSphere() method which will return the surface area of a sphere
   areaTriangle() method that returns the area of a triangle.

7. Build a class of Library. It should be a library management system. In the minimum, it should have the following:
   Constructors
   Accessors and mutators
   Method to borrow
   Method to return
   Late charges
   Test your class with a driver.

8. Write a class to manage text. It should be able to find the number of characters in the text, number of words in the text, find a word in the text, replace all occurrences of a word. Include a driver to read a text from the keyboard and perform any activity that the user selects.

9. Create an application to manage a deli business.

Arrays

7
CHAPTER

7.1   Introduction

Recall that in order to manipulate a value, we use a variable that will be allocated a memory space. This kind of programming approach is fine if there are very few data to be loaded into memory. Recall also that without loading values into memory, there will be no data manipulation in computers. However, this approach has a serious drawback as far as there are huge amounts of data elements to be manipulated (1000 students for example). One solution is to use 1000 variable names, as in the program below (with 10 variables), or use one name but 1000 indices (like 1, 2, 3,...). An array uses the second option.

Is an array needed for data management? Yes, for larger sets of data. Read the following:

Why Arrays		

Challenge	Suppose that you want to read 10 numbers and store them in variables. Without using an array, one simple approach is to declare 10 variables.
	
	Scanner sc = new Scanner (System.in);
	double score1 = sc.nextDouble();
	double score2 = sc.nextDouble();
	double score3 = sc.nextDouble();
	double score4 = sc.nextDouble();
	double score5 = sc.nextDouble();
	double score6 = sc.nextDouble();
	double score7 = sc.nextDouble();
	double score8 = sc.nextDouble();
	double score9 = sc.nextDouble();
	double score10 = sc.nextDouble();
	
	Note that score1 and score2 are two different variables which will be stored in two different memory locations. In memory, those 10 memory spaces are allocated and labeled by each variable, score1, score2, ..., and score10. Notice that they are all different variable names independent of each other.	

	Scale up?	Problem is in defining and accessing as many variables as needed. Can we do this for 1000 names or 1 million names, and type 1 million next() statements?!!!

Solution	Using an array
	But if each student has three courses and each course has 5 quizzes, then we need a two-dimensional array as each student will have 15 scores. Let us begin with one-dimensional arrays. We have a single name "score" but we can change the index using a loop that repeats a million times. We need to type one next statement but repeat it in a loop one million times. Imagine typing 1 million statements like in the code above!

This chapter introduces one of the data structures, called array. Think of a building structure that has several floors. Similarly think of a data structure that has several data in different cells connected to each other. An array is a variable, into which a series of data elements can be loaded. All data elements should be of the <u>same data type</u>. Each array element can be directly accessed by the array variable and its index (number). No matter how many data elements are to be loaded, as far as they are all the same type, either a primitive data type or a user-defined data type (UDT), an array can accommodate all of them.

The length (number of cells in the array) of an array is established when the array is created. Each element of an array can be accessed by an array index, always starting at 0 and ending at the array (length – 1). For example, if score has 10 elements, the index starts at zero and ends at 9. After declaration of an array, the length of an array is determined (see the example below). Array is an important concept of data management.

7.2   One-dimensional Arrays

The example of ten scores is one-dimensional. A spreadsheet is two-dimensional as it will have rows and columns. We can create multi-dimensional arrays in Java. If we consider only the number of students in a class, it will be one-dimensional. But if each student has three exams and 5 quizzes, then we need a two –dimensional array as each student will have eight scores. Let us begin with one-dimensional arrays.

7.2.1.   Creation of Arrays

This section describes the ways of creating one-dimensional arrays. The following three examples will use three different kinds of data types (int, String, UDT):

Example 1: Pictorially, an array called `scores` of `int`values is

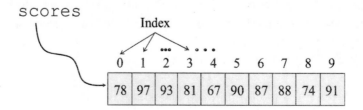

The name of the array is "scores". The figure shows allocated memory and the label "scores". All the values are of the data type int. In Java, the array scores is created by the following statements:

```
int [] scores;              // array scores is declared
scores = new int [10];      // the array length is defined
```

The above two statements can be combined into one:

```
int [] scores = new int [10];
```

[] indicates that "scores" is an array, not a simple variable
The array values are:

```
scores[0] = 78;

scores[1] = 97;

scores[2] = 93;

scores[3] = 81;

scores[4] = 67;

scores[5] = 90;

scores[6] = 87;

scores[7] = 88;

scores[8] = 74;

scores[9] = 91;
```

Note that each element of an array can be accessed by using the index of that element. The index always begins at 0. So, the index of the 5th element is 4 as you can notice above.

An array of integers can also be created as below:

Simple Creation		
Alternative		Another simple way of creating an array is when the array is a small array and you know the values of the array elements. Let us assume that the grades of five students are 93, 45, 81, 67, and 79. We can create "grades" array as below: `int [] grades = {93,45,81,67,79};` Here, `grades[0]` will be 93, `grades[1]` will be 45, and so on. The length of `grades` will be 5.
	Pictorial Structure	Pictorially, `grade` is an array of `int` values is
	Pros & Cons	This creation is simple. However, the values filled from the index 0 with no vacant place, and the size of the array is fixed as the values are initially assigned. For example, the `grades` array holds 5 integers only. This format is not ideal for large number of values.

Example 2: Let us consider another example of an array that can hold non-primitive values. Create an array of 10 names. Each name is a `String`. So, this will be an array of String values. Let us call this array `names`. The statement will be

```
String [] names = new String [10]; //array of names created
names[0] = "John"; //assign John to the first element
names[5] = "Nancy"; //assign Nancy to the 6th element
```

Then, its pictorial structure looks like

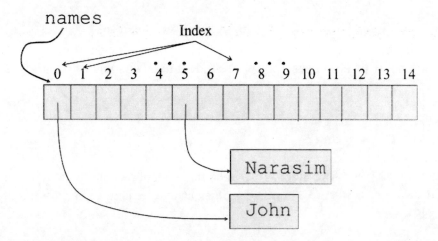

Example 3: Let us consider an array of students. Since students will have several attributes like name, ID, etc., a student object will be an UDT. Let the class for creating student objects be Student. Let us call this array of Student objects stds. Pictorial view of stds could be

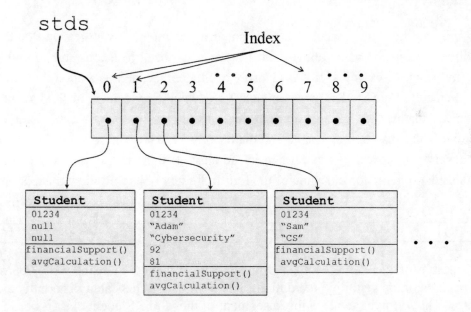

All the elements of this array are of the same type Student. Remember that Student is a class which should be already created before using it as a UDT. When the array is created, memory will be allocated to all the objects of the array and they can be accessed by the label "stds," and appropriate indices. The array stds is created by the following statement:

```
Student [] stds = new Student [10];
```

Before assigning a value to an object of Student.java class, the object should be first constructed. Recall the object construction discussed in Chapter 6 (Coding List 6.3). Remember there were 3 types of constructors to construct objects. Here are three examples using the three different constructors:

```
Student john = new Student();
Student sam = new Student("Sam", "CS");
Student liz = new Student("Liz", "Cybersecurity", 92, 81);
```
Now, we are ready to assign each object of Student to an element of the array, stds:

```
stds[0] = sam;
stds[1] = liz;
stds[2] = john;
```

We created stds[0] in two steps – first creating sam object and then assigning it to stds[0]. We could also create stds[0], or any other array element, directly without using "sam" or "liz" as below:

```
stds[0] = new Student("Sam","CS");
stds[1] = new Student("Liz", "Cybersecurity", 92, 81);
```

7.2.2   Visibility

Visibility will be the way we could access an array element: if public, we could access the variable directly as in the name above and if private, we need to use a method as in java class attributes. In the above example, stds is an array of Student. Student is a class that was defined in chapter 5. Since the type Student is a complex type, which may consist of field variables, name, major, java and mathscores, each element of the array stds is an object which is constituted with those field variables, name, major, java and mathscores. The way these variables in any object is accessed depends on how they are defined in the class. If they are public, they can be accessed directly like stds[3].name for the name of the fourth Student object. Review the example below:

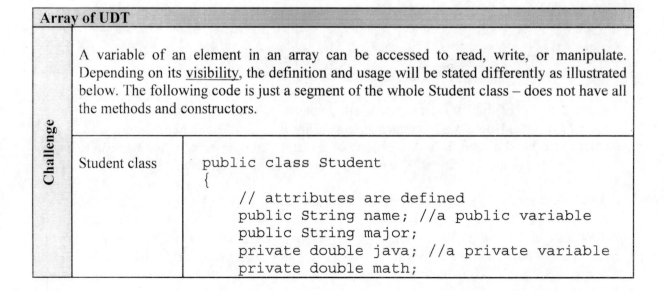

Array of UDT		
Challenge	A variable of an element in an array can be accessed to read, write, or manipulate. Depending on its <u>visibility</u>, the definition and usage will be stated differently as illustrated below. The following code is just a segment of the whole Student class – does not have all the methods and constructors.	
	Student class	``` public class Student { // attributes are defined public String name; //a public variable public String major; private double java; //a private variable private double math; ```

<table>
<tr><td></td><td colspan="2">

```
            public double getMath() {
                return math;
            }

            public intgetJava() {
                return (int) java;
// value release may be manipulated ...
            }

            public void setJava(double num) {
                java = num;
            }
        }
```

</td></tr>
<tr><td></td><td>

StudentDriver

Observe how public and private attributes are accessedclass

</td><td>

```
Student [] stds = {new Student(),new Student("Adam",
"CS")};
```

Since name is public, we could use variable name directly to access the name of any stds[] as below

```
stds[0].name = "sam";
```

Since variable java is a private variable, we cannot assign a value directly as we did for name. We have to use the setJava() method to assign a value and getJava() method to access the value, as shown in the two statements below.

```
stds[0].setJava(82.79);
```

```
intsamJava = stds[0].getJava();
```

Note the type of the value returned from the variable "java"

```
System.out.println ("Sam's Java Score = " + samJava);
// Quiz
```

</td></tr>
<tr><td></td><td>Quiz</td><td>

In the above code segment, what is the output of the statement,
```
System.out.println ("Sam's Java Score = " +samJava);?
```

</td></tr>
</table>

7.2.3. Accessing Arrays and More

Like a spreadsheet, an array has a position number for each array element. The position number called index, in an array starts at 0 and goes up sequentially. Each position in an array can then hold a value of the same type. Recall that an array of integers has one integer value at each position.

7.2.4   Reading Arrays

With a position or an index, each element value in an array can be directly read. The 5-th elements of the arrays scores and names can be printed by

```
System.out.println("The 5th element of scores is " +
scores[4]);
System.out.println("The 5th element of names is " +
names[4]);
```

The output of the above two statements will be

```
The 5th element of scores is 67
The 5th element of names isAdams
```

In a similar manner, we can print an array element of a user-defined class. Consider the array, stds. The 2nd element of stds can be accessed by stds[1].

Read and Print		
Practice	How can we know what we read or what is contained in a variable? For example, what is stored in stds[1]? We can print the value.	
	Solution	1) Using a print method toString() from the class `System.out.println("The 2nd element of stds is " + stds[1]);` 2) Using a debugger. Details are omitted here.

The output of the above statement is a JVM memory address of the object adam, which is the second element, unless the class Student has the method toString() implemented in it. According to Code Listing 6.3 (in Chapter 6), which has the method toString() implemented, the output will be

```
The 2nd element of stds is Adam in Cybersecurity
```

Note that the string "Adam in Cybersecurity" is constituted by the statement return name + " in " + major; in the method toString().

An array can be accessed iteratively.

```
for (int i = 0; i <stds.length; i++)
System.out.println(stds[i]);
```

```
// returns the content of all the elements of studs
```

Observe that as the value of "i" changes in the loop, the index numbers in `stds[i]` keep changing accordingly. Note that an array has the field variable length, which contains the size of that array. In the above example, `stds.length` returns the size of the array `stds`.

Also, if we want to see just the name of the second `Student`, the following statement can be used:

```
System.out.print("Name of the 2nd studentis " + stds[1].name);
System.out.println(" and earns the Math " + stds[1].getMath() + ".");
```

Note that the dot notation is used to access the variable of an array element. The expression `stds[1].name` means the name of the object `stds[1]`. The output of the above two statements will be therefore

```
Name of the 2nd student is Adam and earns the Math 81.
```

	Visibility: Revisited	

Challenge	Consider the following statements:
	
	`System.out.print("The student " + stds[1].name);`
	`System.out.println(" earns the Math " + stds[1].math + ".");`
	
	If it is included in StudDriver class (which is right below, what happens?	

	Answer	The first statement is OK. The second statement causes the error in accessibility. Why?
	Discussion	The variable math is private! If there is an *accessor* method implemented, `getMath()`, we would use that in `stds[1].getMath()`.

Example 1: The following code uses the Student class.

Coding List 7.1: StudDriver.java
``` /* Author: * Date: * Input: * Output: */ ```

```
public class StudDriver
{
  public static void main(String[] args) {
     String [] studs = new String[100];

     studs[0] = new String("Adam");//for String type, we could
     studs[1] = "Brown"; // directly assign value. Both are ok

     Students [] students = { new Student(), new Student("Brown", "CS"),new
Student("Truman", "Math", 87.5,92.5)}; //students is the array name

     students[0].financialSupport();
     students[1].financialSupport(" no reason ");
     students[2].financialSupport(" TAP eligible");
for (int i=0; i<students.length; i++)
System.out.println(students[i] + " earns the average " +
        students[i].avgCalculation());
     }
}
```

```
Here is the output:
null in null: Insufficient message!
Due to  no reason financial support is requested by Brown in CS
Due to  TAP eligiblefinancial support is requested by Truman in Math
null in null earns the average 0.0
Brown in CS earns the average 0.0
Truman in Math earns the average 90.0
MM
```

7.2.5   Writing into Arrays

Values can be assigned to an array element or to its variable (if it is an object). With a position or an index, each element value in an array can be directly written. The 5-th element of the scores array can be written or modified by an assignment statement:

    scores[4] = 99;

In a similar manner, we can modify an array of a user-defined class. Consider the array, stds. Assume that the 2nd element of stds changes the major to CS. It can be done by

    stds[1].major = "CS";

Remember that major is public in the class. Multiple values can also be stored in an array by a bulk assignment. Bulk assignments can be also used to copy an array to another array which contains the same type values.

Example 2: For example, consider the array scores of 10 integers. Assume that we need to double the length of the array. However, as mentioned earlier, the length is fixed when the array is created. To change the length of an array, we need to create another array and then copy the content to a corresponding position.

Coding List 7.2: ArrayCopyDouble.java

```java
/* Author:
 * Date:
 * Input:
 * Output:
*/

import java.util.Random;

public class ArrayCopyDouble
{
  public static void main(String[] args) {
int [] scores = newint [10]; //scores has 10 elements
for (int i=0; i <scores.length; i++)
     scores[i] = i;
// stored 0-9 in the first 10 spaces, to make them different
// from the next 10 grades, which will be random numbers
// double the length of array scores
intlen = scores.length * 2;//len will be 20 now

int [] doubledScore = newint [len];//create array twice the size of the
original

// copy the content of scores to copiedScore
// The first 10 elements of scores, 0-9, are copied into
// doubledScore array in the loop below

for (int i=0; i<scores.length; i++)
doubledScore[i] = scores[i];

// Create a random object using the random generator
   Random randGen = new Random();
// enter random values to the rest 10 elements of copiedScore
// array starting from index scores.length=10
for (int i=scores.length; i<doubledScore.length; i++)
doubledScore[i] = randGen.nextInt(50) + 50;
// The last value of i in this loop is 19.
// Random integers are in the range 50 to 99, both inclusive

// Now display all the content of the array copiedScore
for (int i=0; i<doubledScore.length; i++)
   { System.out.print(doubledScore[i] + "\t");
if(i == 9) System.out.println();
   }
  }
}
```

Here is the output of the doubled array, printed on two linesM

0	1	2	3	4	5	6	7	8	9
74	69	69	51	88	77	59	88	84	52

MM

7.3   Arrays as Parameters and Invoking Methods

Arrays can be passed into methods as parameters. Consider passing an array of integers into the method printArray() to print the numbers. This method should take any array of integers and print the numbers 20 integers per line. Observe that the array parameter will have [] in order to indicate it as an array. Also, observe that there is no length in brackets. So, it should work for any length. Observe that the method will not return any value but will only print the numbers. So, its type is 'void'. The method statement is

```
public static voidprintArray(int x[])
{System.out.println("\n\n");
for (int i=0; i<x.length; i++)
{ System.out.print(x[i]+"\t");
if (i>0 && i%20 == 0)
System.out.println();//to go to the next line after 20
                                    // integers
    }
  }
```

This printArray() is invoked in another method (main() method in this example) by the statement:

```
printArray(nums);
```

Example 3: Observe that printArray() method has one integer array parameter. When we invoke that method, we need to have one integer array argument, nums, without brackets. When the method is invoked, the compiler will be looking for an integer array. nums is an integer array.

We have also included another method, addArray(int x[]), which will receive an integer array, add all the elements of the array, and returns the sum. Here is the complete program with an integer array, generated by a random generator.

Coding List 7.3: ArrayIntMethod.java
```
/* Author:
 * Date:
 * Input:
 * Output:
*/

import java.util.Scanner; // needed to read from a file
import java.util.Random;

public class ArrayIntMethod
{
  public static void main (String args[]) {
    final int MAX=100;
    int nums[] = new int [MAX]; // an array of 100 integers
    Random gen = new Random(); // to generate random integers
    for (int n=0; n<MAX;n++) // generate 30 random integers
    nums[n]=gen.nextInt(100);
    printArray(nums); // print the 100 integers in the actual array nums
```

```
    System.out.println("\n\nSum of the array elements = "+ addArray(nums));
  }

  public static void printArray(int x[]) {
    System.out.println("\n\n");
    for (int i=0; i<x.length; i++) {
      if (i>0 && i%20 == 0)
          System.out.println();
          System.out.print(x[i]+"\t");
    }
  }

  public static int addArray(int x[]) {
    int sum=0;
    for (int i=0; i<x.length; i++)
    sum +=x[i];
    return sum;
  }
}
```

```
Here is the output. First 100 random integers, 10 per line followed by sum
48        83        21        47        12        73        62        48        86        17
87        5         81        79        5         68        16        67        10        11
48        21        14        62        9         97        67        57        45        32
96        16        49        54        56        89        91        9         60        90
65        38        27        53        36        0         87        85        22        82
76        23        86        14        49        30        9         33        83        75
27        73        86        9         33        22        3         60        34        80
0         9         40        42        4         0         63        85        63        75
85        89        13        99        38        89        27        88        72        1
14        25        16        28        17        57        0         8         59        98

Sum of the array elements = 4692
```

Example 4: Here is another example in which we will read data (names) from a text file (in real applications, data are read from databases and processed in applications) into a String array. We again have `printArray()` method but we will pass a String array. Here is the complete program:

```
Coding List 7.4: ArrayFileMethod.java
/* Author:
 * Date:
 * Input:
 * Output:
 */


import java.util.Scanner; // needed to read from a file
import java.io.*;

public class ArrayFileMethod
```

```java
{
  public static void main (String args[]) throws IOException {
    String names[] = new String[10]; // create an array of questions
    String filename = "names.txt";

    Scanner file = new Scanner(new File(filename));
    int n=0;
    while (file.hasNextLine()) {
      names[n] = file.nextLine();
      n++;
    }

    printArray(names);// method call passing names as the argument
  }

  // IOException needed at the  method that reads the file
  public static void printArray(String nm[]) {
    System.out.println("\n\n");
    for (int i=0; i<nm.length; i++)
    System.out.println(nm[i]);
  }
}
```

```
Here is the output. First 100 random integers, 10 per line followed by sum
john
lisa
maria
chris
jose
jorge
mathew
kathy
nancy
ruth
```

Example 5: We discussed reading from and writing into files in section 5.4. It is common to read data from files (text or otherwise) into arrays, process the arrays in applications, and then write data back into files. So, we are repeating the program from section 5.4 but using three arrays and processing these arrays (only printing the data). Here is the code:

Coding List 7.5: ArrayFiles.java

```java
/* Author:
 * Date:
 * Input:
 * Output:
*/

import java.io.*;
import java.util.Scanner;
```

```
public class ArrayFiles
{
  public static void main(String args[]) throws IOException {
    Scanner fl = new Scanner(new File("jobs.txt"));
    PrintWriter flOut = new PrintWriter("jobs2.txt");

    String name;
    String title;
    double salary;

    System.out.println("\n\nData from jobs.txt - read file");
    while (fl.hasNextLine()) {
      name= fl.next();
      salary = fl.nextDouble();
      title = fl.nextLine();
      System.out.printf("%-1s\t%.2f\t%1s\n", name, salary, title);
      flOut.printf("%-1s\t%.2f\t%1s\n", name, salary, title);
    }
    fl.close();
    flOut.close();

    System.out.println("\n\n\n Data from written file - jobs2.txt");

    Scanner fl2 = new Scanner(new File("jobs2.txt"));

    while (fl2.hasNext()) {
      System.out.printf("%-15s\t%10.2f\t%15s\n", fl2.next(),
fl2.nextDouble(), fl2.nextLine());
    }

    fl2.close();
  }
}
```

```
Here is the output:
Data from jobs.txt - read file
smith            83000.00         manager
jones            120000.00         ceo
brown            27800.00         Assistant
Jefferson         125000.00        teacher
gandhi           63000.00         principal

Data from written file - jobs2.txt
smith            83000.00         manager
jones            120000.00         ceo
brown            27800.00         Assistant
Jefferson         125000.00        teacher
gandhi           63000.00         principal
```

7.4   Multidimensional Arrays

An array variable may be able to address a table-like memory space (i.e., conceptually a table). We could also create multi-dimensional arrays. For simple extension of an array as a data structure, consider a two-dimensional array. Again, data in all elements of a two-dimensional array should be the same data type. A two-dimensional array of integers will have rows and columns, like in a spreadsheet of integers. Row is one dimension and column is the second dimension. A multi-dimensional array can be processed by manipulating the array indices efficiently. For example, consider a two-dimensional array:

```
Student [][] s2DS = new Student [3][10];
```

The Student array s2DScan contain the information of 3x10=30 students. We could use an array of 30 students, instead of the above two-dimensional array. By using two indices, we may be able to arrange the students by grouping, e.g., Student[0][10] for the 10 students in group 1, Student[1][10] for 10 for group 2, and for group 3. Pictorially, the first index denotes the row of a table, while the second index refers to the Student[2][10]column numberas illustrated below:

s2DS[0][0]	s2DS[0][1]	s2DS[0][3]	s2DS[0][4]	s2DS[0][5]	s2DS[0][6]	...
s2DS[1][0]	s2DS[1][1]	s2DS[1][3]	s2DS[1][4]	s2DS[1][5]	s2DS[1][6]	...
s2DS[2][0]	s2DS[2][1]	s2DS[2][3]	s2DS[2][4]	s2DS[2][5]	s2DS[2][6]	...

We all know about the average grades, average house prices, and average car sales. Averages (mean) do not always represent the behavior of data, (for example if the data are 5, 10, 30, 8, 3, and 200, then 200 will distort the average). Standard Deviation (SD) is a number which indicates how much each grade (house price or car sale) differs from the average grade (average house price or average car sale). It is easy to find the average, but you will appreciate why an array is needed to find the SD. SD calculation requires both the average and all the data elements. The formula for SD is in the exercises. Consider the following two codes:

```
int x, sum=0;// x is a simple variable with only one memory
location
double mean;
for (int i=0; i<10; i++)
    { x = kb.nextInt();
      sum +=x;
    }
    mean=sum/10.0;
// now we need to find the difference between mean and the
// first value. Does x havefirst, or the second, or the
// ninth value?

int y[] = newint[10];// y is an array with 10 memory
locations
for (int i=0; i<10; i++)
```

```
    { y[i] = kb.nextInt();
      sum +=y[i];
    }
    mean = sum/10.0;
// Since we have all the data values in the array elements,
we could calculate
// the differences between the mean and the data elements
```

	Standard Deviation	
Definition	The Standard Deviation is a measure of how spread out numbers are. [http://www.mathsisfun.com/data/standard-deviation.html] The **standard deviation** measures the amount of variation or dispersion from the average.[http://en.wikipedia.org/wiki/Standard_deviation]	
	Example	The average height for adult men in the United States is about 70 inches, with a standard deviation of around 3 inches.
	Implication	This means that about 68 percent have a height within 3 inches of the mean (67–73 inches) – one standard deviation; about 95% have a height within 6 inches of the mean (64–76 inches) – two standard deviations. If the standard deviation were zero, then all men would be exactly 70 inches tall. Create a text file of thirty heights. Calculate the average height of your data.

Example 6: Standard deviation problem is included in the exercises. We will give a simple example of three survey results and their corresponding averages for six imaginary presidential candidates. This will illustrate the creation of a 2-dimensional array of integer ratings and a 1-dimensional array of the candidate names. It will also show the passing of arrays into methods as parameters and invoking them in other methods. The data (names and the three ratings of each candidate) are read from a text file. Here is the program:

Coding List 7.6: Survey_2D.java

```
/*
 * Author:
 * Date:
 * Input:
 * Output:
 * This program illustrates how arrays are passed into methods
* as parameters and how these methods are invoked in other
 * methods. We are creating two arrays: a one-dimensional
 * array of names of politicians and a two-dimensional
 * array of their popularity rates. The data are read from
 * a text file.
 * Input: an array of names and an array of integer ratings
 * read from a text file
 * Output: a table of the candidates with their ratings and
 * their corresponding average ratings.
 * array names on different line.
```

```
*/

import java.util.Scanner; // needed to read from a file
import java.io.*;

public class Survey_2D
{
  public static void main (String args[]) throws IOException {
    String names[] = new String[6]; // create an array of questions
    int survey[][] = new int[6][4];

    Scanner file = new Scanner(new File("survey.txt"));
    int n=0;
    while (file.hasNextLine()) {
      names[n] = file.next();
      survey[n][0] = file.nextInt();
      survey[n][1] = file.nextInt();
      survey[n][2] = file.nextInt();
      survey[n][3] = (survey[n][0]+survey[n][1]+survey[n][2])/3;
      n++;
    }
    System.out.println("\n\n\n");
    System.out.println("Name\t\tSurvey 1\tSurvey 2\tSurvey 3\tAverage");
    System.out.println("----\t\t--------\t-------\t\t--------\t-------");

    // printArray(names);
    print2_D(names, survey);
  }

// IOException needed at the  method that reads the file
  public static void printArray(String nm[]) {
    System.out.println("\n\n");
    for (int i=0; i<nm.length; i++)
    System.out.println(nm[i]);
  }

  public static void print2_D(String nm[], int x[][]) {
    for (int row=0; row<x.length;row++) {
      System.out.print(nm[row]);
      for (int col = 0; col<x[row].length; col++)
      System.out.print("\t\t"+x[row][col]);
      System.out.println();
    }
  }
}
```

Here is the output:

Name	Survey 1	Survey 2	Survey 3	Average
----	--------	-------	--------	-------
Smith	23	38	16	25
Brown	28	20	19	22
Adams	15	10	9	11
Zhou	8	6	9	7
Gandhi	11	18	31	20
Gomez	15	8	16	13

7.5   Exercises

Concept Understanding

1. Consider the following code segment:
   String name = "Mercy College";

   a) Is the variable name an array?

   b) An array can be accessed by indices. Is name[1]a valid statement? If so, what does it contain? If not, explain why not.

   c) Using a for loop, write a code segment that can print as shown below (one letter per line):

   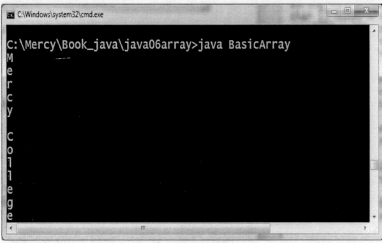

   Hint: look up an API for the class String.

2. Consider the following code segment:

   char [] name2 = new char[13]; // array of characters

   a) Write a code that the variable name2 can hold "Mercy College".

   b) Using a for loop, write a code segment that can print as shown above question 1.c.

   c) Recall question 1 above. Compare 1.c and 2.b. Explain why one uses **length()**and another **length**.

3. Consider the example of student. Each student can be defined over name, major and classes to take, where each class is defined over course title, credit hours and instructor name. There is one implementation requirement that the example structures an array of students and an array of classes.

   a) As shown in Section 7.2.1, draw an array structure for students and classes.

   b) Since each student takes one or more classes, each element of the student array should link a class array. Of course, a class array may be an empty array, if a student takes no class. As an extension of the previous question, draw a student array which links class arrays.

Programming

1. Write a program to create an array of 25 integers.

   a) Print the numbers on one line

   b) Print 5 numbers per line

   c) Print them in reverse order: from the 25th to the first

   d) Print every 5th number in the array

   e) Print the average of the 25 numbers

   f) Print the largest and the smallest of the numbers

   g) Print all the numbers greater than the average

2. Write a method to accept an array of names as a parameter and print the names.

3. Write a method to receive an array of integers and a key integer as parameters and return 'true' or 'false' depending on whether the key is in the array or not.

4. Write a program to generate 100 random integers in the range $0 - 100$ and calculate their mean and standard deviation.

   The formula for SD is

   $$\sigma = \sqrt{\frac{\sum(x1-\mu)^2}{n}}$$

   where σ is the SD and μ is the mean of the numbers.

5. Write a class called Manage Students. Remember that this class must have constructor(s) to create a set of students. Read 25 student names and their average grades from a text file (called "students.txt") into an array of Student objects. Student class has to be created before creating the array.

   a) Add a method to count the number of each grade (A, B, C, D, F). Print a Histogram as shown below with each asterisk representing one student to the ManageStudents class.

   b) Add a method called "printTable" to the class which accepts the Students array and prints a table of student names, average grades, deviations from the class average and the letter grades.

   c) Add a method called "findStudent" to the class which will accept the Students array and a student name. It should search the array for the student name. If the name is found, it should print all the details of that student. If the student is not found, it should print a message stating it.

d) Add a method called "standardDeviation" to calculate and return the standard deviation.

e) Write a driver to let the user choose to 1) print the table of the text file data, 2) print the final roster with "printable", 3) search for a specific student, 4) print the standard deviation, and 5) to print Histogram.

6. Assume that you are doing a survey of popularity of several candidates for the primaries. You should read the names and their vote totals from a text file. It should print a table of the names, votes received, and the percentages of votes received. It should then print the winner of the primaries. Here is the output of one solution:

Name	Survey 1	Survey 2	Survey 3	Average
Smith	23	38	16	25
Brown	28	20	19	22
Adams	15	10	9	11
Zhou	8	6	9	7
Gandhi	11	18	31	20
Gomez	15	8	16	13

The winner is Smith

7. A gene mutation is a permanent change in the DNA sequence that makes up a gene. Mutations range in size from a single DNA building block (DNA base) to a large segment of a chromosome. Write a program to compare two dna sequences of same length to detect any mutation (change) in them and identify the locations of mutations. Thymine (T), Adenine (A), Cytosine (C), and Guanine (G).

8. For each bank account, a variable is created and it holds the information about BankAcct. This approach has a major limitation in creating variables (object references) to construct objects. To overcome this limitation, this assignment needs to use an array.

An array of BankAcct objects is created in the class AcctCollection. BankAcct has variables public intacctNo; public String custName; private double balance = 0.0; and methods, public void deposit (double moneyIn) { ...}, public double withdrawal (double moneyOut) { ... }, public double getBalance() { ... }, etc.

AcctCollection class has two variables, account which is an array of BankAcct, and count: BankAcct[] account; int count; and methods, public void wireTransfer (BankAcct from, BankAcct to, double amount) { ...} and public double revenue() { ... }.

Of course, both BankAcct and AcctCollection classes have overloaded constructors, and toDisplay methods. To run these classes, the AcctDriver class is created.

In the AcctDriver class, we create two banks as an example, chase and boA (bank of america), each of which has 10 and 5 accounts, respectively. Accounts are created and assigned to an array. Objects of account invoke methods, deposit and withdrawal, and then show the states of the objects. At last, money is wire-transferred from one account to another in the same bank (see line (1) in the code segment), and to another in another bank (see line (2) in the code segment). The revenue of each bank is shown in line (3) and (4).

```java
AcctDriver class is given:
public class AcctDriver {

    /**
     * @paramargs
     */
    public static void main(String[] args) {
        // TODO Auto-generated method stub
        AcctCollection chase = new AcctCollection(10);
        AcctCollectionboA = new AcctCollection(5);
        chase.createAcct(100, "Chris");
        chase.createAcct(101, "David");
        boA.createAcct(100, "BChris");
        boA.createAcct(109, "Bob");
        System.out.println("Chase ============");
        chase.display();
        System.out.println("B of A ============");
        boA.display();
        chase.account[0].deposit(500);
        chase.account[1].deposit(600);
        chase.createAcct(102, "David", 1000);
        boA.account[0].deposit(700);
        boA.account[1].deposit(400);
        System.out.println("Chase ============");
        chase.display();
        System.out.println("B of A ============");
        boA.display();
        chase.account[0].withdrawal(211);
        boA.createAcct(102, "Edwin", 1000);
        boA.account[1].withdrawal(177);
        System.out.println("Chase ============");
        chase.display();
        System.out.println("B of A ============");
        boA.display();
        System.out.println("*** Chase revenue: " +
chase.revenue());
        System.out.println("*** BofA revenue: " +
boA.revenue());
        chase.wireTransfer(chase.account[0], chase.account[2],
100);
        chase.wireTransfer(chase.account[0], boA.account[2],
100);
        System.out.println("Chase ============");
        chase.display();
        System.out.println("B of A ============");
        boA.display();
        System.out.println("*** Chase revenue: " +
chase.revenue());
        System.out.println("*** BofA revenue: " +
boA.revenue());
    }
}
```

The sample run is shown
below:

```
C:\Windows\system32\cmd.exe                                    _  □  X

C:\Mercy\131JavaI\prog>java AcctDriver
Chase ============
[100     Chris    0.0]
[101     David    0.0]
B of A ============
[100     BChris   0.0]
[109     Bob      0.0]
Chase ============
[100     Chris    500.0]
[101     David    600.0]
[102     David    1000.0]
B of A ============
[100     BChris   700.0]
[109     Bob      400.0]
Out of the Balance, 500.0: 211.0 withdrawn and the current balance: 289.0
Out of the Balance, 400.0: 177.0 withdrawn and the current balance: 223.0
Chase ============
[100     Chris    289.0]
[101     David    600.0]
[102     David    1000.0]
B of A ============
[100     BChris   700.0]
[109     Bob      223.0]
[102     Edwin    1000.0]
*** Chase revenue: 1889.0
*** BofA revenue: 1923.0
WIRETRANSFER from      [100    Chris    289.0]  :to[102 David   1000.0] :
Out of the Balance, 289.0: 100.0 withdrawn and the current balance: 189.0
100.0 transferred!
WIRETRANSFER from      [100    Chris    189.0]  :to[102 Edwin   1000.0] :
Out of the Balance, 189.0: 100.0 withdrawn and the current balance: 89.0
100.0 transferred!
Chase ============
[100     Chris    89.0]
[101     David    600.0]
[102     David    1100.0]
B of A ============
[100     BChris   700.0]
[109     Bob      223.0]
[102     Edwin    1100.0]
*** Chase revenue: 1789.0
*** BofA revenue: 2023.0
```

9. Write a java program, MultiArray.java, which can generate the following 2-dimensional
   table as specified by a user. The number of rows and columns can be taken from 1) the
   command-line, java MultiArray 5 7, or 2) by asking to enter to a prompt such that "Enter
   the number of rows:" and "Enter the number of columns:". By taking the row and column
   numbers, a table form is generated.

a.   Write a java program, MultiArray.java, that can generate the following:

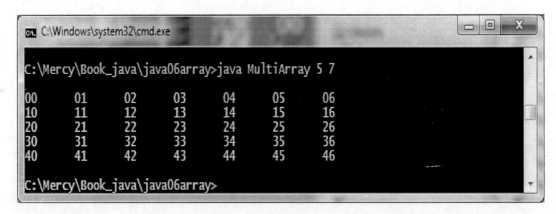

b.   Write a java program, MultiArray2.java, that can generate the following, where the column and row labels are printed:

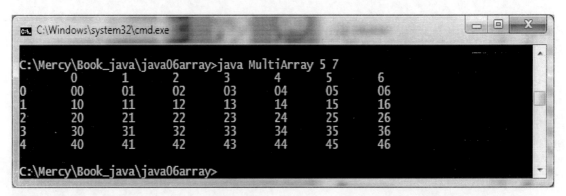

10. Write a program to generate a 2-dimensional array of random integers.

    a.   Print the array in matrix format.

    b.   Print only the diagonal elements

    c.   Print the sum of each row

    d.   Print its transpose (column as rows).

11. Write a program to allocate airline seats. Seats already allocated must have 'x' in the cells and the open seats must have '-' in the cells. If a seat that is already allocated is chosen by a customer, a message must be printed and allowed to enter the location of a different seat.

12. Recall Question 3 in Concept Understanding in this Exercise, write Java programs as follows:

a) Define a Java class for class

b) Define a Java class for student, which has a field variable whose type is the class defined above.

Inheritances

8.1 Introduction

We all know the meaning of the word "inheritance". A son/daughter inherits many things including property from his/her parents. This analogy applies to classes also. We will be creating parent or a superclass and inherit its properties to children or subclasses. This chapter describes the relationships between classes. So far, we have considered classes that are being used by other classes. For example, Student Driverclass (i.e., StudentDriver.java) **has** Studentclass object (i.e., Student.java) in it. Similarly we have written several classes that have Scanner class in them. These are the examples of **has-a** relationship.

One of the strengths of Java is the reuse of code already written: We could use the code already written and add more features to it without rewriting all the code. We can inherit the features of the code already written into the code we want to expand to. Consider a class called Person who has a name and an income. Consider a class called Student. A Student **is a** Personwho also has a name and income. So, instead of re-defining these in Studentclass, we could extend Personclass to Studentclass by inheriting name and income. In addition to the inherited properties, additional properties such as major and gpa can be added to the Student class. In the same manner, we could also add more methods in Studentclass. We call this relationship **is a** relationship as Student **is a** Person. Person is the parent class or superclass and Student is the child class or subclass. There are two relationships between classes:

- Composition relationship. A class can have another class defined in it. Classes are aggregated or composited to form another class. A class "**has-a**" zero or more other classes, each of which is the type of a variable (Student type in Student Driver class).
- Inheritance relationship. There is an inheritance relationship between parent and child classes. A child class can inherit any or all of the "visible" properties (see the box below) from its parent class. Therefore, a child class "**is-a**" relationship to its parent class.

Visible Properties	
Concepts	Recall Section 6.2.3 the visibility modifier that can define the visibility of class property (variables and methods): • public modifier: visible to all classes. • private modifier: visible only within the class, not by inheritors, not by other classes in the package. • protected modifier: visible to classes outside the package that inherit the class, also to all classes in the package. • Default or no modifier: visible to all classes of the package so public.
Question	Consider all classes and objects that are in the same package. Which variables or methods can be inherited?
Answer	All the variables and methods, which are not private, can be inherited.

The *has-a* and *is-a* relationships are depicted in the following UML. Faculty and Student are Persons and hence a Student **is-a** Person and a Faculty **is-a** Person. Assume Dept is a class already defined. As indicated in Figure 1, the classes Student and Faculty have the class Dept as the type of one of their field variables. Faculty and Student exhibit **has-a** relationship to Dept. As discussed in earlier chapters, there is a driver class StudentDriver that uses Student class.

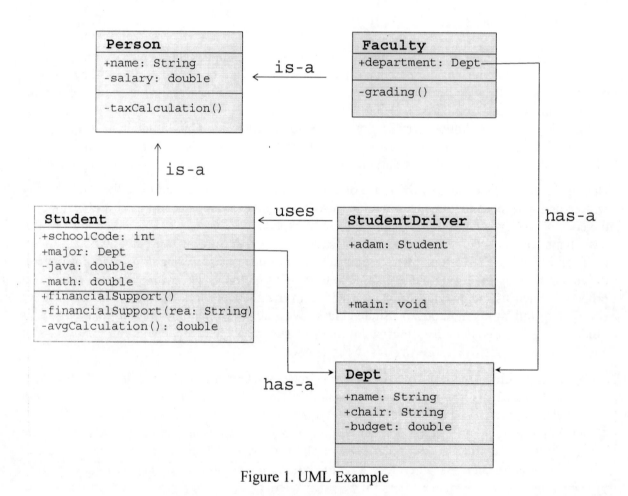

Figure 1. UML Example

8.1.1 Composition Relationship (has-a)

Example 1:

Here is a simple example on **has-a** relationship: Class1 will just print "Hello Java" using print() method. Class2 will create an object of Class1 (Class2 **has** Class1) and invokes its print() method through the object. Also observe that Class1 does not have a constructor. So in Class2, Class1() works as a default constructor.

Coding List 8.1: Classes Example

```
/*
 * Author:
 * Date:
 * Input:
 * Output:
 */

public class Class1
{
    public static void main(String args[]) {
        print();
    }

    public static void print() {
        System.out.println("Hello Java"); }
    }
```

Class2.java

```
/*
 * Author:
 * Date:
 * Input:
 * Output:
 */

public class Class2
{
    public static void main(String args[]) {
        Class1 c1 = new Class1();
        c1.print();
    }
}
```

Example 2:

Here is an example of how variables with public and private modifiers are treated within a class (Class3 with main() method inside it so is a part of Class3) and outside the class (Class4 and Class4Driver: here main() method is in Class4Driver which is outside Class4). name1 is public and name2 is private in both Class3 and Class4. c1 is an object of Class3 in the first case and c1 is an object in Class4Driver in the second case. We will print both c1.name1 and c1.name2 in both cases. When the main() method is inside Class3, it prints both the names, even though name2 is private in Class3. We removed the main method from Class4 and created Class4Driver with the main() method. In this case, main() is in a different class and hence it cannot access c1.name2 directly. You need an access method like getName2(). So, private variables are accessible within the class but need an access method to access them outside the class.

Coding List 8.2: Classes Example Continued

```
/*
 * Author:
 * Date:
 * Input:
 * Output:
 * The main() method is a part of this class. So, it can access name1
   and name2 directly
 */

public class Class3
{
    public String name1;
    private   String name2;

    public Class3(String nm1, String nm2) {
        name1 = nm1;
        name2 = nm2;
    }

    public static void main(String args[]) {
        Class3 cl = new Class3("Washington","Adams");
        System.out.println("public name: "+cl.name1);
        // accessing the private name2 below
        System.out.println("Private name: "+cl.name2);
    }
}
```

Class4.java

```
/*
 * Author:
 * Date:
 * Input:
 * Output:
 * the main() method is outside this class and private
   variables cannot be directly accessed in main()
 */

public class Class4
{
    public String name1;
    private String name2;

    public Class4(String nm1, String nm2)    {
        name1 = nm1;
        name2 = nm2;
    }
}
```

```
Class4Driver.java
/*
 * Author:
 * Date:
 * Input:
 * Output:
 * the main() method is in this class which is outside Class7
   class. So, it cannot access
   the private variable name2 directly. It needs a get method.
   You will get an error message when you run the following class.
*/

public class Class4Driver
{
     public static void main(String args[])  {
          Class4 cl = new Class4("Washington", "Adams");
          System.out.println("Public name: "+ cl.name1);
          System.out.println("Private name: "+cl.name2);
     }
}
```

8.2 Inheritance Relationship

We will now introduce the concept of inheritance. Inheritance is allowed along the *is-a* class hierarchies. It means that a child class can inherit any visible properties from its parent class. Inheritance allows a software developer to derive a new class from an existing one. The existing class is called the *parent class* or *superclass*, which forms the base class for all of its subclasses. The derived class is called the *child class* or *subclass*. So, a parent class should be defined first and then any subclasses can be defined based on the parent class. The keyword to indicate for class declaration over an inheritance hierarchy is "extends." For example, since the class Person is defined as shown in the previous section, one of its subclasses Student can be declared in the following way:

```
public class Student extends Person {
// body of the Student class
}
```

Example 3:

We will give very simple examples of a parent class (Class5) and two child classes (Class6 and Class7). The parent class has the instance variable String name. The child class Class5 does not have the name variable. It means that it will use the variable name in its parent class. Whatever name the child class Class6 assigns will become the parent's name as well. In this case the parent and the child are the same. In the child class Class7, we have String name, that will be the local name. In this case, the parent and the child could be different. We have Class5_6_Driver for classes Class5 and Class6. Class5_7_Driver is the driver for classes Class5 and Class7.

Observe that Class5 is the parent for both Class6 and Class7. If we want the parent name to be different from the child name, we need to have name variable in both the classes. The outputs of the drivers are right below the drivers.

Coding List 8.3: Classes Example Continued

```
/*
 * Author:
 * Date:
 * Input:
 * Output:
 * Observe that Class6 below, subclass of Class5, does not
   have its own name variable. It is getting the name from
   the parent. So, name of both the superclass and subclass
   will be the same as we created in the driver with the
   subclass object. Since Class6 does not have its own name,
   it goes to its parent for the name using super(nm). We
   need the argument "nm" in super() as the constructor in
   Class5 has a String parameter. So, super(nm) will set
   the name for both Class5and Class6.

 This parent class has two constructors. Class7 uses the
 default constructor andClass6 uses the one with the
 String parameter
 */

public class Class5
{
     public String name;

     public Class5() { }
     public Class5 (String nm)  {
         name = nm;
     }
}
```

Class6.java

```
/*
 * Author:
 * Date:
 * Input:
 * Output:
 */

public class Class6 extends Class5
{
     public Class6(String nm) {
         super(nm);
     }

     public void print() {
         System.out.println ("Parent name: "+super.name);
```

```
            System.out.println("Child name: "+this.name);
        }
}
```

Class5_6Driver.java

```
/*
 * Author:
 * Date:
 * Input:
 * Output:
 */

public class Class5_6_Driver
{
    public static void main(String args[]) {
            Class6 child = new Class6("Washington");
            child.print();
    }
}
```

Observe that Class7 below is exactly the same as Class6 except that Class7 has its own name variable. Also observe that the drivers are the same except for the objects. Now, compare the outputs of the two drivers.

Coding List 8.4: Classes Example Continued

```
/*
 * Author:
 * Date:
 * Input:
 * Output:
 *   Class7 below has its own instance variable name. It is using the
     default constructor from Class5. The names of Class5 (Adams) and
     Class6 (Washington) will be different. Here the names of superclass
     and subclass will be different
 */

public class Class7 extends Class5
{
  String name;

  public Class7(String nm) {
      name = nm;
  }

  public void print() {
      System.out.println("Parent name: "+super.name);
```

```
            System.out.println("Child name: "+this.name);
    }
}
```

Class5_7_Driver.java

```
/*
 * Author:
 * Date:
 * Input:
 * Output:
 */

public class Class5_7_Driver
{
    public static void main(String args[]) {
        Class7 child = new Class7("Washington");
        child.print();
    }
}
```

Output

Parent name: Adams
Child name: Washington

Example 4:

Here is a simple example of one superclass and two subclasses: Employee is the superclass, Hourly and Fulltime are its subclasses. They have Employees Driver to test them out. Write an UML to this structure. Observe that the constructors for the subclasses are written in different ways. Also, observe that both the subclasses have the methods salary() and to String() but they work differently. Here are the codes:

Coding List 8.5: Employee.java

```
/*
 * Author:
 * Date:
 * Input:
 * Output:
 * Employee is the super class. There are two types of employees: Hourly
   employees and Fulltime employees. First, the superclass Employee is
   built and compiled. Every employee has a name and an annual income.
 */

public class Employee
{
  private String name, phone;
```

```
    private double age;

    public Employee(String nm, double ag) {
      name = nm;
      age =  ag;
    }

    public Employee(String nm, String phn, double ag) {
      name = nm;
      phone = phn;
      age =  ag;
    }

    public void setName(String nm) {
      name = nm; }

    public String getName() {
      return name; }

    public void setPhone(String phn) {
      phone = phn; }

    public String getPhone() {
      return phone; }

    public void setAge(double ag) {
      age = ag; }

    public double getAge() {
      return age; }
}
```

Coding List 8.6: Hourly.java

```
/*
 * Author:
 * Date:
 * Input:
 * Output:
 */

public class Hourly extends Employee
{

  private double hours;
  private double payRate;

  public Hourly(String nm, double in, double hrs, double pay) {
    super(nm, in);
    // This will make Employee name and age the same as this employee
    hours = hrs;
    // Expanding Employee to Hourly employee by adding hours and payRate
    payRate = pay;
```

```java
    }

  // set and get methods for name and income are available from the
parent
  // Adding them for the extended hours and payRate
  public void setHours(double hrs) {
    hours = hrs; }

  public double getHours() {
    return hours; }

  public void setPayRate(double pay) {
    payRate = pay; }

  public double getPayRate() {
    return payRate; }

  public double salary() {  // calculate hourly salary
    return hours*payRate; }

  public String toString() {
    return (super.getName()+"\n Hours worked = "+hours+" hours \nPay
Rate = $"+payRate+"\nWeekly Salary = $"+salary());
  }
}
```

Fulltime.java

```java
/*
 * Author:
 * Date:
 * Input:
 * Output:
*/

import java.util.Scanner;

public class Fulltime extends Employee
{
  double annualSalary;
  Scanner kb = new Scanner (System.in);

  public Fulltime(String nm, double in) {
    super(nm,in);
  }

  public void putSalary() {
    System.out.print("Enter your annual salary: $");
    annualSalary = kb.nextDouble();
  }

  public double salary() {
```

```
    // both Hourly and Fulltime employees have salaries
    return annualSalary / 52;
  }
    // but are calculated in different ways.

    // appropriate method is used by the object
  public String toString() {
    return (super.getName()+"\n Annual Salary =
$ "+annualSalary+"\nWeekly Salary = $"+salary());
  }
}
```

EmployeesDriver.java

```
/*

 * Author:
 * Date:
 * Input:
 * Output:
 * Employee is the super class. Hourly and Fulltime are its subclasses.
   Both the subclasses have salary() and toString() methods. But they
   work differently. Also, observe how the constructors are built in
   Hourly and Fulltime subclasses.
*/

import java.util.Scanner;

public class EmployeesDriver
{

  public static void main(String args[]) {
    Employee employee1 = new Employee("Kate", "200000", 45);
    Hourly employee2 = new Hourly("Liz", 30, 20, 15.75);
    Fulltime employee3 = new Fulltime("John", 23);

    System.out.println("\nEmployee:\n"+employee1);
    // Employee does not have
    // toString method. So, employee1 object cannot be printed
    // like this. Observe what it prints!
    System.out.println("\nHourly:");
    System.out.println(employee2); // Hourly class has toString method
    System.out.println("\nFulltime:");
    System.out.println(employee3);

    // Observe below that the child objects using their parent methods
    // to print the names of these employees
    System.out.println("Employee is "+employee1.getName());
    System.out.println("Hourly employee is "+employee2.getName());
    System.out.println("Fulltime employee is "+employee3.getName());

  }

}
```

Do You Know the Keyword "super"

In an inheritance hierarchy, a subclass object may need to refer to its superclass object. A reference variable referring to its immediate parent class object is the keyword super. The keyword super can refer to:

- Parent class constructor
- Immediate parent class instance variable
- Immediate parent class method

Consider the following classes

```
/* This parent class has
two constructors. Class7
uses the default
constructor and
Class6 uses the one with
the String parameter
*/


public class Class5
  {
(1) public String name;

(2) public Class5() {
     }



(3) public Class5(String
nm) {
(4)    name = nm; }
}
```

```
/* There is no local instance
variable name in this class.
Whatever name Class6 object
gets will become the name of
both the classes
*/


public class Class6 extends
Class5
  {
(5) public Class6(String nm) {
(6)    super(nm);
     }

   public void print() {
(7)    System.out.println("Parent
name: "+super.name);
(8)    System.out.println("Child
name: "+this.name);
     }
}
```

A driver class is as follows:

```
public class Class5_6_Driver
    {
(9)   public static void main(String args[]) [
(10)      Class6 child = new Class6("Washington");
(11)      child.print();
     }
}
```

Parent name: Washington
Child name: Washington

	Parent class constructor	As an object of Class6 is constructed, the constructor of Class6 invokes the constructor (line 5) of its superclass Class5. The statement super(nm)invokes the constructor of its superclass, Class5 in this case. This will initialize the name variable in Class5 and the subclass Class6 will have the same name.

	Immediate parent class variable	As an object of Class6 invokes the method print(), the method print() in Class6accesses two variables: name in Class6 and name in Class5. But since Class6 does not have its own name variable, it will use its parent's name in Class5. The latter can be accessed by the statement super(nm) as shown on line 8.
		
		 The output of line 10 is
		
		      Parent name: Washington
		      Child name: Washington

Question		Is the following valid in the above driver class? If not, explain why not. `super.print();`
Answer		Invalid because the keyword super is not a variable associated with any object reference and there is no print() in the parent class Class5.

Example 5:

We introduced Person class and its subclasses in the introduction. We will present the completed class hierarchy below. The Person class is defined over two field variables String name and double income. This could be any person in the world as everybody will have a name and income, income could be zero. This could be the superclass for various types of persons like in businesses, education, health, technology, and politics. We will focus on a section of education, namely academic persons: faculty and students. Faculty are persons and students are persons. But, each of them has more information, in addition to name and income. So, the subclasses Faculty and Student will include corresponding data. We will reuse Person in expanding to Faculty and Student. Again we can distinguish between graduate and undergraduate students. Each faculty and each student will belong to some department. So, we will include Dept class as a variable in Faculty and Student classes. Faculty and Student classes will have **has-a** relationship with Dept class. Person class has **is-a** relationship with Faculty and Student classes. We will provide below with complete codes for all the classes. They are simple that can be expanded to a more comprehensive package. Here are the codes:

Coding List 8.7: Person.java

```java
/*
 * Author:
 * Date:
 * Input:
 * Output:
 * Person is the super class. It has subclasses, Student and Faculty.
   There are also a class Dept, which is referenced as the type of a
   field variable by the classes, Student and Faculty.
*/

public class Person
{
    public String name;
    protected double income;

    public Person(){
    }

    public Person (String name) {
      this.name = name;
    }

    public Person(String nm, double in){
      name = nm;
      income = in;
    }

    public double taxCalculation() {
    System.out.println("Person running at " + this.getClass().getName()+"
class");
    double tax , rate = 0.15;// we could read rate from keyboard or a DB
    tax = income *  rate;
    return tax;
    }
}
```

Constructors for a parent class can also be inherited by its subclasses. Consider the constructor of Person. We want to define a constructor for the class Student by exploiting the constructor of Person. One of the constructors for Student is in the form:

```java
public Student (String name, String major) {
    super (name);
// super() is a current variable/object at its parent class
    this.major = major;
}
```

In inheritance along the inheritance hierarchy, a code defined at the parent class can be reused by its child classes. This is what we have done in the blue box for the keyword super() and

Employee-Hourly relationship. In the blue box, Class5 object and Class6 object will have the same name. Employee and hourly employee will be the same person with the same name. We will have this relationship between Person and Student as shown below.

On the other hand, a child class may want to change the field variable already defined at its parent class. This case is illustrated in Class7 above. Class5 (superclass for Class7) and Class7 can have different names. In this case, no super() is stated, and the field variables are directly filled as shown in line (6). Super refers to the immediate parent and this refers to the current class.

Coding List 8.8: Student.java

```java
/*
 * Author:
 * Date:
 * Input:
 * Output:
 * Student is a subclass of the class Person.
   There are field variables and methods defined. Of the methods,
   two methods are defined for constructors.
*/

public class Student extends Person
{
    // variable fields are defined
    public static int schoolCode;
    public Dept major;
        // type of major is Dept
        // Dept is a class defined earlier

    private double gpa;
    protected double stipend;  // visible to classes along the hierarchy

    public Student () {
          // no implementation for the default constructor
        }

    public Student (String name, double in, Dept major) {
          super (name,in);
          this.major = major;
        }
    /* following set and get methods are needed to access gpa outside
this
    this class as gpa is private. */
    public void setGpa(double gp)
    { gpa = gp; }

    public double getGpa()
    { return gpa;   }

    public double financialSupport() {
```

```
            if (this.income > 20000)
              return income * 0.1;
            else {
                    double extra = financialSupport("Insufficient income");
                    return this.income * extra;
                    }
                }

    private double financialSupport (String s) {
            System.out.println("Reason: " + s);
        return -1;
            // underwriter() is omitted here, but returns
            // a reasonable positive floating point number < 1.
            }

    public double taxCalculation() {
            // the method already defined in the superclass is
            // now overridden here

            System.out.println("Student running at "+
this.getClass().getName()+" class");
            double tax, rate = 0.15, deduction = 2000;
              // a deduction may be applied to students

            tax = income *  rate - deduction;
            return tax;
            }
}
```

We have a single constructor for faculty. Each faculty will have the name and income of Person, its superclass. We have also added toString() method to print the information of Faculty objects. The private instance variables have access or methods as they cannot be accessed from outside this class.

Coding List 8.9: Faculty.java

```
/*
 * Author:
 * Date:
 * Input:
 * Output:
 * We have a single constructor for faculty. Each faculty will have
   the name and income of Person, its superclass. We have also added
   toString() method to print the information of Faculty objects. The
   private instance variables have accessor methods as they cannot be
   acceessed from outside this class.
*/

public class Faculty extends Person
```

```
{

  private Dept subjectField;
  private String Id, rank;

  public Faculty(String nm, double in, String id, String rk) {
    super(nm, in); // We are using the third constructor in Person

    Id = id;
    rank = rk;
  }

  /* accessors for the private variables */
  public String getId() {
    return Id;   }

  public String getRank() {
    return rank; }

  public double fedTax(double rate) {
    return this.income*rate/100; }

  /* Observe how Faculty information is printed in the toString() method.
*/
  public String toString() {
    return (this.name +" has an income of $"+ this.income + " and pays fed
tax of $"+this.fedTax(25.5)+"\n");
  }
}
```

Here is the Under class. We skipped the implementation of Grad class. We have left the instance variables public, just for a variation. In a proper implementation, they must be private.

Coding List 8.10: Under.java

```
/*
 * Author:
 * Date:
 * Input:
 * Output:

 * Here is the Under class, a subclass of Student, which is in turn
   a subclass of the class Person. We skipped the implementation of
   Grad class. We have left the instance variables public,
   just for a variation. In a proper implementation, they
   must be private.
*/

public class Under extends Student
{
    // variable fields are defined
    public Dept minor;
```

```java
    public int genEdCredit;

    public Under () {
        // no implementation for the default constructor
    }

    public Under (String name, double in, Dept major, Dept minor) {
        super (name, in, major);
        // super() is a current object at its parent class
        this.minor = minor;
    }

    public double taxCalculation() {
        // the method already overridden in the superclass is
        // again re-overridden here

        System.out.println("Under running at "+ this.getClass().getName()+"
class");
        double tax = 0.0, rate = 0.15, deduction = 1500;
        // a deduction may be applied to students

        tax = this.income *  rate - deduction;
        return tax;
    }
}
```

The last class to be implemented before the driver is the Dept class. This is an independent class that will be used in Student and Faculty classes. The relationship of Student and Faculty to Dept class is **has-a** relationship.

Coding List 8.11: Dept.java

```java
/*
 * Author:
 * Date:
 * Input:
 * Output:

 * Here is the Dept class, which is defined as a stand-alone class.
   This class is used as a field variable type in other classes,
   Student and Faculty.
*/

public class Dept
{
    // variable fields are defined
    public String name;

    private double budget;

    public Dept (String name) {
```

```
            this.name = name;

    }

    public String getName()
    { return this.name;    }

}
```

We will test all the classes defined above in the AppDriver below. We are testing the implementation of taxCalculation() method. Each of the classes Person, Student, and Under has taxCalculator() method, but implemented in different ways. An object of a subclass will execute the method in its class. The output of the AppDriver1 is given below the code.

We are using this to test all the classes in the hierarchy (is-a relation) as well as the class Dept (has-a relation) which is used in Student and Underclasses. We will be using all these classes in Chapter 9 to introduce Polymorphic concepts, using an expanded driver. We will discuss the overriding taxCalculation() method.

Coding List 8.12: AppDriver1.java

```
/*
 * Author:
 * Date:
 * Input:
 * Output:

 * Here is a driver class, which invokes classes, Person, Student,
   Faculty, Under and Dept, directly and indirectly.
*/

public class AppDriver1
{
   // under construction
   public static void main (String [] args) {
     Under stud1_under = new Under ();
     Faculty faculty1 = new Faculty("Jefferson", 200000, "1111111",
"Professor");
     Dept cs = new Dept ("Computer Science" );
     // cs is an object of Dept of Computer Science
     Dept csec = new Dept ("Cybersecurity");
     // csed is an object of Dept of Cybersecurity
     Under stud2_under = new Under ("Brown", 100000, cs, csec);
     // Brown is an undergraduate student  in cs major and in csec minor
     Student student1 = new Student();
     //it is a default constructor, no data is provided
     Person person1 = new Person();
```

```
    System.out.println("Person: "+person1.taxCalculation());
    // executed at Person class
    System.out.println("Student: "+student1.taxCalculation());
    // executed at Student class

    Under under_Jane = new Under ("Kennedy", 200000, csec,cs);

    System.out.println("under_Jane:"+under_Jane.taxCalculation());
    System.out.println(faculty1);

    /* Observe that name and genEdCredit variables are public in Under
class. So, we could directly assign values and print them, or use
whichever way the needs are. */

    stud2_under.genEdCredit = 21;
    stud1_under.name = "Adam";
    System.out.println("Student1 name: "+stud1_under.name);
    System.out.println("Student2 GenEd credits =
"+stud2_under.genEdCredit);
    }
}
```

8.3   Visibility and "Protected" Modifier

There are four possible visibility modifiers. Three of them - "public", "private", and none - have been discussed in earlier chapters. These visibility modifiers can be applied to inheritance hierarchies differently from the structure with no hierarchies. The modifier to restrict the visibility along the inheritance hierarchies is "protected." This section describes about the protected modifier.

Let's consider an extended UML of Figure 1. There is an inheritance hierarchy, starting from the top, "Person" to "Student" and "Faculty" which are subclasses to Person. Student is extended to "Under" and "Grad" in Figure 2. Traverse the links with the is-a label from Person to Under. As you might examine, there are more inheritance hierarchies available in the UML.

In UML, the symbols, +, − and 0, appearing before variables or method tokens, denote the modifiers "public", "private" and "protected", respectively. Recall that the public modifier on variables, methods, and objects allows them to be accessed by any objects or classes, while the private modifier does not. However, the protected modifier allows objects or classes along its inheritance hierarchy, but does not from outside of its hierarchy.

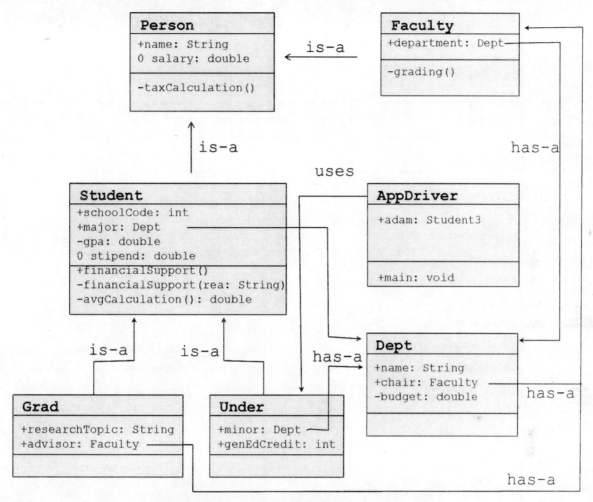

Figure 2. Revised UML Example from Figure 1

Now, consider a driver program. A driver program may be able to use any classes shown in UML of Figure 1. However, the visibility of an object constructed in a driver program is determined based on its visibility modifier and the class relationship. Assume that the driver program, AppDriver.java in the following example, uses the classes Under and Dept.

To the classes defined as above, a driver program may try to access the properties. The way of accessing classes and the restriction due to the visibility of class properties will remain the same as before except those with the new modifier "protected" along the new class relationships such as *is-a* or *has-a* hierarchies.

Table 1. Visibility with respect to Modifier

Modifier	Class	Package	Subclass	World
public	Y	y	y	y
protected	Y	y	y	n
None	Y	y	n	n
private	Y	n	n	n

Note that "y" and "n" denote accessible and not accessible, respectively.

<table>
<tr><td colspan="3">How to fix an error from
<code>System.out.println (under_K.gpa);</code></td></tr>
<tr><td rowspan="4">Challenge</td><td>Add the methods, <code>setX()</code> and <code>getX()</code>, into the class <code>Student</code>, where X could be gpa or major.</td><td>Use <code>setX()</code> and <code>getX()</code> to access the variable gpa of the object <code>under_K</code></td></tr>
<tr><td>

```
public class Student extends
Person
{
(1) public static int schoolCode;
(2) public Dept major;

(3) private double gpa;
(4) protected double stipend;

// line (5) - (13) omitted

(14) public double getGpa () {
        Return gpa;
     }

(15) public void setGpa (double
gpa) {
        this.gpa = gpa;
     }
}
```

</td><td>

```
public class AppDriver
{

 public static void main (String []
argv) {

  Under under_K = new Under();

  under_K.name = "Kelly";

  System.out.println
  (under_K.getGpa());

  }
}
```

</td></tr>
<tr><td>Question</td><td>Why the accessor <code>getX()</code> and mutator <code>setX()</code> methods are modified as public?</td></tr>
<tr><td>Answer</td><td>Unless otherwise, it cannot be invoked from AppDriver.</td></tr>
</table>

8.4 Abstract Classes and Interfaces

Abstract classes and interfaces are a special case of classes. More precisely speaking, they are generic classes which are yet another placeholder in a class hierarchy. Unlike regular classes that we have discussed so far, abstract classes and interfaces cannot be instantiated. They cannot be instantiated mainly because they are a class but not yet fully implemented. They are literally a description at an abstract level and they describe the way of interfaces.

Unlike an interface, the abstract modifier must be applied to each abstract method. An abstract class should have at least one fully defined method and could have more.

Interfaces are similar to abstract classes, but they do contain methods which are unimplemented.

8.5 Exercises

Concept Understanding

1. Consider a New York City political hierarchy, which you may refer to the web, hierarchystructure.com.

   a) List all possible entities that are mentioned on the webpage.

   b) Draw a structure of the New York City political hierarchy.

   c) Add static and behavioral elements to the class on the top second level in your hierarchy.

   d) Explain the inheritance that are applied to all classes along the hierarchy.

2. Consider the class A and SubA:

class A	class SubA extends A

``c++
class A
{
 	
  public int b;
 	
  private int c;
 	
  protected int d;
 	
  int e;
 	
public A (int b, int c){
 	
    }
``
	``c++
	class SubA extends A
	{
	    public int f;
	
	    public SubA (f) {
	      this.f = f;
	    }
	
	    SubA (intf,int b) {
	        this.f = f;
	        this.b = b;
	    }
	
	    SubA (int f, int b, int d){
	        this (f,b);
	        this.d = d;
	    }
	
	    SubA (int f, int b, int c, int
	    d){
	``

| `}` | ```
    this (f):
        this.d = d;
        super(b,c);
    }

    SubA (int f, int b, int c, int
d, int e){
        this (f,b):
        this.d = d;
        this.c = c;
        this.e = e;
    }
}
``` |

Which of the following construction statements are valid? Explain each answer.

1) SubA subA1 = new SubA(0);

2) SubA subA2 = new SubA(1,2);

3) SubA subA3 = new SubA(3,4,5);

4) SubA subA4 = new SubA(6,7,8,9);

5) SubA subA5 = new SubA(6, 7, 8, 9, 10);

Programming

1. Consider publications of books and magazines. Write a class called Publication. Let Publication have attributes title, price and year. Include Book and Magazine as subclasses of Publication. Let an author be an attribute of Book while Magazine has periodical information such as monthly, biweekly, or weekly. Book and Magazine classes should have Publisher class to use. Let the attributes of Publisher be company name and location. Book has Textbook and Reference as subclasses. Textbook has subject and title as its attributes. Reference has its type such as url address and title as its attributes. Use appropriate modifiers like public, private or protected. Include a separate driver class called AppDriver.

   a. Draw a UML with has-a and is-a hierarchies among the classes clearly marked.

   b. Write all the above classes with attributes and methods. Use appropriate modifiers for all the attributes and methods.

   c. Include short explanation of each method by identifying input parameters and return types if applicable.
```

d. Each class should show method overriding and overloading. Be creative to create methods for each class. Those methods may be used by the driver class. As used, the driver class should display

e. What method is being invoked e.g., "method mnm() in class uvw is invoked by an object opq" and then invoke the method.

f. Make sure that all the features of all the classes are used and properly displayed in the output.

2. Write a management system for a furniture store. Furniture class should be the superclass with name of the manufacturer as the attribute. It has LivingRoom, BedRoom, and DiningRoom as the subclasses of Furniture. Living room should have sofas, tables, and futons. Bed room should have beds, headboards, and dressers. Dining room needs dining table and dining chairs. Each subclass should include (a) a default constructor and other appropriate constructors as needed, (b) 'get' and 'set' methods, (c) a method to print the list of furniture and the corresponding prices, (d) a method that allows the selection from the list and returns the total price for all the items selected.

3. Write a program to represent an athletic department of a college. Athletics should be the superclass. Its attributes are name of the college and the athletic division it is in. (In August 1973, the current three-division setup of Division I, Division II, and Division III was adopted by the NCAA membership in a special convention. Under NCAA rules, Division I and Division II schools can offer scholarships to athletes for playing a sport. Division III schools may not offer any athletic scholarships.) This should have two subclasses: Mens and Womens. Both the subclasses should have number of athletes in the program, number of scholarships given (zero for Division III), the total amount of scholarship, and the list of sports offered in the school. Assume Football, Baseball, and Basketball are subclasses of Mens and Softball, Volleball, and FieldHockey are the subclasses of Womens. Each sport event should have a list of the players and their GPAs. Each of these subclasses must include (a) a default constructor and other appropriate constructors as needed, (b) 'get' and 'set' methods, (c) a method to print the information of the athletes, and (d) a method to calculate the average GPA of the team and return it. The driver class should allow a user to select any of these objects and their features, like want to see the list of women athletes in softball and their average GPA.

4. Create a program to compare different auto companies for their products.

5. Create a store management system. Each store has departments, each department has items to sell, employees, prices of items, salaries. Or we could go the other way, Sales, Finance, Procurement, HR,…

6. Write a program to solve math problems: Algebra, Trig, Stat,...

7. Consider Q1 in Concept Understanding in this Exercise, and write a Java program as follows:

   a) Choose a hierarchy that includes the first child class and its descendent classes. Define all those classes in a right sequence that no unknown classes are found.

   b) Define a driver class that can demonstrate the class inheritance at your best. Hint: refer to Q2 in Concept Understanding in this Exercise.

Polymorphisms

9.1 Polymorphic References

We know what a polynomial is: an algebraic expression with several monomials. Polymorphism is many forms or shapes. For example, human beings have two forms: male and female. Human could be superclass, male and female subclasses. Polymorphism is used in various subjects including chemistry, biology, and programming. In an *is-a* hierarchy in object-oriented programming, a super class and one of its subclasses may have the same method name but may exhibit different behaviors. A single method can take different forms in different classes in the hierarchy. The method in the subclass may override the method in its superclass if it is used by an object of the subclass.

Example 1:

For example, let us consider the Employee, Hourly, and Fulltime class hierarchy from Chapter 8. Employee is the superclass and Hourly and Fulltime are its subclasses. Let us create an object of type Employee:

```
Employee empl3;
```

Let us now make empl3 variable reference to an Employee object.

```
empl3 = new Employee("Dave", 60000);
```

It has been our practice to create a variable of one class type and make it reference to an object of the same class. In the example above, Employee variable empl3 is referencing to the Employee object with the name "Dave" and income 60000.

In an *is-a* relation, we could also make a variable of the superclass reference to an object of any subclass. Let us create empl4 as an Employee variable:

```
Employee empl4;
```

Let us make this reference to Hourly object:

```
empl4 = new Hourly("Kate", 160000, 37.5, 23.80);
```

This is possible and does not contradict the requirement of assigning a value of the same type as the variable (remember type mismatch) – Hourly is also an Employee, so Hourly can be assigned to an Employee variable. Let us also create empl5 which will be Hourly type and will reference Hourly object:

```
Hourly empl5 = new Hourly("Maria", 73000, 43, 25);
```

Both empl3 and empl4 are of type Employee. But empl3 (object of Employee) and empl4 (object of Hourly) use methods in different ways. Hourly object can access all the methods of Employee as it inherited its parent's features, but will execute methods in its own Hourly class if those methods are also defined in Hourly. If any of these methods are not defined in Hourly, then the methods from Employee will be executed. These actions are taken at the time of execution. The method publicdouble FedTaxes (double rate) is in the Employee (parent or superclass) class but not in Hourly (child or subclass). The Hourly object empl4 (of Employee type) and the Hourly object empl5 (also Hourly type) can both access and execute FedTaxes() method. The method publicdouble salary()is in the Hourly class but not in its parent Employee class. Empl4, even though it is a Hourly object, cannot executesalary() method as empl4 is an Employee type.

Observe that Hourly objects are getting their names from their parent Employee super(nm, in); in Hourly class is referring to the constructor in Employee which takes name and income. So, there are nosetName(), getName(), setIncome(), and getIncome() methods in Hourly class. These will not work in Hourly class even if you add them in that class as name and income are private in Employee class. They cannot be accessed directly outside of Employee, even if the class is a subclass of Employee. So, whenever an Hourly object executes getName() method, it will execute the getName() method from the Employee class.

The following code illustrates all these concepts:

Coding List 9.1: Employee.java which illustrates polymorphic classes

```
/*
 * Author:
 * Date:
 * Input:
 * Output:

 * Employee is the super class. There are two types of
   employees: Hourly employees and Fulltime employees. First,
   the superclass Employee is built and compiled. An employee
   has a name and an annual income.
*/

public class Employee
{
```

```
  private String name;
  private double income;

  public Employee(String nm, double in) {
    name = nm;
    income = in;
  }

  public void setName(String nm) {
    name = nm+"E"; }

  public String getName() {
    return name; }

  public void setIncome(double in) {
    income = in; }

  public double getIncome() {
    return income; }

  public double FedTaxes( double rate) {
    return income*rate/100; }
}
```

Hourly.java

```
/*
 * Author:
 * Date:
 * Input:
 * Output:

 * Hourly is a subclass of Employee.
*/

public class Hourly extends Employee
{
  private double hours;
  private double payRate;

  public Hourly(String nm, double in, double hrs, double pay) {
    super(nm, in); // This will make Employee name and income the
                   // same as this employee
    hours = hrs;   // Expanding Employee to Hourly employee by adding
                   // hours and payRate
    payRate = pay;
  }

  // set and get methods for name and income are available from the
  // parent. Adding them for the extended hours and payRate
  public void setHours(double hrs) {
```

```java
    hours = hrs; }

  public double getHours() {
    return hours; }

  public void setPayRate(double pay) {
    payRate = pay; }

  public double getPayRate() {
    return payRate; }

  public double salary() {  // calculate hourly salary
    return hours*payRate; }

  public String toString() {
    return (super.getName()+"\n Hours worked = "+hours+" hours \nPay
Rate = $"+payRate+"\nWeekly Salary = $"+salary());
  }
}
```

PolyDriver.java

```java
/*
 * Author:
 * Date:
 * Input:
 * Output:

 * This driver has three types of objects: empl3 is an Employee type
   Employee objectempl4 is an Employee type Hourly object and empl5
   is an Hourly type Hourly object.The way they execute methods from
   different classes are different. Study the following program.
*/

public class PolyDriver
{

  public static void main(String args[]) {
    Employee empl3 = new Employee("Dave", 60000);
    Employee empl4 = new Hourly("Kate", 160000, 37.5, 23.80);
    Hourly empl5 = new Hourly("Maria",73000, 43, 25);

    /* Observe that empl3 cannot execute any method that is not in
     Employee. Even empl4 of type Employee cannot execute salary()
     method. Observe below System.out.println(empl4.salary()); This
     will produce the error  PolyDriver.java:9: error: cannot find
     symbol.
    */

    //System.out.println(empl4.salary());
    /* Warning: since the above statement causes an error, if you want
to run
```

```
              this entire program without that statement, comment it out. Then,
              you can see an example of the polymorphism.
         */

         System.out.println("empl5 executing salary() method:
"+empl5.salary());
         System.out.println("empl5 executing its parent class Employee
FedTaxes(): "+empl5.FedTaxes(10));

         /* Check what is printed by empl3, empl4 and empl5. They all
         execute the methods intheir objects, honoring method binding.
         */

         empl3.setName("Jose");
         empl4.setName("Tao");
         empl5.setName("Mary");
         // emp15, an Hourly type object, will use setName() from Employee

         System.out.println("empl3: "+empl3.getName());
         System.out.println("empl4: "+empl4.getName());
         System.out.println("empl5: "+empl5.getName());
     }
}
```

Output with an error:

```
PolyDriver.java:19: error: cannot find symbol
System.out.println(empl4.salary());
```

Output with the error statement commented out:

```
empl5 executing salary() method: 1075.0
empl5 executing its parent class Employee FedTaxes(): 7300.0
empl3: JoseE
empl4: TaoE
empl5: MaryE
```

9.2   Polymorphism via Inheritances

In this section, we will discuss about overriding methods at different hierarchies. How is method binding resolved? With objects in subclasses (like Under) referencing their superclasses (like Student or Person), taxCalculation() method is in the hierarchy of Person class. We find out how they are executed.

Consider again the Person class defined in Chapter 8. We will add

```
System.out.println("running    at"   +   this.getClass().getName()+"
class");
```

to the `taxCalculation()` method to identify where this method is executed at. The method `taxCalculation()` is in all the three hierarchies. The codes of their implementations are different from one another. So, the calculations will be different depending on which of those `taxCalculation()` methods will be executed. Depending on how the object is created (type and reference), `taxCalculation()` method will be executed in the appropriate class. We are using `getClass()` method from Java library. This will return the object of the runtime class of the object, the class the object is executing in. If an object is executing in Student class, `this.getClass()` will return a `Student` object. Please refer to the codes for all the classes in chapter 8.

In *is-a* hierarchy, polymorphic references can be defined as follows:

```
Student stud_S = new Under();
// On the right hand side, an object reference is constructed
// The object reference is assigned to the reference stud_S.
// The type of stud_S is Student and referencing Under.
```

It means that the variable type of stud_Sis Student, but stud_Srefers to the object constructed by an Under constructor. What is accessed by the variable is not from its type, but it is only what is available in the object that is referred to by the variable (if all the classes in the hierarchy have overriding methods). As taxCalculation()method is in all the three classes (Person, Student, and Under), let us find out which of them will be executed by various objects with different types and references. Let's start with the following statement, to see which method is executed.

```
stud_S.taxCalculation();
// Which version of method is executed?
// the version of Student or the version of Under?
```

The version of Under is executed as you may see the output! It is the type of the object being referenced, not the type of the variable, that determines which method is invoked.

Polymorphic References	
	Consider the method overriding along the inheritance hierarchy from the classes Person, Student and Under. The method taxCalculation() has been rewritten and therefore there are the method in the version of Person, the on in the version of Studentand the one in Under. Three objects are constructed from the same constructor of Underand each is assigned to a reference variable in different types.
Challenge 1 — Reference variable in the Undertype – line	`Under under_Jane = new Under ("Kennedy", 200000, csec,cs);`

(8) below	Let under_Janeinvoke the method taxCalculation(). `under_Jane.taxCalculation();` Which method in what class is invoked? What is the output on the screen?

Reference variable in the Studenttype
   -   Line (9)
	`Student student_Jane = new Under ("Reagan",`
	`300000, cs,csec);`
	
	Let student_Janeinvoke the method taxCalculation().
	
	`student_Jane.taxCalculation();`
	
	Which method in what class is invoked? What is the output on the screen?

Reference variable in the Persontype – line (10)	`Person person_Jane = new Under ("Clinton", 400000,`
	`cs, csec);`
	
	Let person_Janeinvoke the method taxCalculation().
	
	`person_Jane.taxCalculation();`
	
	Which method in what class is invoked? What is the output on the screen?

Answer?	Under running at Under class Study AppDriver2 class below. Observe the corresponding lines (12), (13), and (14). Then observe the output lines (a), (b), and (c). All of them are executed as Under. Note that a super class type can create a subclass object and become capable of executing the overriding method in the subclass.

Example 2:

Please refer to Person, Student, and Under classes in chapter 8. Here we are including AppDriver2 class. This is using the same classes as AppDriver1 has in chapter 8 with additional statements to explain the concepts discussed above. We are using toString() method from Faculty class to print facutly1 information on line (15).

```
Coding List 9.2: AppDriver2.java
/*
 * Author:
 * Date:
 * Input:
 * Output:


 * We would like to show the difference in how we create objects.
   We have under_Jane, student_Jane, and person_Jane all defined
   as Under, Student, and Person types. But they are all referencing
```

```
        Under objects. So, all these objects will be executing Under
        methods, unless the method does not exist in Under. To contrast
        this with student_Bob who is a Student type and also referencing
        to Student object. So, student_Bob will execute taxCalculation()
        method in Student class where as student_Jane will execute
        taxCalculation() method in Under class. So, the method an object
        will execute will depend on which class it is referring to.
*/


import java.io.PrintWriter;
import java.io.FileWriter;
import java.io.IOException;

public class AppDriver2Ex {

        public static void main(String[] args) {//throws ClassCastException
{
                Student stud1 = new Student();
                Person stud2 = new Student();
                    stud1.age = 500;
                //Student stud3 = new Person();
                Under under1 = new Under();
                stud1.comp(stud1);
                stud2.comp(stud1);
                //stud3.comp(stud1);
                stud1.comp((Student) stud2);
                        //type of stud2: Person
                        // comp() expects Student variable
                stud1.comp(under1);
                under1.comp(stud1);

                stud1.interview();
                under1.interview();


                try {
                            writeList();
                        Under under5 = (Under) stud2;
                        under1.comp(under5);

                } catch (ClassCastException cce) {
                        System.out.println("* Clas case error");
                        //cce.printStackTrace();
                        } catch (IOException ie) {
                            System.out.println("--------> IO error");
                        } finally {   }
            }

            public static void writeList() throws IOException {
                    // because there is a check exception, e.g., FrileWriter,
                    // the checked exception IOException should be thrown
                    // This thrown exception should be caught by the main
method !!
```

```
                    System.out.println(" *** called ***");
                    PrintWriter out = new PrintWriter(new
FileWriter("OutFile.txt"));
                    out.append('c');
                    out.close();
                }
}
```

Here is the output. Observe all the Jane's are running as Under objects whereas Bob is running as a Student object:

```
at Person - The invoking object: Student@7852e922
== The input parameter Student@7852e922: in the type of Student
 at Student - The invoking object: Student@7852e922
== The input parameter Student@7852e922: in the type of Student
at Person - The invoking object: Student@4e25154f
== The input parameter Student@7852e922: in the type of Student
 at Student - The invoking object: Student@4e25154f
== The input parameter Student@7852e922: in the type of Student
at Person - The invoking object: Student@7852e922
== The input parameter Student@4e25154f: in the type of Student
 at Student - The invoking object: Student@7852e922
== The input parameter Student@4e25154f: in the type of Student
at Person - The invoking object: Student@7852e922
== The input parameter Under@70dea4e: in the type of Under
 at Student - The invoking object: Student@7852e922
== The input parameter Under@70dea4e: in the type of Under
at Person - The invoking object: Under@70dea4e
== The input parameter Student@7852e922: in the type of Student
 at Student - The invoking object: Under@70dea4e
== The input parameter Student@7852e922: in the type of Student
Student@7852e922: Introduce yourself first, please.
Under@70dea4e: Introduce yourself first, please.
 *** called ***
* Clas case error
```

Polymorphic References

Challenge2

As a continuation of the above blue box, consider the following code segment, which will constitute a driver class, AppDriver3.java. This has a pay() method taking a Student object as a parameter. Three objects are created in the main() method. Answer the questions that follow:

```java
public class AppDriver3 {

  public static void pay(Student s) {
System.out.println("Now PAY:: " + s.getClass().getName());
  }
```

```
public static void main(String[] args) {
Under under_Jane = new Under ();
Student student_Jane = new Under ();
Person person_Jane = new Under ();
}
}
```

Reference variable in the Undertype	Let under_Janeinvoke the method pay(). pay(under_Jane); Which method in what class is invoked? What is the output on the screen?
Reference variable in the Studenttype	Let student_Janeinvoke the method pay(). pay(student_Jane); Which method in what class is invoked? What is the output on the screen?
Reference variable in the Persontype	Let person_Janeinvoke the method pay(). pay(person_Jane); Which method in what class is invoked? What is the output on the screen?
Answer?	Since the method pay() defined in the class AppDriver takes an input parameter which is in the Student type, only an object of Student can be passed. • student_Jane is an object of Student. So, the invocation pay(student_Jane) returns Now PAY::: Under • under_Janeis an object of Under, which is a Student. So, the invocation pay(under_Jane) returns Now PAY::: Under • person_Janeis an object of Person, which is NOT a Student. Person is a superclass. Person could be a Student or Faculty. It means that we cannot pass a Person as Student. So, the invocation pay(person_Jane) gives an error. The error message is " reason: actual argument Person cannot be converted to Student by method invocation conversion".

Recall that a variable in one type can be converted to another type by assignment. There are two type conversions: 1) narrowing conversion and 2) widening conversion. Consider the following type conversions.

```
int a = 3;
//short b = a;    //  impossible narrowing conversion
short b = (short) a;   // type casting needed for narrowing

double c = a;            // widening conversion OK
```

It is natural to convert to widen types. As shown above, int is 32 bits and double is 64 bits. Conversion of a smaller space into a larger one is possible.

However, conversion to a smaller space is impossible. Short uses 16 buts whereas int uses 32 bits. So a conversion to squeeze in a bigger space into a smaller space is called a narrowing conversion. Narrowing conversion becomes possible by type casting as shown above. Similarly, conversion process can be applied to objects along the inheritance hierarchies.

Assigning a child object to a parent reference is considered to be a widening conversion, and assigning to a child reference is considered to be a narrowing conversion. Back to the running example, widening conversion is possible. It is okay for an object of Under to be converted to Person reference.

```
Person person_J3 = new Under();
```

Narrowing conversion is impossible. There will be a compile error.

```
Under person_P3 = new Person();
// cannot do narrowing conversion
```

Similar to type conversion, the type casting is needed as follows:

```
Person under_P = new Under();
Under under_K3 = (Under)under_P;
```

The following example is also narrowing conversion, and therefore the type casting looks fine. There is no syntax error.

```
Under person_P3 = (Under) (new Person());
```

However, there will be a run-time error. What should we do to deal with run-time errors?

Run-time Errors

Exception handling is needed, and it will be introduced in Chapter 10. Exceptions are handled by using the following block statement:

```
try {

    // general business logic here

} catch (Exception e) {
}
```

Challenge

```
try {
Under person_P3 = (Under) (new Person());
} catch (ClassCastExceptioncce) {
System.out.println(cce.getClass() + "\t" + cce.getMessage());
}
```

9.3   Polymorphism via Interfaces

A Java *interface* is a collection of abstract methods and constants. An abstract method is a method header without a method body. All the methods of an interface are declared but not implemented. It implies that those methods are modified by the modifier abstract. Since all the methods in an interface are just declared with no implementation, i.e., "*abstract*", usually those methods are not explicitly modified by the modifier abstract, and "abstract" word is left off.

An interface is used to establish a set of methods in itself. No methods declared in an interface should be implemented. Since there is no implementation of the methods of an interface, there will be no object to be instantiated from an interface. If there exists a class that is a subclass to an interface, then the subclass should implement all of those methods. If there is any method left out to be unimplemented, a subclass cannot be a regular class but an abstract class. Since any subclasses of an interface need to implement methods of an interface, the methods in an interface have public visibility by default. A class that implements an interface can implement other methods as well. It turns out that through interface hierarchies there will be multiple inheritances. When a class implements an interface, it gains access to all its constants.

Example 3:

Suppose that the class Secretary is a subclass of the interface Employment. Secretary should *implement* all the methods declared in Employment. The Secretary class is defined as *Secretary implements Employment*. We will first define an interface called Employment and then implement it in the class Secretary. Here is the complete code and its output:

Coding List 9.3: Interface Employment

```
/*
 * Author:
 * Date:
 * Input:
 * Output:

  Here is an interface with two abstract methods. There is no
  need to use "abstract" modifier. We have give one example of
  implementation of this interface in the Secretary class below.
*/


public interface Employment {
     final String name = "HR";
     public void interview();
}
```

Secretary.java implementing Employment interface

```
/*
 * Author:
 * Date:
 * Input:
 * Output:

 * This class implements the Employment interface. There could be
   other classes which could be implementing Employment interface
   with different implementations of callFromHR() and techInterview()
   methods. As you can observe the Secretary class other methods
   in addition to implementing the interface methods.
*/

public class Secretary extends Person implements Employment
{
  public String name;
  private int age;

  public Secretary(String nm, int ag) {
    name =nm;
    age = ag;
  }

  public int getAge() {
```

```java
      System.out.println("getAge() is invoked at Secretary by "+ this);
      return age;
  }

  public void setAge(int n) {
    System.out.println("setAge() is invoked at Secretary by "+ this);
    age = n;
  }

  public String toString() {
    System.out.println("toString() from Student");
    return"name: " + name + "\tage " + age+"\nMessage is:
"+techInterview("Can you code in Java");
}

  public void callFromHR() {
    System.out.println("Can I call you "+this+ "?");
  }  // "this" in the print statement will print whichever the object
    // isusing the toString() method! Observe the output.

  public void interview() {
    // this method was declared in the interface Employment.jave.
    // As this class implements Employment in the first line of this
class,
    // the method should be implemented here.
    String interviewMsg = "The interview begins with HR officer, followed
by tech officers";
    System.out.println(interviewMsg);
  }

  public String techInterview(String msg) {
    String returnMsg = "";
    this.interview();
    returnMsg += msg;
    return returnMsg;
  }

  public static void main(String args[]) {
    Secretary s1 = new Secretary("Gandhi", 67);
    s1.callFromHR();
    System.out.println(s1);
    Secretary s2 = new Secretary("Sandy", 27);
    s2.callFromHR();
    System.out.println(s2.techInterview("This lady is capable..."));
  }
}
```

```
Here is the output:
toString() from Student
The interview begins with HR officer, followed by tech officers
Can I call you name: Gandhi  age 67
Message is: Can you code in Java?
toString() from Student
```

```
The interview begins with HR officer, followed by tech officers
name: Gandhi      age 67
Message is: Can you code in Java
toString() from Student
The interview begins with HR officer, followed by tech officers
Can I call you name: Sandy    age 27
Message is: Can you code in Java?
The interview begins with HR officer, followed by tech officers
This lady is capable...
```

A class can implement multiple interfaces and it must implement all methods in all interfaces listed in the header. The Java standard class library includes multiple useful interfaces. For example, the Comparable interface[1] is declared over an abstract method called compareTo(), which compare two objects. The Iterator interface has the methods hasNext(), next() and remove(). A subclass can extend only one superclass but can implement multiple interfaces separated by commas.

9.4   Exercises

Concept Understanding

1. In the hierarchy of the US government, each position along the hierarchy has one more roles. The positions that you may consider include Chief of State, Chief Executive, Chief Administrative, Chief Diplomat, Commander in Chiefs, Chief Legislative, etc. This hierarchy begins with People. People can be split into Employed and Self_Employed. Employed has FedEmp as its child, which has WHEmp, so-called White House Employed, one of the objects in WHEmp is the president. Consider the hierarchy of People.

    a) Draw the hierarchy of People on top and president at the bottom. Note that president is an object.

    b) Consider the roles of president. Take three classes along the hierarchy and discuss on the inheritance to the president object.

    c) Furthermore, discuss the roles of the president object.

---

[1] API for Java SE7: http://docs.oracle.com/javase/7/docs/api/java/lang/Comparable.html; or API for Java SE8: http://docs.oracle.com/javase/8/docs/api/java/lang/Comparable.html

Programming

1. Consider the Athletics problem from Chapter 8, problem #3. Include toString() method and cost() method to all the classes (Athletics, Mens, Womens, Basketball, Baseball, Football, FieldHockey, Softball, and Volleyball). toString() methods should print the information of the corresponding object. Cost() object will calculate and return the cost of scholarhips given in that object. In order to calculate this cost, each class should have an instance variable for number of athletes for that object. For example, Athletics class will have the number of athletes from all the sports offered in the institution. A Basketball object should have the number of scholarship players on the basketball team. Test polymorphism by creating different combinations of class types and class references. For example, you could have MensMteam = new Football(); The constructors need not be default constructors only. Include a application driver to test all the polymorphic constructs.

2. Consider bookstores where the printed matters are being sold. Note that for simplicity, all classes here are written as a singular entity. There are hierarchies in publications. On the top, there will be a class called Publication. Publication has attributes title, price, and year. The price variable is private. Subclasses to the class Publication include Book and Magazine. Book has an author, while Magazine has a periodical information such as monthly, biweekly, or weekly. For each book or magazine, there is a variable publisher which is the type of Publisher. Publisher has company name and location. Book has subclasses, Textbook and Reference. Textbook has class information, while Reference has its type such as url address, etc. Make sure that some of those variables reasonably modified as public, private or protected. There is also a driver class called PublisherDriver. In this scenario, we will illustrate a few cases of polymorphism.

    a. Create an object of Book and assign the Book object to an object reference, book1, whose type is Book.

    b. Create another object of Book and assign the Book object to a polymorphic object reference, book2, whose type is Publication.

    c. In Publication, create a method called price(), which returns the price.

    d. Override the method price() in Book and also in Textbook. The price() in Book returns the price after 5% the price off, and the method in Textbook takes an integer ($>= 0$ and <100) and returns the one after the given number percent off.

    e. In PublisherDriver, the following invocations are performed.

        i. book1 to invoke the method price() of Book.

    ii. book1 to invoke the method price() of Publication. (Hint: the method of superclass can be invoked within the overridden method. Recall Text Ch8 pages 5-7!)

    iii. book2 to invoke the method price() of Book.

    iv. book2 to invoke the method price() of Publication.

f. In Publication, create a method called invoice(), which returns the price based on the object which invokes.

    i. If the invoking object is in Publication, the method returns the same as the price.

    ii. If the invoking object is in Book, the method returns the price plus 10, and if it is in Textbook, the method returns the price plus 25.

g. In PublisherDriver, create another polymorphic object reference book3 in Textbook type for an object of Book. If type casting is needed, please do so. Do the following invocations:

    i. book1 to invoke the method invoice() of Book.

    ii. book1 to invoke the method invoice() of Publication.

    iii. book2 to invoke the method invoice() of Book.

    iv. book2 to invoke the method invoice() of Publication.

    v. book3 to invoke the method invoice() of Publication.

    vi. book3 to invoke the method invoice() of Book.

    vii. book3 to invoke the method invoice() of Textbook.

h. In Publication, create another method called comp(Book opp), which takes an object of Book to compare the price of the invoking object. Perform the following statement. If error occurs, fix it.

    i. book1.comp(book2); //

    ii. book3.comp(book1);

    iii. book2.comp(book3);

3. Consider Q1 in Concept Understanding in this Exercise.

  a. Define classes, FedEmp and WHEmp, with their field variables.

  b. Add their behavioral elements, including ruleAppointed().

  c. Define a driver class that can demonstrate the polymorphism over the People hierarchy.

  d. Run the driver class and discuss the polymorphism to your best.

Exceptions

10.1 Why Exceptions

As a Java program is executed, we know that there are numerous situations that may lead to serious errors. For example, we may try to read from a non-existing file (file not found error, either <u>checked</u> at the compile time if not thrown or <u>unchecked</u> until the runtime if IOException is thrown), or we may try to read a decimal value into a String variable (type mismatch error, runtime exception). Exception is an object in Java which will deal with such exceptional events. The action could result in termination of the program.

Some situations are not known because they occur outside Java programs and other exceptions may occur only when the Java programs are executed. An exception is an action that can interrupt the normal flow of a program.

There are two types of exceptions, checked exceptions and unchecked exceptions.

- <u>Checked Exceptions</u>: Checked exceptions are the exceptions <u>checked</u> at the compile time. An exception in reading from a file could be a checked exception if we do not throw IOException. Listing 10.1 below is an example of this. Checked exceptions are subclasses of the class Exception as shown in Figure 10.1.

- <u>Unchecked Exceptions</u>: Unchecked exceptions are<u>unchecked</u> at the compile time but checked during runtime. In Listing 10.2, we have included "throws IOException" to read from java file. If the input file is not present nor appears valid, it will lead to a runtime exception, an unchecked exception. These are subclasses of the class RuntimeException.

When an exception occurs, a Java program generates compile errors or its execution gets terminated without completion. Advanced programming languages, including Java, have facilitated the handling capability of exceptions. If an exception is raised, it is handled so that program execution will not terminate and that the system generates a user friendly error message.

Example 1:

Consider the following Java program, FileReadingIOProb.java, which reads a file called FileIO.java and adds line numbers to statements. The exception here is that the Java program cannot find the file. In this case we are not throwing an IOException and hence the method from

Scanner class will throw a checked exception at the compile time. The error message is below the code.

Coding List 10.1: FileReadingIOProb.java

```
/*
 * Author:
 * Date:
 * Input:
 * Output:

  This program tries to read a file.
  At the compile time, application programs have no way of
  verifying the existence of external resources. Application programs
  and their compilation process does not matter whether the file
  exists or not.

  However, when you compile this program, the compiler identifies the
  exception. In Java, several exceptions are already expected and defined.
  This type of exceptions is identified by the Java compiler.
  This is checked at the compile time, so it is a checked exception.
  Execution is halted with an error.
*/

import java.io.File;
import java.util.Scanner;

class FileReadingIO
{
  public static void main (String [] args) {
    File myFile = new File("FileReadingIO.java");
    Scanner fileScn = new Scanner(myFile);
    intlineCnt = 0;
    while (fileScn.hasNextLine())
       System.out.println(++lineCnt + "\t" + fileScn.nextLine());
  }
}
```

Below is a sample run. There is an error at compile time.

```
FileReadingIOProb.java:15: error: unreported exception
FileNotFoundException; must be caught or declared to be thrown
     Scanner fileScn = new Scanner(myFile);
```

```
1 error
```

We can avoid this error by "throwing" an IOException in the code. This will compile without an exception. If the file exists, the program will run successfully. If the file does not exist, an IOException error will be thrown. We have changed "import java.io.File; to import java.io.*". This will enable us to deal with files and also to throw exceptions. Observe the change in main() statement, where "throws IOException" is added. When we compile a program that reads from a file, it will not know if that file exists or not. So, it should compile without checking whether the input file exists or not. It should throw an error when it finds out that the input file is not to be found during the run time. So, we have made the above changes for the IOException to throw an error message at the runtime. This file compiles free of any error.

Example 2:

The exception error is below the program in Code List 10.2.

Coding List 10.2: FileReadingIOProb2.java

```
/*
 * Author:
 * Date:
 * Input:
 * Output:
 * Here we are throwing IOException. So, there will be no compile-
   time error. But, the FileIO.java does not exist. So, there
   will be a run-time error. We have the error message below this
   Box.
   We created the FileIO.java file. Now, there is no error. So, we
   provided the output of this program below the error box.
*/

import java.io.*;
import java.util.Scanner;

class FileReadingIOProb
{

  public static void main (String [] args) throws IOException {
    File myFile = new File("FileReadingIO.java");
    Scanner fileScn = new Scanner(myFile);
    intlineCnt = 0;
```

```
    while (fileScn.hasNextLine())
        System.out.println(++lineCnt + "\t" + fileScn.nextLine());
    }
}
```

Below is a sample run generating a run-time error:

Exception in thread "main" java.io.FileNotFoundException: FileIO.java (The system cannot find the file specified) at java.io.FileInputStream.open0(Native Method)

at java.io.FileInputStream.open(FileInputStream.java:195)

at java.io.FileInputStream.<init>(FileInputStream.java:138)

at java.util.Scanner.<init>(Scanner.java:611)

at FileReadingIOProb.main(FileReadingIOProb.java:30)

Example 3:

Consider another example below. The Java program, DivideByZeroExProb.java, takes two integers from users and returns the result of their ratio. The program will not know the integrity of user input data until the program runs and receives the input. A user may enter zero for denominator or a non-numeric value. If such exceptions take place, the program will terminate or returns a wrong answer. Notice that depending on the Java compiler version, the division by zero may result in different answers, e.g., infinity. When the input is a non-numeric value, the runtime error will throw a "typemismatch" exception. Since such an exception is not checked by jdk, the error occurs at runtime. The output box below the code has three runs covering three different cases. The exception thrown at the runtime due to non-numeric input is also included. InputMismatchException will be thrown only when the numbers are integers. It will not work for decimal values. In that case, we have to create our own exception class as a subclass of Exception class.

Coding List 10.3: DivideByZeroExProb.java

```
/*
 * Author:
 * Date:
 * Input: Two integers
 * Output: Division result
*/

import java.util.Scanner;

public class DivideByZeroExProb {
```

```java
  public static float quotient (int numerator, int denominator) {
    return (float) numerator / denominator;
  }

  public static void main (String args[]) {
    Scanner scanner = new Scanner (System.in);
    System.out.print ("Enter an integer numerator: ");
    int numerator = scanner.nextInt();
    System.out.print ("Enter an integer denominator: ");
    int denominator = scanner.nextInt();
    float result = quotient (numerator, denominator);
    System.out.println(numerator + "/" + denominator + "= " + result);
  }
}
```

Below are three sample runs: without any error, with division by zero, and third with run-time error.

```
C:\Windows\system32\cmd.exe

C:\Mercy\231JavaII1\prog\exception>javac DivideByZeroExProb.java

C:\Mercy\231JavaII1\prog\exception>java DivideByZeroExProb
Enter an integer numerator: 15
Enter an integer denominator: 2
15/2= 7.5

C:\Mercy\231JavaII1\prog\exception>java DivideByZeroExProb
Enter an integer numerator: 15
Enter an integer denominator: 0
15/0= Infinity

C:\Mercy\231JavaII1\prog\exception>java DivideByZeroExProb
Enter an integer numerator: 15
Enter an integer denominator: zero
Exception in thread "main" java.util.InputMismatchException
        at java.util.Scanner.throwFor(Unknown Source)
        at java.util.Scanner.next(Unknown Source)
        at java.util.Scanner.nextInt(Unknown Source)
        at java.util.Scanner.nextInt(Unknown Source)
        at DivideByZeroExProb.main(DivideByZeroExProb.java:14)

C:\Mercy\231JavaII1\prog\exception>
```

10.2 · Exception Class Hierarchies

Exceptions are checked or unchecked in Java. The Java exception class hierarchy is shown in Figure 10.1 and Figure 10.2. Figure 10.2 is an API screen capture for the exceptions from the URL, http://docs.oracle.com/javase/7/docs/api/java/util/package-tree.html. Errors and exceptions are subclasses of the class Throwable, which is in turn a subclass of the top superclass Object. In the figure, red colored are *checked* exceptions. Any checked exception that may be thrown in a method must either be caught or declared in the method's throws clause. Checked exceptions must be caught at compile time. Checked exceptions are so called because both the Java compiler and the Java virtual machine check to make sure this rule is complied with. If not caught, a checked exception error is generated as shown in Coding List 10.1.

On the other hand, *unchecked* exceptions are blue colored. They are exceptions that are not expected to be recovered and they are unchecked by jdk. Examples include the exception of null pointer, divide by 0, as shown in Coding List 10.2, etc. Unchecked exceptions do not generate errors at compile time but generate errors at runtime. They can be thrown to make the Java program more robust and proper error messages can be provided.

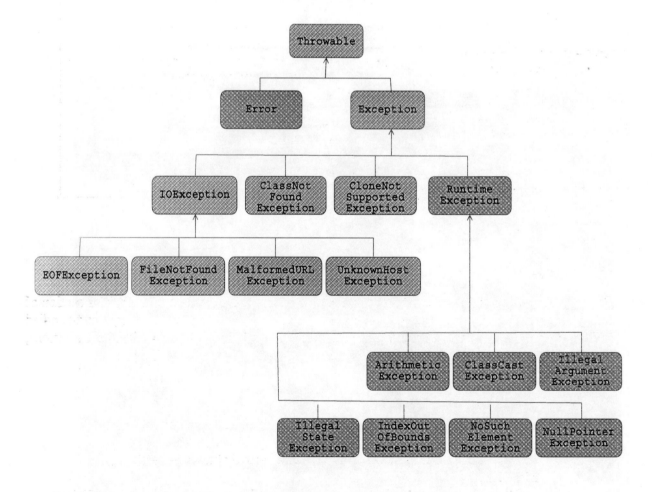

Figure 10.1 Exception Class Hierarchy

```
o java.lang.Throwable (implements java.io.Serializable)
    o java.lang.Error
        o java.util.ServiceConfigurationError
    o java.lang.Exception
        o java.io.IOException
            o java.util.InvalidPropertiesFormatException
        o java.lang.RuntimeException
            o java.util.ConcurrentModificationException
            o java.util.EmptyStackException
            o java.lang.IllegalArgumentException
                o java.util.IllegalFormatException
                    o java.util.DuplicateFormatFlagsException
                    o java.util.FormatFlagsConversionMismatchException
                    o java.util.IllegalFormatCodePointException
                    o java.util.IllegalFormatConversionException
                    o java.util.IilegalFormatFlagsException
                    o java.util.IllegalFormatPrecisionException
                    o java.util.IllegalFormatWidthException
                    o java.util.MissingFormatArgumentException
                    o java.util.MissingFormatWidthException
                    o java.util.UnknownFormatConversionException
                    o java.util.UnknownFormatFlagsException
            o java.lang.IllegalStateException
                o java.util.FormatterClosedException
            o java.util.IllformedLocaleException
            o java.util.MissingResourceException
            o java.util.NoSuchElementException
                o java.util.InputMismatchException
        o java.util.TooManyListenersException
```

Figure 10.2 Exception Class Hierarchy

10.3   Exception Handling

Exception handling is a mechanism that can handle exceptions described in the earlier section of this chapter. As an exception occurs, the exception event should be thrown, caught and handled in Java programs. We cannot catch an exception without it being thrown. To handle exceptions, Java provides the exception handling block, try – catch – finally as shown below:

```
try {
      // code free of exception to be executed
} catch ( an exception object ) {
    // code in response to the exception event
} finally {
    // code that works at the end of exception handling
}
```

In the try-catch-finally blocks, one try block can be associated with one or more catchblocks. This could build a chain of exceptions. The finally block is optional.

Before a try catches an error, an exception should be thrown. An exception to be thrown would be either from Figures 10.1 and 10.2 or a runtime exception that may be defined by the coder. An exception can be thrown by the statement with the keyword "throw". The way of creating exceptions on your own will be discussed in the following section. We will provide the codes for file reading and division by zero to illustrate try-catch combination and how the execution of the code terminates normally. In the following Coding List 10.4, the try block executes if no exception is thrown and thecatch block is executed ifFileNotFoundExceptionis thrown. In either case, the execution continues and ends normally with "Program ends!" output. Each exception has a system message associated with it. We can retrieve this message by using the method getMessage().

Example 4:

In the following code we have our own error message printed first and then followed by the message of the corresponding Exception (FileNotFoundException e)caught in the catchstatement. Notice that we do not have throwsIOExceptionhere in themain(String args[]) statement as we have added try-catch combination.

Coding List 10.4: FileException1.java

```java
/*
 * Author:
 * Date:
 * Input:
 * Output:
 */

import java.io.*;
import java.util.Scanner;

public class FileException1
{
  public static void main(String args[]) {

    Scanner inputFile;
    try {
      inputFile = new Scanner(new File("inputFile.txt"));
      System.out.println("Input file is found");
    } catch (FileNotFoundException e) {
      System.out.println(e.getMessage());
      System.out.println("Program ends!");
    }
  }
}
```

Below is a sample run.

Input file is found
Program ends!

Example 5:

The following Coding List 10.5 deals with division by zero. We need to use integer division in order for ArithmeticException to work. Again try-catch combination will catch the exception but will still runthe program normally. When we divided by zero in Coding List 10.2, the result was Infinity, without an exception. As we mentioned earlier, it was dependent on the compiler. Now, we are actually catching the exception and printing an error message.In the following code we have our own error message printed first and then followed by the message of the corresponding Exception (ArithmeticException e)caught in the catchstatement. Again, observe that if there is no error, the tryblock is executed and the catch block is executed if there is an exception.

Coding List 10.5: DivideException.java

```java
/*
 * Author:
 * Date:
 * Input:
 * Output:
 */

import java.io.*;
import java.util.Scanner;

public class DivideException
{
  public static void main(String args[]){
    Scanner keyboard = new Scanner(System.in);
    int numerator, denominator, ratio;// for integer division

    System.out.print("Enter numerator: ");
    numerator = keyboard.nextInt();
    System.out.print("Enter denominator: ");
    denominator = keyboard.nextInt();

    try {
      ratio = numerator/denominator;
      System.out.println(numerator+"/"+ denominator+"="+
ratio);
    } catch (ArithmeticException e) {
      System.out.println("Division by zero, ratio not defined");
      System.out.println(e.getMessage());
    }

    System.out.println("Program ends normally");
  }
}
```

Below is a sample run. #1 is with non-zero denominator. #2 is with zero denominator. Notice that this compiler is giving a / by zero message.

```
#1
Enter numerator: 87
Enter denominator: 23
87/23=3
Program ends normally

#2
Enter numerator: 87
Enter denominator: 0
Division by zero, ratio not defined
/ by zero
Program ends normally
```

10.4   Creating Exception Classes

Here is another example to illustrate integration of exceptions into applications:

Consider the example of salaries of employees in a business. Let us create a file of salaries. Let us read the salaries into an array of decimals. Let us have the following methods:

1. read() method to read from a text file

2. average() method that calculates the average salary

3. count() method to count the number of employees below theaverage

4. main() method to test all these.

Example 6:

The goal is to include appropriate exceptions into the methodsso that exceptions will be handled and the program completesnormally. Some needed exceptions are in the Exception class hierarchyand some are not in the Exception class hierarchy. For example, salaries cannot be negative. So we have created NegativeSalaryExceptionclass and throw that exception object in the driver. This program illustrates different exceptions with one of two try blocks having two catch blocks. We have included one negative salary (-5200) and one non-numeric (String value "Gandhi") in the text file. The array is defined to have ten elements. The text file attached below has 12 values, but two of the invalid values will be skipped from the array. You can observe this from the output of the print() method. If we add more values, a java.lang.ArrayIndexOutOfBoundsException: 10 will be thrown. We are not catching this exception.

Coding List 10.6: EmployeeExceptions2.java

NegativeSalaryException.java created by us as a subclass of Exception

```java
/*
 * Author:
 * Date:
 * Input:
 * Output:
 */
public class NegativeSalaryException extends Exception
{
  public NegativeSalaryException() {
    System.out.println("Negative Salary - invalid entry"); }
}
```

```java
/*
 * Author:
 * Date:
 * Input:
 * Output:

 *Here is the ExployeeExceptions2 code. This uses
   NegativeSalaryException. Note that We are reading data as String
   values and parsing into Double as we could be dealing different
   types of data.
 */

import java.util.*;
import java.io.*;

public class EmployeeExceptions2
{
  private double salary[] = new double[10];
  private double ave;
  private intnumEmployees=0;

  public EmployeeExceptions2() {
    //default constructor
  }

  public void read() {
    System.out.println("Start read()*******");
    int n=0;
    try { // try #1
      Scanner file = new Scanner (new File("empExceptions.txt"));

      while (file.hasNextLine()) {
        String dataIn = file.next();
```

```java
        try {          // try #2
            Double numberIn = Double.parseDouble(dataIn);
            if (numberIn>= 0) {
                salary[n] = numberIn;
                n++;
            } else throw new NegativeSalaryException();

        } catch (NumberFormatExceptionnfe) {// catch #1 for try #2
            System.out.println("non-numeric value: "+nfe.getMessage());
        } catch (NegativeSalaryException e) {// catch #2 for try #2
            System.out.println(e.getMessage()+"\t"+dataIn);
        }
    }// end of while loop
  }// catch #1 for try #1
    catch (InputMismatchException | FileNotFoundException e) {
        System.out.println(e.getMessage());   }
        numEmployees=n;
        System.out.println("End read()******");
}

public intgetNumEmployees() {
  return numEmployees;   }

public double average(){
  System.out.println("Start average()********");
  double sum=0;
  for (int i=0; i<numEmployees; i++)
     sum += salary[i];

  System.out.println("End average()*******");
  return sum/numEmployees;
}

public int count() {
  System.out.println("Start count()*********");
  intnumBelowAve=0;

  double ave = this.average();
  for (int i=0; i<numEmployees; i++)
  if  (salary[i] <ave)
      numBelowAve++;

  System.out.println("End count()********");
  return numBelowAve;
}

public void print() {
    for (int i=0; i<numEmployees; i++)
    System.out.println("$"+salary[i]);
}
}
```

Coding List 10.7: EmployeeExceptionsDriver.java

```java
/*
 * Author:
 * Date:
 * Input:
 * Output:
*/

import java.io.*;

public class EmployeeExceptionsDriver
{
  public static void main(String args[]) throws NegativeSalaryException{
    EmployeeExceptions2 business = new EmployeeExceptions2();

    business.read();

    System.out.println("Average Salary = $"+business.average());
    System.out.println("\n\nNumber of employees below average salary =
"+business.count());
    System.out.println("\n\nNumber of employees at and above average
salary = "+(business.getNumEmployees()-business.count()));
    business.print();
  }
}
```

```
#1 output without the salary file. The exception is thrown by
FileNotFoundException.
Start read()*******
empExceptions3.txt (The system cannot find the file specified)
End read()******
Start average()********
End average()*******
Average Salary = $NaN
Start count()*********
Start average()********
End average()*******
End count()********

Number of employees below average salary = 0
Start count()*********
Start average()********
End average()*******
End count()********
```

```
Number of employees at and above average salary = 0

#2 The salary file is supplied. Everything worked without exceptions.
Since the count() method calls average() method, look at the order in
which these two methods executed (A) - (B).
Start read()*******
End read()******
Start average()********
End average()*******
Average Salary = $136650.0
Start count()*********                              (A)
Start average()********
End average()*******
End count()********                                 (B)
Number of employees below average salary = 9
Start count()*********
Start average()********
End average()*******
End count()********
Number of employees at and above average salary = 9
$23500.0
$87000.0
$102000.0
$45000.0
$800000.0
$73000.0
$52000.0
$36000.0
$50000.0
$98000.0

#3 We have added a negative salary (-52000) and a string ("gandhi") to
the text file. These two values will be skipped storing in the array
and appropriate exception messages are printed. The program will
complete normally. Observe the output lines (C) and (D).

Start read()*******
Negative Salary - invalid entry -52000             (C)
non-numeric value: For input string: "gandhi"      (D)
End read()******
Start average()********
End average()*******
Average Salary = $136950.0
```

```
Start count()*********
Start average()********
End average()*******
End count()********


Number of employees below average salary = 9
Start count()*********
Start average()********
End average()*******
End count()********


Number of employees at and above average salary = 1
$23500.0
$87000.0
$102000.0
$45000.0
$800000.0
$73000.0
$36000.0
$50000.0
$98000.0
$55000.0
```

```
Here is the text file of salaries:
23500
87000
102000
45000
800000
73000
-52000
36000
50000
gandhi
98000
55000
```

Here is another example with Illegal Input class created by us. Observe how we include this to Coding List 10.3: DivideByZeroExProb.java and how we "throw" this exception. We are going to include try-catch blocks to Coding List 10.3. We need to create IllegalInputclass (Coding List 10.7) and then throw its object (observe "new" in creating the object) as in the statement below:

```
if ((numerator < 10) || (numerator > 100)) {
System.out.println("Exception Error ");
```

```
throw new IllegalInput ("Bad numerator: Out of the range "
+ numerator);
```

A Java code that might throw certain exceptions must be enclosed by either of the following:

- A try statement that catches the exception. The try must provide a handler for the exception.

- A method that specifies that it can throw the exception. The method must provide a throws clause that lists the exception.

Back to the example thrown above, the Java program segment can be enclosed by try-catch clause as follows:

```
try {
System.out.print ("Enter an integer numerator: ");
try {
int numerator = scanner.nextInt();
if ((numerator < 10) || (numerator > 100)) {
System.out.println("Exception Error - catched");
throw new IllegalInput ("Out of the numerator range:" + numerator);
}

System.out.print ("Enter an integer denominator: ");

int denominator = scanner.nextInt();
if ((denominator < 10) || (denominator > 100)) {
System.out.println("Exception Error - catched");
throw new IllegalInput ("Out of the numerator range:" + denominator );
}

System.out.print (numerator + "/" + denominator + "=" +numerator/denominator
);

} catch ( InputMismatchExceptionie ) {
System.out.println ("Runtime Error: just out!!");
ie.printStackTrace();
}
} catch ( IllegalInput bi ) {
bi.printStackTrace();
}
```

Example 7:

Here isIllegalInput exception class which extends Exception class. We will create IllegalInput objects in Coding List 10.8 to throw exceptions in try-catch block.

Coding List 10.8: IllegalInput.java

```
/*
 * Author:
 * Date:
 * Input:
 * Output:
*/

public class IllegalInput extends RuntimeException {
  public IllegalInput (String s) {
    super(s);
  }
}
```

The following Coding Lists 10.9 and 10.10 are the classes completed as explained so far. Before they are compiled, the exception in Coding List 10.8 should be compiled.

Coding List 10.9: DivideByZeroEx.java

```
/*
 * Author:
 * Date:
 * Input:
 * Output:
*/

import java.util.InputMismatchException;
import java.util.Scanner;

public class DivideByZeroEx {

// (1)
  public float ratio (int numerator, int denominator) throws
ArithmeticException {
    return numerator / denominator;
  }

  public static void main (String args[]) throws IllegalInput {
    DivideByZeroEx de = new DivideByZeroEx();
    int numerator, denominator;
    float result;
    Scanner scanner = new Scanner (System.in);
    booleancontinueLoop = true;
    System.out.print ("Enter your name: ");
    String name = scanner.nextLine();
```

```
      if ( name.compareTo( "Adams") != 0 ) {
        throw new IllegalInput("Bad Login: Quick Kicked out!" + name);
      }
    do {
      try {
            System.out.print ("Enter an integer numerator: ");
            try {
                numerator = scanner.nextInt();
                if  ((numerator < 10) || (numerator > 100)) {
                    System.out.println("Exception Error - caught");
// (16)
                    throw new IllegalInput ("Bad numerator: Out of the
range " + numerator);
                }
                System.out.print ("Enter an integer denominator: ");
                denominator = scanner.nextInt();
                if  ((denominator < 10) || (denominator > 100)) {
                    System.out.println("Exception Error - caught");

// (21)

                    throw new IllegalInput ("Bad numerator: Out of the
range " + denominator );
                }
                result = de.ratio (numerator, denominator);
                System.out.print (numerator + "/" + denominator + "="
+result);
// (24)

            } catch ( InputMismatchExceptionie ) {
                System.out.println ("Runtime Error: just out!!");

// (26)

                ie.printStackTrace();
            }
            continueLoop = false;

// (28)

            } catch ( IllegalInput bi ) {

// (29)

                bi.printStackTrace();
            }
      } while ( continueLoop );
    }
  }
```

```
Here is the output:
_____                    _____


Enter your name: Adams
Enter an integer numerator: 40
Enter an integer denominator: 0
```

```
Exception Error - caught
IllegalInput: Bad numerator: Out of the range 0
        at DivideByZeroEx.main(DivideByZeroEx.java:43)
Enter an integer numerator: 40
Enter an integer denominator: 20
40/20=2.0
```

Unchecked exceptions can be handled in different ways as illustrated in Coding List 10.6. As explained above,IllegalInputis an object of Exception. We are throwing exceptions on lines (16) and (21) with IllegalInput exception object. At the same time, the checked exception, ArithmeticException, which is provided by jdk, is thrownon line (1). Note that IllegalInput throw statement appears in a try block, and ArithmeticException is included in the header line of the method. Those exceptions can bethrown with a message as shown on lines (16) and (21). We can also stack messages on JVM memory space so that we will be able to extract, as we have done on lines (26) and (29).

For the thrown exceptions, the program can catch as many exception objects as needed. For example, line (24) catches an objectof InputMismatchExceptionexception and generates a message on line (26), while line (28) catches an object bi of IllegalInputexception on line (29). The messages stacked on lines (16) and (21) use the method invocation printStackTrace() to extract and to provide user-kind error messages.

The Coding List 10.9 extends Coding List 10.2 and catches an object of the exception FileNotFoundException. Note that the input file is the same as the Java program file, the program open the file itself and prints lines.

Example 8:

Here is an example on FileNotFoundException.

Coding List 10.10: FileReadingIO.java

```
/*
 * Author:
 * Date:
 * Input:
 * Output:

*This program tries to read a file.
 At the compile time, application programs have no way of
 verifying the existence of external resources. Application programs
 and their compilation process does not matter whether the file
 exists or not.
```

```
   However, when you compile this program, the compiler identifies the
   exception. In Java, several exceptions are already expected and defined.
   This type of exections is identified by the Java compiler.
   This is checked at the compile time, so it is a checked exception.
   Execution is halted with an error.
*/

import java.io.File;
import java.io.FileNotFoundException;
import java.util.Scanner;

public class FileReadingIO
{
  public static void main (String [] args) {
    try {
      File myFile = new File("FileReadingIO.java");
      Scanner fileScn = new Scanner(myFile);
      intlineCnt = 0;
      while (fileScn.hasNextLine())
        System.out.println(++lineCnt + "\t" + fileScn.nextLine());

    } catch (FileNotFoundExceptionfnf) {
          fnf.printStackTrace();
    } finally {
        System.out.println("- in this way, an exception is handled.");
    }
  }
}
```

```
It is reading itself. So, it is reproducing the code with line numbers
added. Here is the output:
1      /*
2       * Author:
3       * Date:
4       * Input:
5       * Output:
6
7         This program tries to read a file.
8         At the compile time, application programs have no way of
9         verifying the existence of external resources. Application
programs
10        and their compilation process does not matter whether the file
11        exists or not.
12
13        However, when you compile this program, the compiler identifies
the
14        exception. In Java, several exceptions are already expected and
defined.
15        This type of exections is identified by the Java compiler.
16        This is checked at the compile time, so it is a checked
```

```
exception.
17      Execution is halted with an error.
18    */
19
20    import java.io.File;
21    import java.io.FileNotFoundException;
22    import java.util.Scanner;
23
24    public class FileReadingIO
25    {
26      public static void main (String [] args) {
27        try {
28          File myFile = new File("FileReadingIO.java");
29          Scanner fileScn = new Scanner(myFile);
30          intlineCnt = 0;
31          while (fileScn.hasNextLine())
32            System.out.println(++lineCnt + "\t" + fileScn.nextLine());
33
34        } catch (FileNotFoundExceptionfnf) {
35            fnf.printStackTrace();
36        } finally {
37            System.out.println("- in this way, an exception is
handled.");
38        }
39      }
40    }
- in this way, an exception is handled.
```

10.5   Exercises

Concept Understanding

1. Explain compile-time errors and run-time errors.

2. Explain what would happen if there is no except handled.

    a. Why there is a compile error even if an appropriate exception is already available?

    b. Why there is no compile error even if an appropriate exception is undefined?

3. Explain the differences between checked and unchecked exceptions

4. How run-time errors and unchecked exceptions are in common?

Programming

1. Assume that a company requires that their employees be older than 29 years and younger than 69 years of age. Write a program, MyEmployees.java, that takes 10 valid data of 10 employees. If the age is out of valid range, print an error message, and continue receiving data until 10 employees with valid data are read. Write the valid employee data into a new data file. Includeappropriate exceptions (for example, out Of Range exception for age, type mismatch exception for non-numeric value).

2. A broker in an investment bank will be given two types of orders to buy or sell your shares. They are to stop order and limit order. With a stop order, your trade will be processed only when the share price reaches the price you have specified. The trading will stop when the price reaches the stop price. On the other hand, a limit order is an order that sets price range – minimum price and maximum price.

   Write MyInvestment.javaprogram to perform the stop order application. You are required to implement stop order only, not limit order.The program must first receive the stop price and then keep buying (reading stock prices,limiting to buying only for simplicity) until the stop price is reached. Print the total value of all the valid stocks bought. When it comes to stop order, your program stops automatically by generating exceptions. Include relevant exceptions.

3. Consider a random number generation. Assume that the stock share price is in the range 100 and 200. A current price is in the range and the prices ticks randomly will be in the range as well. Write a java program, MyInvestment2.java, which continues receiving a randomly generated price only if it does not violate the preset stop order. Other details remain the same as Question 2 above.

4. Modify the definition of stop order: instead of giving a specific price, we can set a percentage. Your trading continues as far as the price change (i.e., change from the initial current price) remains within the percentage. Redo Question 3 for this stop order.

5. Consider problem #2 in Chapter 8. Add appropriate exceptions (for text file reading, checking the validity of prices) and try-catch block.

6. Consider problem #3 in Chapter 8. Add appropriate exceptions (file reading, number of athletes, and costs) to try - catch exceptions.

7. Recall Q3in Concept Understand in Chapter 7 Exercise. Assume that each student object has the classes already taken, and each class object may have aprerequisite course. One course has at most one prerequisite. Now, consider a prerequisite exception handling.

   a) Define an exception Prerequisite Check that verifies whether the prerequisite course has been taken.

   b) Define a driver class with a try-catch block so that can check whether Prerequisite Check is satisfied when a class is inserted into a student.

Graphical User Interfaces

11.1   GUI Components and Class Hierarchies

Most high level programming languages provide numerous Graphical User Interface (GUI) components. It means that we do not have to program any graphical components from scratch, but use or modify the GUI components provided in the language. Java GUI components are very similar to Java classes that are provided by jdk, as such, can be simply instantiated in our GUI application programs. GUI programming is nothing but looking up the GUI components, aka Java classes to instantiate and modify to our needs. Before looking up a GUI component from jdk, let us consider a simple GUI app below.

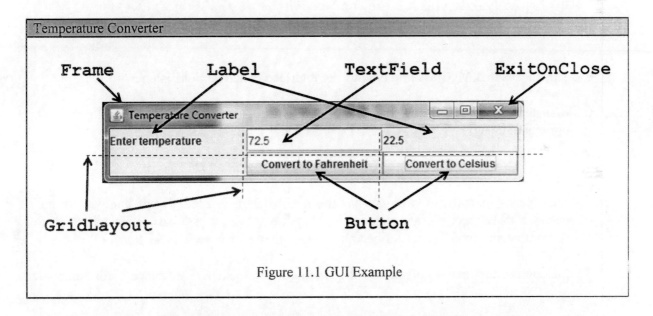

Figure 11.1 GUI Example

In GUI, there is a relationship between GUI components and containers. In the above figure, the outer container is aFrame, which is in the package called java.awtprovided byjdk. Note that there is an extended version ofjava.awt,which is called javax.swingpackage. Many graphical components of java.awt are extended to those in java.swing. For example, JFrame in java.swingis the corresponding component of Frame which is in java.awt. In fact, the swing components are used in the GUI above.

The Frame in the above figure contains Labels, TextFields and Buttons, each of which respectively expresses text label, editable field, and clickable button. Detailed description of the GUI components can be found at http://docs.oracle.com/javase/7/docs/api/javax/swing/package-summary.html.

One of the benefits of developing GUI applications is to combine GUI components with various event-related actions. Event-related actions are either driven by users or devices (including network communications). To an event that may take place in a GUI component, one or more proper actions are to be implemented. In the figure above, as the button "Convert to Fahrenheit" is clicked, the corresponding action, i.e., a calculation of temperature conversion, needs to be taken (could be executing a method). Button clicking is an event, and the calculation is an event handler. For an event handler to be activated in response to an event occurring, the GUI component, i.e., the button should listen to event occurring (pressing the button). We need to implement the interface called ActionListenerin such a GUI application.

To write an Action Listener, follow the steps given below:

1. Declare an event handler class and specify that the class either 1) implements an ActionListenerinterface or 2) extends a class that implements an ActionListenerinterface. Recall that the former is to implement one or more interfaces and the latter is to extend a class which will be its superclass. For example:

```
public class MyClass implements ActionListener {

// body of the class here

}
```

This means that MyClass implements the interface called ActionListener.

2. Register an instance of the event handler class as a listener on one or more components. For example:

```
aButton.addActionListener(instanceOfMyClass);
```

This means that a Button object has the event handler added. Event handler instance, instanceOfMyClass, is an instance of MyClass, which is also an instance of the ActionListener interface as defined above. Detailed is discussed in Section 11.3.

3. Include code that implements the methods in listener interface. For example:

```
public void actionPerformed(ActionEvent e) {

// implement a series of the actions ...

}
```

Since the instance of MyClass was implemented for the interface ActionListener, more particularly the method called actionPerformed() of the ActionListener interface is implemented against the action event which is the button clicking in this case, a series of the corresponding actions should be implemented in the body.

Example 1:

With this in mind, let us start from the simple GUI application that creates a window with the title "Welcome to Mercy Cyber Science" and size zero length and zero height. As you can see in (a) below, there is no white area. But, you can enlarge it as in (b). You could also size it as you please, say for example (350,100) with length=350 and height=100.

Coding List 11.1 Simple Windows

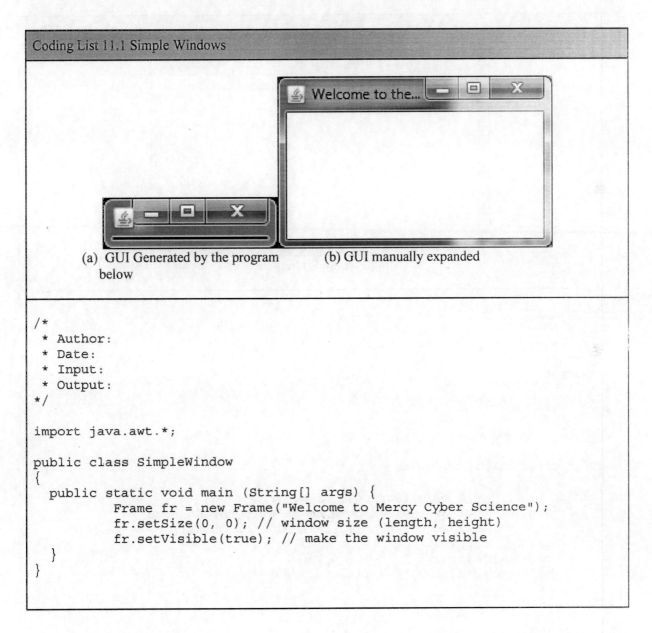

(a) GUI Generated by the program below

(b) GUI manually expanded

```
/*
 * Author:
 * Date:
 * Input:
 * Output:
*/

import java.awt.*;

public class SimpleWindow
{
  public static void main (String[] args) {
        Frame fr = new Frame("Welcome to Mercy Cyber Science");
        fr.setSize(0, 0); // window size (length, height)
        fr.setVisible(true); // make the window visible
  }
}
```

Note that the above code is written in java.awt. Since the GUI program has no event handler for window closing, clicking the 'x' button will not close the window, it can only be closed by pressing ctrl + x.

Example 2:

The following coding list is written in javax.swing, which provides the method fr.setDefaultCloseOperation (JFrame.EXIT_ON_CLOSE); to close the GUI window. This method is invoked by the JFramefr.We have set the size at (350,150) and also made it fixed without allowing any resizing by adding the method fr.setResizable(false).

Coding List 11.2 Simple Swing Window

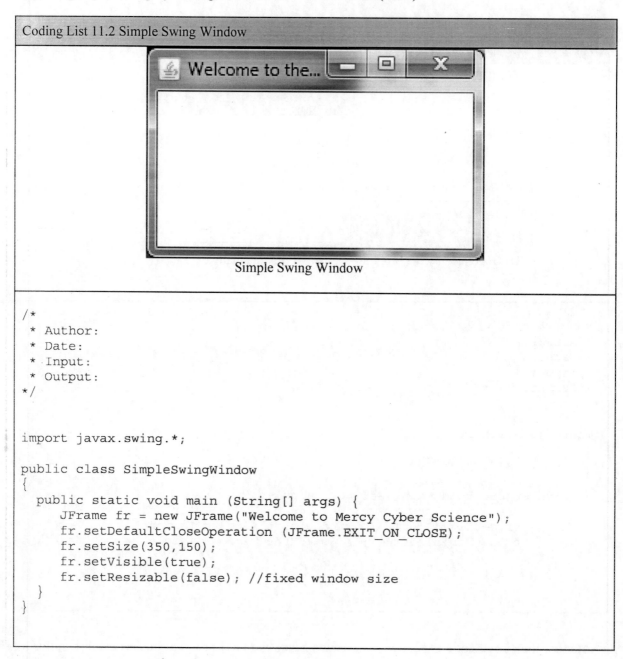

Simple Swing Window

```
/*
 * Author:
 * Date:
 * Input:
 * Output:
 */

import javax.swing.*;

public class SimpleSwingWindow
{
  public static void main (String[] args) {
     JFrame fr = new JFrame("Welcome to Mercy Cyber Science");
     fr.setDefaultCloseOperation (JFrame.EXIT_ON_CLOSE);
     fr.setSize(350,150);
     fr.setVisible(true);
     fr.setResizable(false); //fixed window size
  }
}
```

Now, let us build the Temperature Converter in stages:

<u>Example 3:</u>

1. First we will create the frame with window size (250,100). This will be the container.

2. We will add the label "Enter Temperature" to the frame. We will create a JLabelobject and add it to the frame. The window created is below.

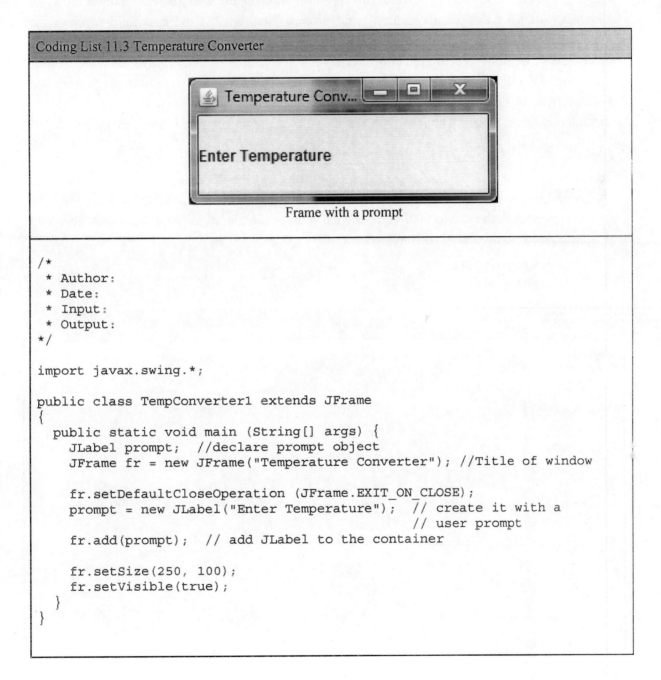

Coding List 11.3 Temperature Converter

Frame with a prompt

```java
/*
 * Author:
 * Date:
 * Input:
 * Output:
*/

import javax.swing.*;

public class TempConverter1 extends JFrame
{
  public static void main (String[] args) {
    JLabel prompt;  //declare prompt object
    JFrame fr = new JFrame("Temperature Converter"); //Title of window

    fr.setDefaultCloseOperation (JFrame.EXIT_ON_CLOSE);
    prompt = new JLabel("Enter Temperature");  // create it with a
                                               // user prompt
    fr.add(prompt);  // add JLabel to the container

    fr.setSize(250, 100);
    fr.setVisible(true);
  }
}
```

11.2   Layout Managers

If we have several GUI components in our application, we need to set up a layout manager. There are several layout managers. More detailed information can be found at https://docs.oracle.com/javase/tutorial/uiswing/layout/visual.html.

Example 4: Now let us add a TextField for the user to enter the Celsius temperature. Now the container will have two components: 1) the prompt label and 2) the text field to enter the temperature. Hence, we will consider using a layout manager. Since we have two components in the container, we need to setup the container layout. We do this with GridLayout. GridLayout is in awt. So, we will import both javax.swing and java.awt. We want to have both the prompt and the text field in one row making two columns. Of several layout managers, GridLayout is illustrated in this example. The layout object of two columns in one row is constructed below:

```
GridLayoutgLayout = new GridLayout(1,2);
```

OncegLayout is created it is then inserted into the frame fr. Since the layout defined is ready to display 1x2 GUI components, each such component should be defined prior to the insertion. The object references to those two GUI components in this example are prompt and input, and each of them is added to the frame fr. Here is the code:

```
fr.add(prompt);
fr.add(input);
```

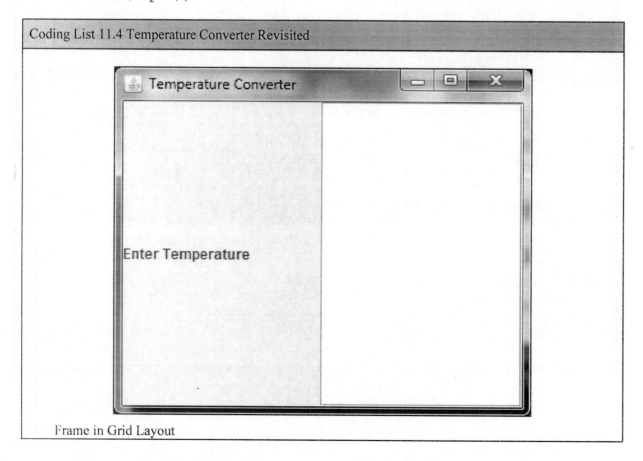

Coding List 11.4 Temperature Converter Revisited

Enter Temperature

Frame in Grid Layout

```
/*
 * Author:
 * Date:
 * Input:
 * Output:
*/

import java.awt.*;
import javax.swing.*;

public class TempConverter2 extends JFrame
{
  public static void main (String[] args) {

  JLabel prompt;
  JFrame fr = new JFrame("Temperature Converter");
  JTextField input = new JTextField(); // a text field where you
                                       // can enter a text
  GridLayout gLayout = new GridLayout(1,2); // grid with 1 row and
                                            // 2 columns
  fr.setLayout(gLayout);   // we will see one row with first label
                      //and then text field
  fr.setDefaultCloseOperation (JFrame.EXIT_ON_CLOSE);
  prompt = new JLabel("Enter Temperature");
  fr.add(prompt);
  fr.add(input);
  fr.setSize(350, 300);
  fr.setVisible(true);

  }
}
```

Example 5:

In this example we will add all the needed components without the event handlers. The button will not react to pressing the button. We will add the action in the next example. So, we will have

    a. A prompt label

    b. A text field for entering the Fahrenheit temperature

    c. A label to put the converted Celsius temperature. This is an event that has to occur in order to get the text entered in the text field to be taken and put in the output label. We need an event handler which will be added in the next example.

    d. A button to click and get the converted Celsius temperature in the answer label. It will not be active yet: when you click it, nothing will happen. It needs an ActionListener to listen to clicking the button and take appropriate action. It will be added in the next example.

We will have one row and four columns. The components will not look very elegant as we are not sizing them appropriately. We will postpone that to a later time.

To start a more appropriate coding practice, we will create TempConverter4 class with a constructor and create its object in the main() method (could be in the same class at the bottom or could be in a different driver.) Here is the code:

Coding List 11.6 Temperature Converter Extended

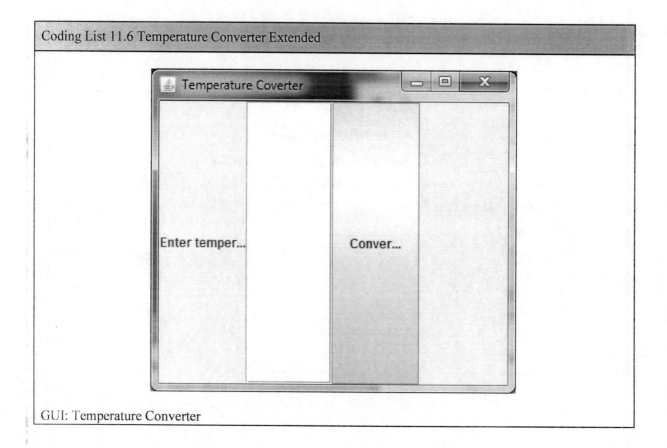

GUI: Temperature Converter

```java
/*
 * Author:
 * Date:
 * Input:
 * Output:

 * Creates four components: prompt, text field for the Farhenheit
temperature, a converter button which when clicked temperature
conversion occurs, and a label to enter the converted Celsius
temperature. No action will work as the button is not activated and
the text entered in the text field will notbe processed. The
actions will be included in the next example.
*/

import java.awt.*;
import javax.swing.*;

public class TempConverter4 extends JFrame
{
   JTextField input;
   JLabel answer, prompt;
   JButton convert; // declare the button object
   GridLayout gLayout; //declare the layout object

   public TempConverter4() {
     JFrame fr= new JFrame("Temperature Coverter"); //create the Frame,
                                                     // the container
     fr.setDefaultCloseOperation (JFrame.EXIT_ON_CLOSE);

     gLayout = new GridLayout(1,4); // container with 1 row & 4
                                    // components
     fr.setLayout(gLayout);

     answer = new JLabel(); // create the 4 component objects
     input = new JTextField();
     prompt = new JLabel("Enter temperature");
     convert = new JButton("Convert to Celsius");

     fr.add(prompt); // add the objects to the frame in the order they
                     // need to
     fr.add(input);   // appear in the contaner.
     fr.add(convert);
     fr.add(answer);

     fr.setSize(350, 100);
     setResizable(false); // fix the size of the window
     fr.setVisible(true);
   }

   public static void main (String[] args) {
     TempConverter4 converter = new TempConverter4(); // test the class
   }
}
```

11.3   Event Handling

We need to make the convert button work. When we click on the convert button, the action should be to calculate the Celsius equivalent and place it in the answer label field. We need to notice that whatever 'number' we enter in the textField will be a text value, not a numeric value. So, in order to convert to Celsius, we need to first parse the text value to numeric value and then use the conversion formula.

The GUI components laid out according to a layout manager may lead to some actions. An event occurs when a user interaction runs through a GUI component. In other words, an action takes place in response to an event of a GUI component. User interactions through a GUI component should be listened by Java program. Luckily, a few of the listener classes or interfaces are provided by jdk which could be added to GUI components.

Example 6:

We have created the convert button in TempConverter4 class. Let us activate it: when we press the button, it should calculate the Celsius temperature and place it in the answer label. For all these actions, jdk provides an ActionListener class. This provides us the **actionPerformed** (ActionEvent e) method in which we could code all the actions that we want to perform for the specific application. In our example, we want to parse the text number to numeric value, convert it to Celsius, and then set it in the answer label. The method should 'listen' (respond to pressing the button in this example) to user action and execute the action. We will do all this in TempConverter class in the following example. First look at just the statements related to this:

```java
public class TempConverter extends JFrame implements
ActionListener
{

    JButton buttn = new JButton("Convert to Celsius");
    bttn.addActionListener(this);


    public void actionPerformed (ActionEvent e) {
      // converter code will go here
   }
 }
```

Here is the complete code for the temperature converter class:

Coding List 11.7 Temperature Converted with Event Handler

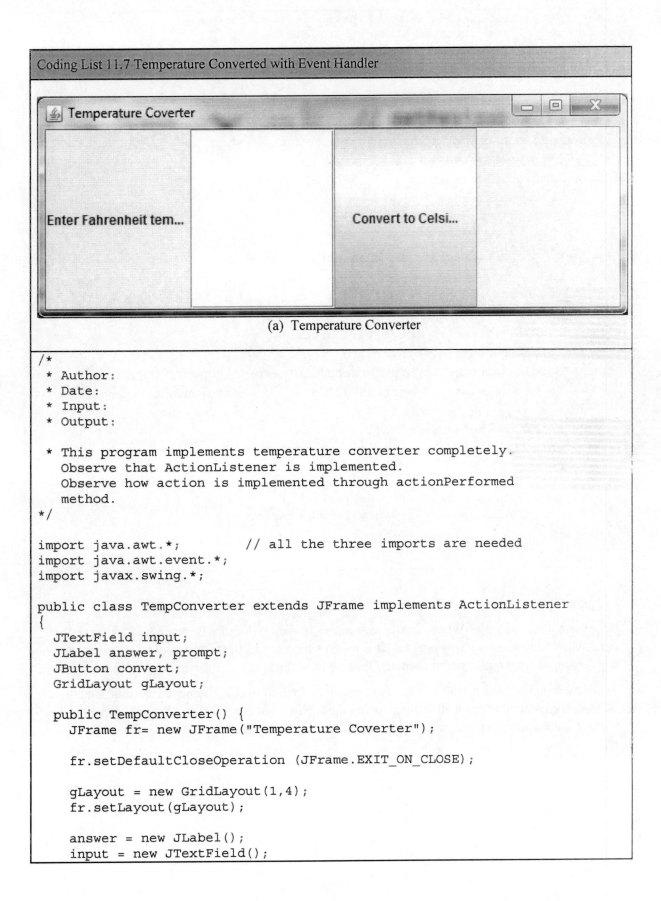

(a) Temperature Converter

```
/*
 * Author:
 * Date:
 * Input:
 * Output:

 * This program implements temperature converter completely.
   Observe that ActionListener is implemented.
   Observe how action is implemented through actionPerformed
   method.
*/

import java.awt.*;          // all the three imports are needed
import java.awt.event.*;
import javax.swing.*;

public class TempConverter extends JFrame implements ActionListener
{
  JTextField input;
  JLabel answer, prompt;
  JButton convert;
  GridLayout gLayout;

  public TempConverter() {
    JFrame fr= new JFrame("Temperature Coverter");

    fr.setDefaultCloseOperation (JFrame.EXIT_ON_CLOSE);

    gLayout = new GridLayout(1,4);
    fr.setLayout(gLayout);

    answer = new JLabel();
    input = new JTextField();
```

```
    prompt = new JLabel("Enter Fahrenheit temperature");
    convert = new JButton("Convert to Celsius");

    fr.add(prompt);
    fr.add(input);
    fr.add(convert);
    fr.add(answer);
    convert.addActionListener(this);
    fr.setSize(550, 100);
    setResizable(false);
    fr.setVisible(true);
}

public void actionPerformed (ActionEvent e) {

  String temp = input.getText();
  System.out.println(temp);
 // check if it is the converter button
  if (e.getSource() == convert){
     double farhen = Double.parseDouble(temp);//convert to numeric
     double celsius = 5*(farhen-32)/5;          //formula to convert to
                                                // Celsius
  // enter in the answer label
     answer.setText(celsius+" degrees Celsius");      }
}

public static void main (String[] args) {
  TempConverter converter = new TempConverter();
}
}
```

Example 7:

Here is another example: Whatever the user enters in the textField will be echoed in the output label when the Echo button is pressed. It is much simpler than the temperature converter and no conversion of text to number is needed. Observe how the two actionPerformed()methods differ.

The button bttn has the method addActionListener() added to itself. Whenever the button is clicked, the method addActionListener() is invoked. Note that the interface ActionListenerhas one method called actionPerformed(), which should be implemented in the class Echo2.java.

Coding List 11.8 Echo Event Handling

```java
/*
 * Author:
 * Date:
 * Input:
 * Output:
 */

import java.awt.*;
import java.awt.event.*;
import javax.swing.*;

public class Echo extends JFrame implements ActionListener
{
  JButton bttn;
  JTextField input;
  JLabel output;
  GridLayout gLayout;

  public Echo() {

    JFrame fr = new JFrame("Copy Cat");
    fr.setDefaultCloseOperation (JFrame.EXIT_ON_CLOSE);

    gLayout = new GridLayout(1,3);
    fr.setLayout(gLayout);

    input = new JTextField();
    bttn = new JButton("Echo");
    output = new JLabel();

    bttn.addActionListener(this);

    fr.add(input);
    fr.add(bttn);
    fr.add(output);

    fr.setSize(250, 100);
    fr.setResizable(false);
    fr.pack();
    fr.setVisible(true);
  }

  public void actionPerformed (ActionEvent e) {

    String temp = input.getText();
```

```
      System.out.println(temp);
      if (e.getSource() == bttn)
         output.setText(temp);
   }

   public static void main (String[] args) {
      Echo convert = new Echo();
   }
}
```

11.4 Revisit GUI Components

Swing components are provided in jdk for Java programs to include GUI components. The AWT and Swing classes provided by jdk can be found in packages http://docs.oracle.com/javase/7/docs/api/javax/swing/package-summary.html and they are shown in a tree formathttp://docs.oracle.com/javase/7/docs/api/javax/swing/package-tree.html. We will not be able to use most of them in this chapter. We have introduced some popular features (labels, text fields, checkboxes, buttons, and radio buttons) and you could expand on it (combo boxes, sliding bars, etc.) as you find the need for.

Using a few of those GUI components, a GUI program can be defined as shown in Figure 11.1. The container JFramecontains JLabel, JBotton, JTextField, etc.

The GUI components used in a java program are organized in a nested manner so that a component contains one or more other components. At the top level, a container contains components, each of which may in turn contain other components, and so on. The top-level container classes provided by Swing are: JFrame, JDialogand JApplet. Each container may contain one or more GUI components. Once components and containers are defined, inner components are added to an outer component or its container.

As GUI components are contained in containers, there will be a containment hierarchy. The containment hierarchy is a tree of GUI components that has a top-level container as its root and each GUI component is contained in its container. Each GUI component can be contained only once. If a component is already in a container and if you try to add it to another container, the component will be removed from the first container and then added to the second. In this way, GUI components can form a containment hierarchy.

We will now implement a complete program which will have several panels containing several components (like buttons, check boxes, and radiobuttons). Panels are invisible containers into which several components can be added. Each of these panels can be made visible by adding them to a frame container, for example. Here is an example which implements these ideas.

Example 8: Let us create an application to place a restaurant dinner order. The requirements are

- Choose between Take Out or Eat In (two radio buttons)
- Choice of appetizers (three choices, 3 checkboxes)
- Choice of main course (four choices, 4 checkboxes)
- Choice of desert (three choices, 3 checkboxes)

- Calculating the total bill and presenting it to the patron (submit the order or cancel, two buttons)

Each bullet above is a group. Each group will be created in a panel. All these panels will be added to a frame. A customer will select either Eat In or Take Out option. Then checks any number of boxes in the three food groups. Finally presses the appropriate button to either place the order or cancel it. We can draw a rough window design and then create the frame. Each panel will be a class, except the button panel which will be in the final order class. Pressing a button has to activate an action. Here is the code with internal documentation:

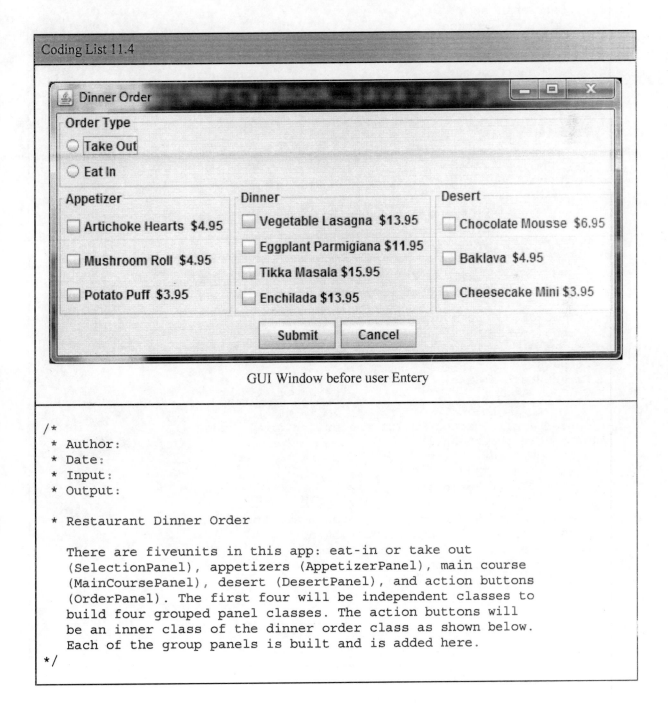

Coding List 11.4

GUI Window before user Entery

```
/*
 * Author:
 * Date:
 * Input:
 * Output:

 * Restaurant Dinner Order

   There are fiveunits in this app: eat-in or take out
   (SelectionPanel), appetizers (AppetizerPanel), main course
   (MainCoursePanel), desert (DesertPanel), and action buttons
   (OrderPanel). The first four will be independent classes to
   build four grouped panel classes. The action buttons will
   be an inner class of the dinner order class as shown below.
   Each of the group panels is built and is added here.
*/
```

```java
import java.awt.*;
import javax.swing.*;
import java.awt.event.*;

// The main class which puts together all different classes
public class DinnerOrder extends JFrame
{

  AppetizerPanel ap ;        // declare the four objects of panels
  DesertPanel dp ;
  MainCoursePanel mcp ;
  SelectionPanel sp ;
  JButton submit, cancel;
  JPanel op;

  public DinnerOrder() {                          //constructor
    JFrame fr = new JFrame("Dinner Order");
    fr.setDefaultCloseOperation(JFrame.EXIT_ON_CLOSE);

    fr.setLayout(new BorderLayout());

    ap= new AppetizerPanel();  // create all the four objects
    dp = new DesertPanel();
    mcp = new MainCoursePanel();
    sp = new SelectionPanel();

    orderPanel();   //void method below

    fr.add(sp,BorderLayout.NORTH); // add 5 panels to frame
    fr.add(ap,BorderLayout.WEST);
    fr.add(mcp,BorderLayout.CENTER);
    fr.add(dp,BorderLayout.EAST);
    fr.add(op,BorderLayout.SOUTH);

    fr.pack();
    fr.setVisible(true);
  }

  // orderPanel() method builds the button group panel
  public void orderPanel() {
    op = new JPanel();
    submit = new JButton("Submit");
    cancel = new JButton("Cancel");

    // ButtonListener and CancelListener are inner classes below
    ButtonListener bl = new ButtonListener();
    CancelListener cl = new CancelListener();
    submit.addActionListener(bl);
    cancel.addActionListener(cl);

    op.add(submit);
    op.add(cancel);
  }
```

```
  /* when submit button is pressed, charges are added and
     placed in a separate window - JOptionPane
     OBSERVE THAT THIS IS AN INNER CLASS. THIS CLASS IS INSIDE THE
     DinnerOrder CLASS
  */
  public class ButtonListener implements ActionListener {
    // actionPerformed(), like the main() method, provided by jdk.
    // we can fill-in our own code as needed

    public void actionPerformed(ActionEvent ae) {
      double charge;

      charge = dp.desertCharge()+ap.appetizerCharge()+mcp.dinnerCharge();
      JOptionPane.showMessageDialog(null,"Total =$"+charge);
      //JOptionPane creates a new window
    }
  }

  // when cancel button is pressed, "Order Cancelled" will
  // be displayed in a different window. THIS IS ANOTHER
  // INNER CLASS
  public class CancelListener implements ActionListener {
    public void actionPerformed(ActionEvent ae) {
      JOptionPane.showMessageDialog(null,"Order Cancelled");
      System.exit(0);
    }
  }

  // this main method creates DinnerOrder object. Its constructor
  //will execute OrderPanel().
  public static void main(String args[]) {
    new DinnerOrder();
  }
}
```

SelectionPanel.java

```
/*
 * Author:
 * Date:
 * Input:
 * Output:

 * This panel lets the user select either eat-in
   or take-out. Each of these two is a button. In the
   real world, the eat-in should allocate a table and
   serve the patrons. This app does not implement
   those actions.
*/

import java.awt.*;
import javax.swing.*;

public class SelectionPanel extends JPanel
```

```java
{
  JRadioButton takeOut, eatIn;
  GridLayout selectionLayout = new GridLayout(2,1);

  public SelectionPanel() {
    takeOut = new JRadioButton("Take Out");
    eatIn = new JRadioButton("Eat In");

    ButtonGroup bGroup = new ButtonGroup();
    bGroup.add(takeOut);
    bGroup.add(eatIn);
    setLayout(new GridLayout(2,1));
    setBorder(BorderFactory.createTitledBorder("Order Type"));

    add(takeOut);
    add(eatIn);
  }
}
```

AppetizerPanel.java

```java
/*
 * Author:
 * Date:
 * Input:
 * Output:

 * The next three panels are checkBox panels for
   allowing the patrons to make their selections.
*/

import java.awt.*;
import javax.swing.*;

public class AppetizerPanel extends JPanel
{
  JCheckBox artichoke, mushroom, potato;
  GridLayout selectionLayout = new GridLayout(3,1);

  public AppetizerPanel() {
    artichoke = new JCheckBox("Artichoke Hearts  $4.95");
    mushroom = new JCheckBox("Mushroom Roll  $4.95");
    potato = new JCheckBox("Potato Puff  $3.95");
    setLayout(new GridLayout(3,1));
    setBorder(BorderFactory.createTitledBorder("Appetizer"));

    add(artichoke);
    add(mushroom);
    add(potato);
  }

  public double appetizerCharge() {
    double charge=0.0;
```

```
      if (artichoke.isSelected() )
         charge +=4.95;
      if (mushroom.isSelected())
         charge +=4.95;
      if (potato.isSelected())
         charge += 3.95;

      return charge;
   }
}
```

MainCoursePanel.java

```
/*
 * Author:
 * Date:
 * Input:
 * Output:
 */


import java.awt.*;
import javax.swing.*;

public class MainCoursePanel extends JPanel
{
  JCheckBox lasagna, parmigiana,tikkaMasala,enchilada;
  GridLayout selectionLayout = new GridLayout(4,1);

  public MainCoursePanel() {
    lasagna = new JCheckBox("Vegetable Lasagna  $13.95");
    parmigiana = new JCheckBox("Eggplant Parmigiana $11.95");
    tikkaMasala = new JCheckBox("Tikka Masala $15.95");
    enchilada = new JCheckBox("Enchilada $13.95");
    setLayout(new GridLayout(4,1));
    setBorder(BorderFactory.createTitledBorder("Dinner"));

    add(lasagna);
    add(parmigiana);
    add(tikkaMasala);
    add(enchilada);
  }

  public double dinnerCharge() {
    double charge=0.0;

    if (lasagna.isSelected())
       charge +=13.95;
    if(parmigiana.isSelected())
       charge += 11.95;
    if (tikkaMasala.isSelected())
       charge += 15.95;
```

```java
        if (enchilada.isSelected())
            charge += 13.95;

    return charge;
    }
}
```

DesertPanel.java

```java
/*
 * Author:
 * Date:
 * Input:
 * Output:
*/

import java.awt.*;
import javax.swing.*;

public class DesertPanel extends JPanel
{
  JCheckBox chocolate, baklava,cheeseCake;
  GridLayout selectionLayout = new GridLayout(3,1);

  public DesertPanel() {
    chocolate = new JCheckBox("Chocolate Mousse  $6.95");
    baklava = new JCheckBox("Baklava  $4.95");
    cheeseCake = new JCheckBox("Cheesecake Mini $3.95");
    setLayout(new GridLayout(3,1));
    setBorder(BorderFactory.createTitledBorder("Desert"));

    add(chocolate);
    add(baklava);
    add(cheeseCake);
  }

  public double desertCharge() {
    double charge=0.0;

    if (chocolate.isSelected())
       charge +=6.95;
    if (baklava.isSelected())
       charge += 4.95;
    if (cheeseCake.isSelected())
       charge += 3.95;

    return charge;
  }
}
```

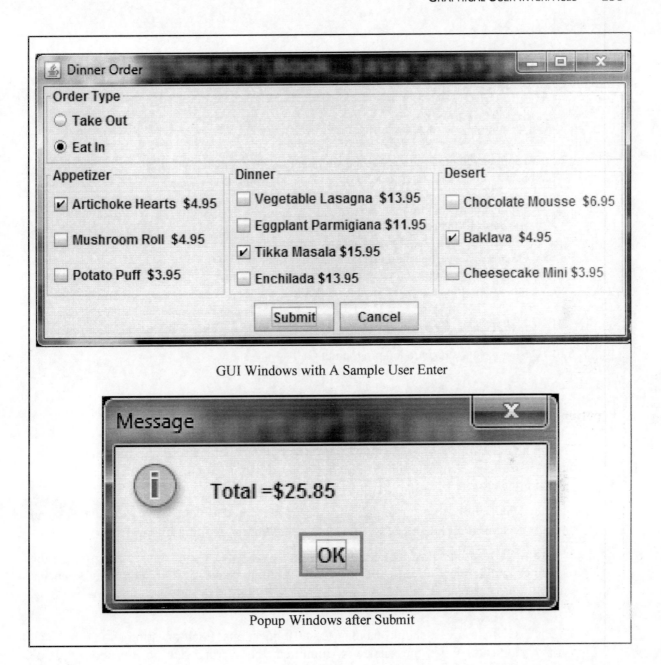

GUI Windows with A Sample User Enter

Popup Windows after Submit

11.5   Exercises

Concept Understanding

1. Consider computer application programs.

    a) An application program may or may not interact with human users. Discuss the pros and cons between a user-interactive program and one without.

    b) An application program may interact with uses by dialog-based-interface (DBI) or by a graphical-user-interface (GUI). Discuss the effectiveness of GUI over DBI.

2. Recall Q3 in Concept Understanding and Q12 in Programming in Chapter 7 Exercise, and Q7 in Chapter 10 Programming Exercise. Consider a class registration program. Note that this is not a programming question, but you may use a UML.

    a) Design the class registration program in DBI

    b) Design the class registration program in GUI

Programming

1. Create a GUI application to receive a number in a text field and output the square of the number in a label. You should have a prompt for the user to enter a decimal number and a label for the answer.

2. Create a GUI application which should accept two integer values in two text fields and output the sum of all the integers between and including the input integers.

3. Create a GUI based sales application. It should list at least five items with prices. The customer could select any number of them. It should have a submit button. When the submit button is clicked, the app should print the total price that includes a sales tax of 8%.

4. Create a GUI survey. It should have at least 10 questions. Each question should be rated on a 1 – 3 scale. When the survey is submitted, the average rate per question must be presented in a window.

5. This programming assignment aims at creating a graphical user interface (GUI) program. Your GUI program displays in the JTextField two integer operands which are randomly generated between 0 and 10000. The operations performed in your program are four arithmetic operations, e.g., +, -, * and /. There will be an equal sign JButton, which can listen to user's clicking event and actuates an appropriate action and display the result on the last column. Meanwhile, users can make a guess and enter the guess on the 5th column. The following figure illustrates a plus operation: two given numbers, 45 and 23, are added and displayed the outcome at the CorrectAnswer column. Your guess appears as well.

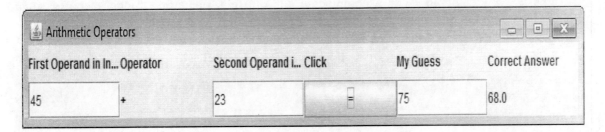

Your Java GUI program should extend the sample GUI above to align the text in GUI components. For example, using the following statements,

```
JFrame.EXIT_ON_CLOSE
setHorizontalAlignment(JTextField.RIGHT)
setHorizontalAlignment(javax.swing.SwingConstants.RIGHT)
```

your program will has a different text alignment and the frame which can exit by clicking the red "X" button on the upper right corner.

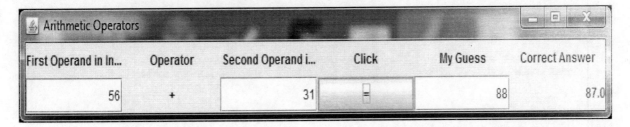

Now your program will be extended to give an option to enter random numbers for the two operands. By clicking the button on the bottom, random numbers are generated to fill in the two boxes. If not clicking, you may enter those numbers manually.

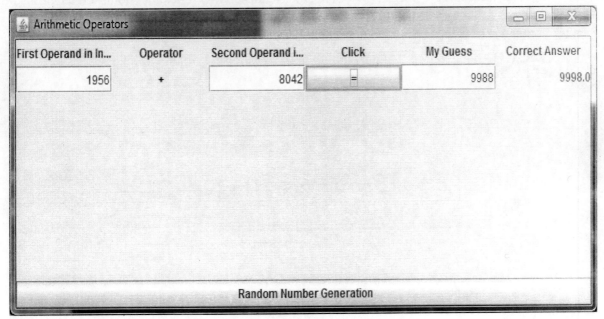

Finally, your program will accommodate for all four operators. Since there is some computation that may generate an exception, your program should handle it. For example, a division by zero denominator may cause a run-time error. Please use try-catch blocks in your program.

Arithmetic Operators					□ ▣ X
First Operand in In...	Operator	Second Operand i...	Click	My Guess	Correct Answer
2777	+	3472	=		6249.0
2777	-	3472	=		-695.0
2777	*	3472	=		9641744.0
2777	/	3472	=		0.7998271889400...
			Random Number Generation		

Extra Bonus: if your program make a judgement to see if MyGuess is the same as CorrectAnswer, or wrong or close enough.

6. Create a GUI application for students to select their course schedule. The selections are made from three groups: General Education, major, and open electives. Each group must have at least three choices. "My Schedule" button, when clicked, should either print the selected schedule or print the message "Exceeded 12 credits, get dean's approval" if the total credits exceed 12. All courses are three credit hours.

7. Recall Q2.b in Concept Understanding in this Exercise. Implement the GUI in Java.

Introduction to Recursion and Graphics

12.1 Introduction

We have used and also created so many methods. We have used methods calling other methods. <u>Recursion is a method calling **itself**</u>. Anytime a method is executed, there will be extra work to be done. There are several applications where recursive solutions are more simple and logical than iterative solutions. We will introduce recursion in this chapter and then recursion's advantage will be exploited in searching and sorting algorithms in the next chapter.

<u>Example 1:</u>

Let us start with an example in which main() method invokesmethodA() and in turn methodA() invokesmethodB(). Let us look at the order of execution of the code. Here is the code and its output:

Coding List 12.1 Method Example

```
/*
 * Author:
 * Date:
 * Input:
 * Output:

 * Here is a very simple class with three methods: main(),
   methodA(), and methodB(). main() invokes methodA() and
   methodA() invokes methodB(). Can you trace their
   executions? the output? When main() invokes methodA(),
   the control is passed on to methodA(). methodA() will
   first print "methodA() - before" and then invokes
   methodB(). The control is now passed onto methodB().
   methodB() will complete the loop and then control is
   returned to methodA(). methodA() will complete after
   printing "methodA() - after".
*/


public class MethodExample
{

  public static void main(String args[]) {
```

```
    System.out.println("main()- before");
    methodA();
    // #1
    System.out.println("Back to main()"); }

  public static void methodA() {
    System.out.println("methodA()- before");
    methodB();
    // #2
    System.out.println("methodA() - after");
  }

  public static void methodB() {
     for (int i=0; i<5; i++)
       System.out.println("methodB()");
  }

}
```

```
main() - before
methodA()- before
methodB()
methodB()
methodB()
methodB()
methodB()
methodA() - after
Back to main()
```

12.2   Recursion

Example 2:

Now consider a method invoking itself. This will be a recursion example. Trace it by hand and write the output. We have given only a part of the output. It prints lots of "Hello" and then error messages.

Coding List 12.2 Recursion 1

```
/*
 * Author:
 * Date:
 * Input:
 * Output:

 * This program creates an infinite loop using recursion.
   Observe that the method infinite() invokes itself in
   its body.
*/
```

```
public class Recursion_1
{
  public static void main(String args[]) {
    infinite();
    System.out.println("Back to main()");
  }

  public static void infinite() {
    System.out.println("Hello");
    infinite();  // recursive invocation
  }
}
```

```
Hello
Hello
Hello
Hello
Exception in thread "main" java.lang.StackOverflowError
at sun.nio.cs.SingleByte.withResult(SingleByte.java:44)
at sun.nio.cs.S
```

Once the control is passed from main() method to the infinite() method, it will never return to the main() method and thus "Back to main()" is never printed. infinite() method will print "Hello" and calls itself. This repeats forever, infinitely. So the recursion acts like an infinite loop except in how recursion (with several method calls) is handled when compared to the way iterative loops are handled.

Now let us go back to the MethodExample. When the main() method invokes methodA(), the address of the location where the control has to return to (#1 in the code) has to be saved and then the control should be passed to the address where methodA() starts. When methodA() invokes methodB(), the address of the location in methodA() where the control has to return to (#2) after completing methodB() has to be saved first and then control passed to the address of methodB(). The order in which the control should be returned has to be preserved. This is achieved in using a data structure called "stack". This is similar to a stack of dinner plates: The last plate we place on the stack (#2 in this case) has to come out first (last-in first-out). In addition to addresses, local variables will also be pushed on the stack. When a method completes, all its local variables will be removed from the stack. Now think of the way infinite() method uses the stack. Each infinite() method call is different from the previous one. So, this recursion creates infinitely many method calls leading to stack overflow.

Example 3:

Let us modify the infinite() method so that it will end after five calls. Let us call this method finite(). Here is the code:

Coding List 12.3 FiniteRecursion

```
/*
 * Author:
 * Date:
 * Input:
 * Output:

 * The recursion is controlled by the parameter n in
   the finite(int n) method. The base case is n=1 at
   which the recursion ends. Each invocation finite(n-1)
   is a method with a reduced number. n starts at 5 and
   keeps decreasing through 4, 3, 2, and 1.
*/

public class FiniteRecursion
{
  public static void main(String args[]) {
    finite(5); // recursion starts with n=5
    System.out.println("Back to main()");
  }

  public static void finite(int n) {
    if (n==1)   // base case
      System.out.println("Hello-Done at n="+n);
    else {
      System.out.println("Hello at n="+n);
    finite(n-1); // reduced case
    }
  }
}
```

```
Hello at n=5
Hello at n=4
Hello at n=3
Hello at n=2
Hello - Done at n=1
Back to main()
```

12.2.1 Recursive requisites

Notice the following steps that made recursive method finite() to end successfully:

1. A base case should be stated. For example, in Coding List 12.3, there is a base case n=1 when the recursion ends

2. The argument to a recursive method invocation should be converged. For example, in Coding List 12.3, every call will invoke a reduced problem from n to n-1 so that it will ultimately reduce to the base case.

These are essential for all recursive solutions. A recursive solution is very similar to mathematical induction where we know the answer for the base case (say when n=1), we assume that there is a solution for a reduced case (when n is reduced to n-1), and prove the result for the general case (for n). Every coding problem which satisfies these requirements can be solved recursively. Every problem that can be solved recursively can also be solved using iterative loops. But, as we discussed earlier, methods require the use of stacks and its management will be extra overhead in recursion when compared to iterative solutions. In spite of the overhead, many problems can be solved with more meaningful logic and generally less coding.

Example 4:

Let us consider a very simple problem of adding all the integers 1 through n. Let

sum(n) = 1+2+...+(n-1)+n
sum(1) = 1   base case
sum(n) = (1+2+...+(n-1)) + n = sum(n-1) + n   recursive case

Here is the code:

```
Coding List 12.4 RecSum

/*
 * Author:
 * Date:
 * Input:
 * Output:

 * sum(int n) is the recursive method here. It is invoked
   with n=5. So, it adds 1 through 5.
*/


public class RecSum
{

  public static void main(String args[]) {
    System.out.println("n="+5+"\tsum="+sum(5));
  }
  public static int sum (int n) {
```

```
      if (n==1) return 1; // base case, sum of 1 is 1
      else {
        System.out.print(n+"\t");
        return n+sum(n-1); // recursive case
      }
    }
  }
}
```

```
n=5    sum=15
```

```
Here is the sequence of the method calls:
main()
      sum(5)
            sum(4)
                  sum(3)
                        sum(2)
                              sum(1)  =  1
                        2+sum(1)  =  3
                  3+sum(2)=3+3  =  6
            4+sum(3)=4+6=10
      5+sum(4)=5+10=15
n=5    sum=15
```

Example 5:

The code above prints the final sum only. Here is the code to print all the intermediate results:

Coding List 12.5 RecSum2

```
/*
 * Author:
 * Date:
 * Input:
 * Output:

 * sum(int n) is the recursive method here. It is invoked
   with n=5. So, it adds 1 through 5. */

public class RecSum2
{
  public static void main(String args[]) {
    System.out.println("n="+5+"\tsum="+sum(5));
  }

  public static int sum (int n) {
    if (n==1) return 1; // base case, sum of 1 is 1
    else {
      int s=sum(n-1);
      System.out.println("n="+(n-1)+"\tsum="+s);
      return n+s; // recursive case
    }
  }
}
```

```
n=1        sum=1
n=2        sum=3
n=3        sum=6
n=4        sum=10
n=5        sum=15
```

12.2.2 Towers of Hanoi

Example 6:

Now we will introduce a classical problem called Towers of Hanoi. It is also called Towers of Brahma (https://en.wikipedia.org/wiki/Tower_of_Hanoi). The problem is to move a set of disks from a source peg to a destination peg using an intermediate peg. Some of you may have played this game when you were kids. The conditions are:

1. Move only one disk at a time

2. Only a smaller disk may be placed on a bigger disk

3. All the n disks should be moved from the source disk to the destination disk using an intermediate disk.

Let us try it for three disks (n=3):

```
|                          |                                              |
#                          |                                              |
###                        |                                              |
#####_____|_____|
Source          Intermediate          Destination
```

Fist move - move disk 1 from source to destination:

```
|                          |                                              |
|                          |                                              |
###                        |                                              |
#####_____|_____#
Source          Intermediate          Destination
```

Second move – move disk 2 from source to intermediate:

```
|                          |                                              |
|                          |                                              |
|                          |                                              |
#####                     ###                                             #
Source          Intermediate          Destination
```

Third move – move disk 1 from destination to intermediate: (Observe now that we moved 2 = n-1 disks from source to intermediate)

```
|                         |                              |
|                         |                              |
|#                        |                              |
#####      ###_____|_____|
Source            Intermediate        Destination
```

Fourth move – move disk 3 from source to destination:

```
|                         |                              |
|                         |                              |
|              #          |                              |
|_____###|_____#####
Source            Intermediate        Destination
```

Fifth move – move disk 1 from intermediate to source:

```
|                         |                              |
|                         |                              |
|                         |                              |
#_____###_____#####
Source            Intermediate        Destination
```

Sixth move – move disk 2 from intermediate to destination:

```
|                         |                              |
|                         |                              |
|                         |                            ###
#_____|_____#####
Source            Intermediate        Destination
```

Seventh move – move disk 1 from source to destination: (Notice the step in Fourth move: we had 2=n-1 disks on intermediate. We have now successfully moved those n-1 disks from intermediate to destination.)

```
|                         |                              |
|                         |                              #
|                         |                            ###
|_____|_____#####
Source            Intermediate        Destination
```

The whole algorithm to solve the Towers of Hanoi problem is stated in moves Third, Fourth, and Seventh:

1. Move n-1 disks from Source to Intermediate (Third move)

2. Move n[th] disk from Source to Destination (Fourth move)

3. Move n-1 disks from Intermediate to Destination(Seventh move)

It all looks so complicated to code, right? But, in terms of recursion, it looks simple. You will see how powerful recursion is in the basic code below that solves this problem with clear moves to make for any number of disks. Here is the simple code:

Coding List 12.6 Towers of Hanoi

```
/*
 * Author:
 * Date:
 * Input:
 * Output:

 * move() is a recursive method. It receives number of
   disks and names of the three pegs. The base case is
   when there is only one disk, it has to be moved to
   the destination peg. The method prints the moves as
   well.
*/

public class TowersOfHanoi
{
  public static void main(String args[]) {
    move(3,"source","intermediate","destination");
  }

  public static void move(int n, String s, String i, String d) {
    if (n==1)  // base case
      System.out.println("Move disk "+n+" from "+s+" to "+d);
    else {
      move(n-1, s,d,i);  // move n-1 disks from source to intermediate
      System.out.println("Move disk "+n+" from "+ s + " to "+ d);
      move(n-1, i, s, d);  // move n-1 disks from intermediate to
                           // destination
    }
  }
}
```

```
Move disk 1 from source to destination
Move disk 2 from source to intermediate
Move disk 1 from destination to intermediate
Move disk 3 from source to destination
Move disk 1 from intermediate to source
Move disk 2 from intermediate to destination
Move disk 1 from source to destination
```

12.3   Graphics

We will introduce only a small part of graphics to enable us to do some recursions and also have some fun. Just like we need the main() method to execute a class, we need the paint() method to draw some graphics. Since graphics will show up in frames of windows, we need to extend JFrame class and set up the frame. Just a reminder: the windows origin (0,0) is the top-left corner of the window and the y-coordinate increases downward. We will create a simple boilerplate program that can be used for all the problems in this chapter. Here is the boilerplate with comments:

Coding List 12.7   TEMPLATE TO USE FOR ALL GRAPHICS PROBLEMS

```
/*
 * Author:
 * Date:
 * Input:
 * Output:
 */

import java.awt.Graphics; // needed to draw graphics
import java.awt.Color;    // needed to use different colors
import javax.swing.JFrame;// needed to create the window

public class IntroGraphics extends JFrame  // create your class
{
  public IntroGraphics() {      // set up the window in the constructor
    setTitle("Introduction to Graphics");
    setSize(1200,1200);
    setVisible(true);
    setDefaultCloseOperation(EXIT_ON_CLOSE);
  }

  // THE paint() METHOD IS NEEDED TO DRAW GRAPHICS
  public void paint(Graphics g) {
    // PLACE ALL YOUR DRAWINGS HERE. IT COULD BE METHOD CALLS
  }

  // main() method to execute. JUST CREATE AN OBJECT OF THE CLASS
  public static void main(String args[]) {
    IntroGraphics ig = new IntroGraphics(); // object of the class
  }
}
```

Example 7:

Without much details let us look at the code to draw <u>a line in red, a rectangle in blue, an oval in green</u>. We will copy the boilerplate above and add new code to it, the new code in red to make it explicit and to show how simple it is to write your programs.

Coding List 12.8 FirstGraphics.java   non-recursive

```java
/*
 * Author:
 * Date:
 * Input:
 * Output:
*/

import java.awt.Graphics; // needed to draw graphics
import java.awt.Color;    // needed to use different colors
import javax.swing.JFrame;// needed to create the window

public class FirstGraphics extends JFrame  // create your class
{

  public FirstGraphics() {      // set up the window in the constructor
     setTitle("Introduction to Graphics");
     setSize(1800,1800);
     setVisible(true);
     setDefaultCloseOperation(EXIT_ON_CLOSE);
  }

  // THE paint() METHOD IS NEEDED TO DRAW GRAPHICS
  public void paint(Graphics g) {
    g.setColor(Color.RED);
    // Draw line with first point(100,100), (300,300) end point
    g.drawLine(100,100,300,300);
    g.setColor(Color.BLUE);
    // Draw rectangle (350,100) top left corner, 200=len, 400=width
    g.drawRect(350,100,200,400);
    g.setColor(Color.GREEN);
    //oval inscribed in a rectangle with(600,500) top left corner,
    // 200=length, 400=width
    g.drawOval(600,500,200,400);

    // PLACE ALL YOUR DRAWINGS HERE. IT COULD BE METHOD CALLS
  }

  // main() method to execute. JUST CREATE AN OBJECT OF THE CLASS
  public static void main(String args[]) {
    FirstGraphics fg = new FirstGraphics(); // object of the class
  }
}
```

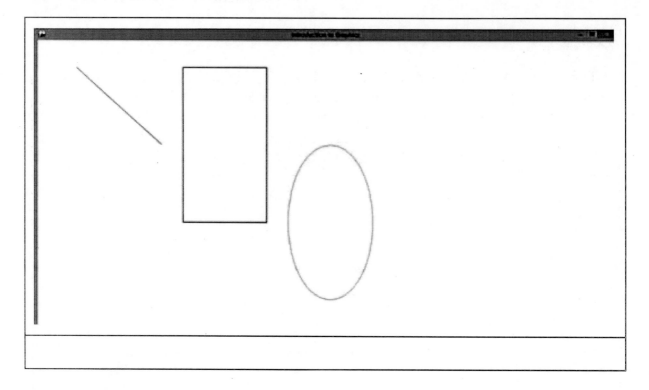

Example 8:

We drew the figures in the paint() method. It may not be always possible to draw all graphics in the paint() method. We may have to write methods to draw different graphics. In that case, we will call those methods in the paint() method. In order to illustrate this point, we will do the same code as above except that we will remove all the graphics code from paint, put them in drawFigures() method and invoke drawFigures() method in the paint() method. We changed the name of the class to FirstGraphicsB.It will be the same graphics as above. Here is the code:

Coding List 12.9   FirstGraphicsB.java   drawing with a method

```java
/*
 * Author:
 * Date:
 * Input:
 * Output:
*/

import java.awt.Graphics; // needed to draw graphics
import java.awt.Color;    // needed to use different colors
import javax.swing.JFrame;// needed to create the window

public class FirstGraphicsB extends JFrame  // create your class
{
  public FirstGraphicsB() {  // set up the window in the constructor
    setTitle("Introduction to Graphics");
    setSize(1800,1800);
```

```
    setVisible(true);
    setDefaultCloseOperation(EXIT_ON_CLOSE);
}

// THE paint() METHOD IS NEEDED TO DRAW GRAPHICS
public void paint(Graphics g) {
    drawFigures(g);
    //(500,500) top left corner, 200=length, 400=width
    // PLACE ALL YOUR DRAWINGS HERE. IT COULD BE METHOD CALLS
}

public void drawFigures(Graphics g) {
    g.setColor(Color.RED);
    g.drawLine(100,100,300,300);
    g.setColor(Color.BLUE);
    g.drawRect(350,100,200,400);
    g.setColor(Color.GREEN);
    g.drawOval(600,300,200,400); //oval inscribed in a rectangle
}

// main() method to execute. JUST CREATE AN OBJECT OF THE CLASS
public static void main(String args[]) {
    FirstGraphicsB ig = new FirstGraphicsB(); // object of the class
}
}
```

You may be familiar with RGB (R=red, G=green, B=blue) system in which these three colors can be mixed in different proportions to create new colors. You may have enjoyed that fun by mixing different color paints when you were children. Computer graphics works on the same principle. The max color code is 250. It will be white if all the colors are 250 and black if all of them are zero. If R=250 and the other two are zeros, it will be completely red. We will make the background color a light grey (R=234, G=231, B=231) by drawing a rectangle that covers the whole window. You can find different color systems and their codes at http://www.color-hex.com/. If you click on any color, you will get a table of codes. There are lots of other places where you can find the codes. We will use these numbers in setColor() method as shown below. Just add

```
    g.setColor(new Color(234,231, 231);
    g.fillRect(0,0,1200,1200); //NOTICE IT IS "fillRect", not
    "drawRect"
```

to the beginning of the drawFigures() method and run the program. As you may have already realized, you can draw a circle using drawOval() method with length and width the same.

Draw axes: Write a program to draw coordinate axes with its origin at the center of the window.

We know that we need the coordinates of the starting point and the ending point to draw a straight line. We are given the coordinates of the origin of the axes. We need to figure out the coordinates of the end points of both the x-axis and the y-axis. If the window size is set to length=1200 and width=1200, then the mid-point of the window will be (600,600). So the starting point of the x-axis is 600 to the left of the origin. Its coordinates will be (0,600). The right end of the x-axis is (1200,600). The end points of the y-axis will be (600,0) and (600,1200). Let us write a method, call it drawAxes() that will take the size of the window and Graphics as the parameters. Here is the method:

```java
public void drawAxes(int x, int y, Graphics g)
   { intoriginX = x/2, originY=y/2;
g.drawLine(0, originY, x, originY);
g.drawLine(originX,0, originX, y);
   }
```

We could just replace drawFigures(Graphics g)method by drawAxes(int x, int y, Graphics g)method in FirstGraphicsB. We may want to change the name of the class though.

Now that we have set up the boiler plate, we could write some recursive codes in graphics.

Example 9:

StepLines: Use a recursive method to draw segments of lines which would look like steps. Let the length of the step be 50. Let us start the steps at (100,100). First we should draw a horizontal line segment starting at (100,100) and ending at (150,100). We should move the line 50 units to the right and 25 units down, and keep doing it. We have also drawn the baseline of the staircase. Here is the code:

Coding List 12.10 RecursiveSteps.java   recursive graphics

```java
/*
 * Author:
 * Date:
 * Input:
 * Output:
*/

import java.awt.Graphics; // needed to draw graphics
import java.awt.Color;    // needed to use different colors
import javax.swing.JFrame;// needed to create the window

public class RecursiveSteps extends JFrame  // create your class
{
  public RecursiveSteps() {    // set up the window in the constructor
    setTitle("Introduction to Graphics");
    setSize(1800,1800);
    setVisible(true);
```

```
    setDefaultCloseOperation(EXIT_ON_CLOSE);
  }

  // THE paint() METHOD IS NEEDED TO DRAW GRAPHICS
  public void paint(Graphics g) {
    g.setColor(new Color(234,230,230));
    g.fillRect(0,0,1800,1800);
    drawSteps(50,100,100,g);
  }

  public void drawSteps(int len, int x, int y,Graphics g) {
    g.setColor(Color.RED);
    if (x == 1000) {              // BASE CASE
       g.drawLine(100,100, 1000,y); // base line below the steps
       g.drawLine(100,100, 100+len,100);//first step at the top
    }
    else {
      x +=len;            // OBSERVE THAT BOTH X AND Y ARE MOVED FORWARD
      y +=len/2;                 // UNTIL X BECOMES 1000
      g.drawLine(x,y, x+len,y);
      drawSteps(len,x,y,g);   // RECURSIVE CASE
    }
  }

  // main() method to execute. JUST CREATE AN OBJECT OF THE CLASS
  public static void main(String args[]) {
    RecursiveSteps rs = new RecursiveSteps(); // object of the class
  }
}
```

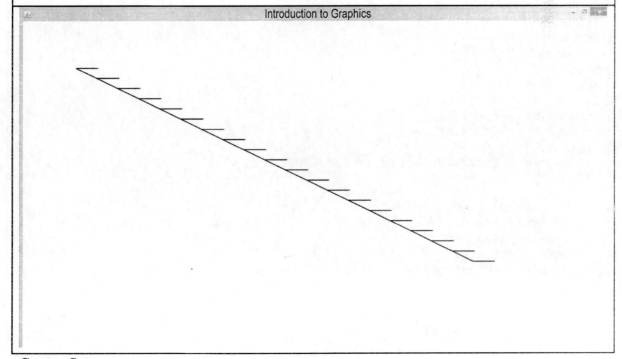

Cantor Set:

Example 10:

(https://en.wikipedia.org/wiki/Cantor_set): In mathematics, the **Cantor set** is a set of points lying on a single line segment that has a number of remarkable and deep properties. It was discovered in 1874 by Henry John Stephen Smith[1][2][3][4] and introduced by German mathematician Georg Cantor in 1883.[5][6]

Through consideration of this set, Cantor and others helped lay the foundations of modern point-set topology. Although Cantor himself defined the set in a general, abstract way, the most common modern construction is the **Cantor ternary set**, built by removing the middle thirds of a line segment. Cantor himself only mentioned the ternary construction in passing, as an example of a more general idea, that of a perfect set that is nowhere dense.

Let us build Canter ternary set: Draw a line of length 1. Remove the middle $1/3^{rd}$ of the line. Repeat this to the remaining two segments. Continue this recursively. This will be the Cantor ternary set in graphics. Let us start with line of length 1000. The recursive steps are

1. If length =1, draw the last line
2. Else, remove the middle 1/3 of the line and draw the left segment and then draw the right segment
3. Repeat step #2 recursively

Here is the code:

Coding List 12.11 Recursive Cantor

```
/*
 * Author:
 * Date:
 * Input:
 * Output:
*/

import java.awt.Graphics;
import java.awt.Color;
import javax.swing.JFrame;

public class RecursiveCantor extends JFrame
{

  public RecursiveCantor() {
    setTitle("Cantor Ternary Set");
    setSize(1800,1800);
    setVisible(true);
    setDefaultCloseOperation(EXIT_ON_CLOSE);
  }

  public void paint(Graphics g) {
    g.setColor(Color.GREEN);
```

```
        drawCantorSet(50,50,1200,g);
    }


    public void drawCantorSet(int x, int y, int len, Graphics g) {
        if (len == 1)                   //BASE CASE
            g.drawLine(x, y, x+1, y);
        else {
            g.drawLine(x, y, x+len, y); // DRAW THE LINE
            y += 20;                    // MOVE DOWN 20 UNITS TO DRAW THE NEXT SET
            g.setColor(Color.BLUE);
            // NOTICE THAT THE LENGTH IS CUT TO 1/3RD
            drawCantorSet(x,y,len/3,g); // CANTORIZE THE LEFT SEGMENT

            drawCantorSet(x+2*len/3, y,len/3 ,g); // CANTORIZE THE RIGHT
                                        // SEGMENT STARTING AT X+2/3RD LENGTH

        }
    }

    public static void main(String args[]) {
        RecursiveCantor rc = new RecursiveCantor();
    }
}
```

Here is the trace of method calls. We will use dcs for drawCantorSet. The first call is in the paint() method. That is where we will start. Since at each step, there will be two recursive calls, the trace will be a binary tree. We have shown only three left nodes in orrage which will be executed only after each of the corresponding right node is completed. We have shown the left branch of the tree in black. To see what this branch will graph, comment out the second recursive call drawCantorSet(x+2*len/3,y,len/3,g) and run the code. We have the graph below. Observe that trace has 7 calls in the left branch and the graph has 7 line segments.

dcs(50,50,1200,g)
dcs(50,70,400,g)dcs(850,70,400,g)
dcs(50,90,133,g)   dcs(94,90,133,g)
dcs(50,110,44,g)
dcs(50,130,14,g)   dcs(64,130,14,g)
dcs(50,150,4,g)
dcs(50,170,1,g)

12.4 Exercises

Concept Understanding

1. Consider the following two definitions:
       PHP: PHP Hypertext Preprocessor
       GNU: GNU is Not Unix
   Explain how the above definitions are defined recursively.

2. Consider the number counting system.
   1) Decimal numbers are counted 0,1,2,3,..., 9, 10, 11, 12, ..., 20, 21, ..., 99, 100, 101. Do count the number in the binary system. Hint: It begins 0,1, 10, 11, 20. Please continue.
   2) Read https://en.wikipedia.org/wiki/hexadecimal. Count decimal numbers from 0 to 100 in hexadecimal.
   3) Explain a recursion while counting in various different counting systems.

Programming

In all the problems below, you need to write the working codes and then trace the method calls. Submit both the working code and the trace.

1. Write a program to read two sides of a right triangle and calculate the length of the hypotenuse. This is to trace the sequence of method calls.

2. Write a recursive program to calculate factorial of an integer. If you add integers 1 through n, it will be sigma(n)=1+2+...+n. Factorial is the product of the integers 1 through n. So, factorial(5)=1x2x3x4x5=120. The notation is 5!. Print all the intermediate factorials as well.

3. Write a recursive program to generate Fibonacci numbers (https://en.wikipedia.org/wiki/Fibonacci_number). For example, the first six Fibonacci numbers in the sequence are 1, 1, 2, 3, 5, 8. Print all the numbers in the sequence for any given index and then draw the following graph (HINT: Fibonacci() method should be recursive. Print the sequence of numbers and draw graphs in paint() method using a loop for the given index.)

Fibonacci Squares

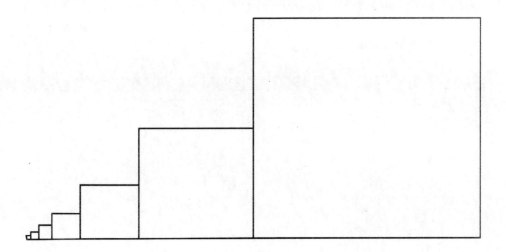

4. Read a sentence from the keyboard and print it in the reverse order. You need to use a recursive method that accepts the sentence as a parameter and print the characters.

5. Write a program to draw concentric circles as shown below. It should use a recursive method until the radius of circles reach a maximum size that you choose. Remember circles are ovals inscribed in rectangles.

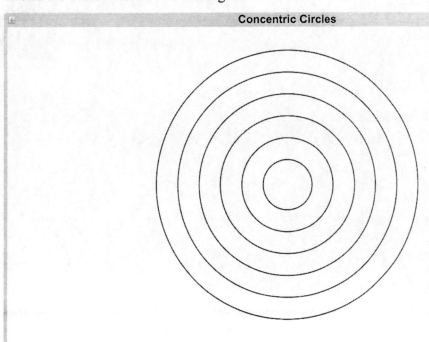

Concentric Circles

6. Write a program with a recursive method that draws circles that fills the plane like tiles. We have pasted a very simple graph and fully developed plane. (HINT: As you know circles are ovals. Ovals are inscribed in rectangles that accepts coordinates of left-top corner, length and width of the rectangle. So, the circles are drawn as ovals going in four directions with reduced lengths.)

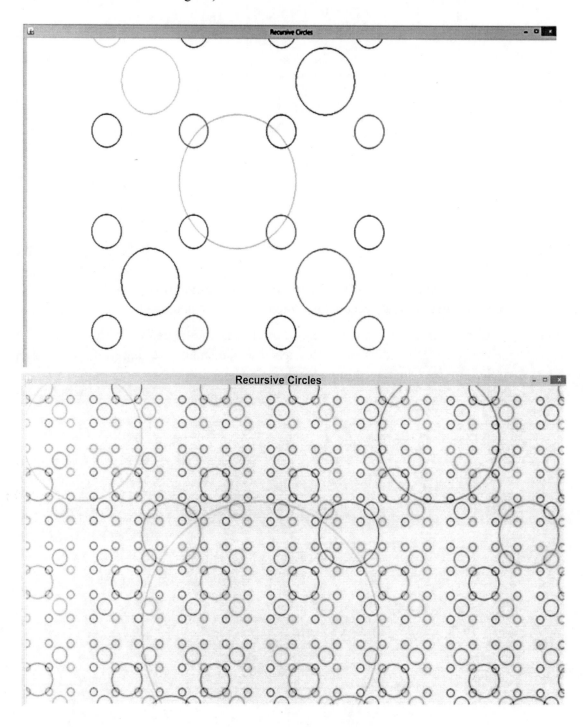

7. Write a program to calculate payments of a loan. For example, if you borrow a ten year loan of $10,000, you will be asked to pay a fixed amount every month (assume $200). The loan will be charged a fixed rate of interest (assume 6%). So the interest amount will be added to borrowed amount and your payment will be deducted from the loan amount. This will continue every month for 10x12=120 months. This can be done very easily with a loop. This can also be solved by recursion. Let us write two steps for the example given here:

Principle = 10000, interest per month = 6/12 = 0.5%, number of months =120

First month: 10000+10000*0.005 – 200 = 9850

Second month: 9850+9850*0.005-200 = 9699.25. This can be written as 9850*1.005-200.

The recursive formula will be:

When n=1, mortgage = 10000.

mort(n) = mort(n-1)*1.005-200   recursive

8. Write a program to convert a given integer into a binary number. The integer is given from the command line argument. The conversion uses division and modulo operations. A sample coding list is shown partially:

```
public class Convert2Bin
{


    public static void convert (intnum) {
    if (num< 2) System.out.print (num);
    else {
            // implement here
}
}
    public static void main (String args[]) {
    System.out.println("The given integer "+args[0]+ " = ");
    convert(Integer.parseInt(args[0]));
    System.out.println(" in binary");

    }
}
```

Sample runs are shown below.

```
C:\Windows\system32\cmd.exe

C:\Mercy\Book_java\recursion>javac Convert2Bin.java

C:\Mercy\Book_java\recursion>java Convert2Bin 35
The given integer 35 =
100011 in binary

C:\Mercy\Book_java\recursion>java Convert2Bin 11
The given integer 11 =
1011 in binary

C:\Mercy\Book_java\recursion>java Convert2Bin 8
The given integer 8 =
1000 in binary

C:\Mercy\Book_java\recursion>
```

9. (Coding Challenge) Recall Coding List 12.4. Write a Java program that can display the output shown below. The computation logic remains the same as Coding List 12.4, however this new program requires a careful sequence of print statements.

```
C:\Windows\system32\cmd.exe

C:\Mercy\Book_java\recursion>javac RecSum.java

C:\Mercy\Book_java\recursion>java RecSum
sum(5)
        |sum(4)
        |       |sum(3)
        |       |       |sum(2)
        |       |       |       |sum(1)
        |       |       |       |=1
        |       |       |=2+sum(1)=3
        |       |=3+sum(2)=6
        |=4+sum(3)=10
=5+sum(4)=15
n=5      sum=15

C:\Mercy\Book_java\recursion>
```

10. Recall Q2.b in Concept Understanding of this Exercise. Write a Java program that takes a non-negative integer and returns the hexadecimal counting system from 0 to the given integer.

   a) Do it in a for-loop.

   b) Do it in a recursion.

2.5 Course Project Problems:

The whole class will choose one of the problems (class project) from the list below or create a new problem of your choosing with approval from the professor. This class project will be coded in stages in the class as we keep learning more and more instructions as the course progresses. The class project will be complete in the class two weeks before the end of the term. Each student group will choose its own project and develop a complete program to its chosen problem (student project). Each of the student groups will submit completed student project during the last two weeks of the term. All completed projects must be GUI based applications.

1. Create a student management system. The application should be able to perform the following tasks:

   - Print student information (Name, ID, address, phone numbers, email address, major, tuition, number of credits, GPA,...)

   - Search for students by name or ID

   - Manage tuition payments

   - Update GPA

   - Print current student schedule

2. Create a bank account management system. The application should be able to perform the following tasks:

   - Print a customer's information (Name, bank balance, kind of account, address, phone numbers, email address, ...)

   - Search for a customer by name or phone number

   - Manage at least two types of accounts (checking and savings accounts, for example)

   - Manage deposits and withdrawals

   - Manage bill payments

3. Create a business management system. There could be a variety of applications which could include auto dealership, restaurant management, and retail stores. The application should be able to perform the following tasks, applicable to your project:

   - Print the business's information (Name, address, phone numbers, staff and department directories,...)

- Print inventory

- Search for a product by number or key word

- Manage sales and purchases

- Print financial information

- Print daily sales revenue figures

4. Create a calculator application. The calculator should be able to perform the following tasks:

    - Perform arithmetic operations

    - Perform exponentiation, logarithms, basic trigonometric functions

    - Compute the sum of integers in a given range and step value

    - Calculate percentages

5. Create an application for an Internet business. There are a massive number of examples to imitate or to design new ones.

    Create an application to conduct various surveys. It should be able to collect data and present it in a meaningful format.